THE DIFFERENCE WITHIN: FEMINISM AND CRITICAL THEORY

CRITICAL THEORY
Interdisciplinary Approaches to
Language, Discourse and Ideology

Volume 8

Elizabeth Meese and Alice Parker (eds)

THE DIFFERENCE WITHIN:
FEMINISM AND CRITICAL THEORY

THE DIFFERENCE WITHIN: FEMINISM AND CRITICAL THEORY

edited by

ELIZABETH MEESE and ALICE PARKER
University of Alabama

JOHN BENJAMINS PUBLISHING COMPANY
AMSTERDAM/PHILADELPHIA

1989

Library of Congress Cataloging-in-Publication Data

The Difference within.

(Critical theory, ISSN 0920-3060; v. 8)
Papers presented at the 13th Annual University of Alabama Symposium on Literature and Language, held in 1986.
Bibliography: p.
1. Feminist literary criticism -- Congresses. 2. Feminism and literature -- Congresses. 3. Women in literature -- Congress. I. Meese, Elizabeth A., 1943- . II. Parker, Alice, 1937- . III. Alabama Symposium on English and American Literature (13th : 1986 : University of Alabama) IV. Series.
PN98.W64D5 1988 801'.95'088042 88-7916
ISBN 90 272 2415 3 (Eur.)/1-55619-043-3 (US)(pb., alk. paper)
ISBN 90 272 2414 5 (Eur.)/1-55619-042-5 (US)(hb., alk. paper)

Contents

Acknowledgments

We extend our thanks and appreciation to all of those who helped with this volume: David L. Miller and Gregory S. Jay for having started it all in Alabama with the 1982 symposium "After Strange Texts: The Role of Theory in the Study of Literature"; Claudia Johnson, Chair of the Department of English, for unwavering support; the University of Alabama Language and Critical Theory Group for advice, even when not taken; and Elliot Adams, Andrea Cumpston, Alicia Griswold, and Peggy Kissinger for their word processing, research, printing, transcriptions and enthusiasm.

Further, we appreciate permission to reprint the following essays previously published: Catharine Stimpson, "Nancy Reagan Wears a Hat: Feminism and Its Cultural Consensus," *Critical Inquiry* 14,2 (Winter 1988): 223-243 (also in Stimpson, *Where the Meanings Are*, New York, Methuen, 1988); Hortense Spillers, "Notes on an Alternative Model — Neither/Nor," *The Year Left II: An American Socialist Yearbook, Toward a Rainbow Socialism: Essays on Race, Ethnicity, Class, and Gender*, ed. Mike Davis, Manning Marable, Fred Pfeil and Michael Sprinker (London: Verso/NLB, 1987): 176-194. In the essay by Jane Marcus, Plate 1 is taken from the cover of Andrew Rosen's *Rise Up Women* (Routledge, 1974), and Plate 2 is provided through the generosity of the Jill Craigie Women's Suffrage Collection (London).

Acknowledgments

[illegible]

Notes on contributors

HOUSTON A. BAKER, JR., Albert M. Greenfield Professor of Human Relations at the University of Pennsylvania, is the author of many works on Afro-American literature and culture, including *Journey Back: Issues in Black Literature and Criticism* (Chicago: University of Chicago Press, 1980), and more recently *Blues, Ideology, and Afro-American Literature: A Vernacular Theory* (Chicago: University of Chicago, 1984), his third volume of poetry, *Blues Journeys Home* (1985), and *Modernism and the Harlem Renaissance* (Chicago: University of Chicago Press, 1987).

MICHÈLE BARRETT, Senior Lecturer in Sociology at the City University of London, has done extensive research on the relationship between feminist and Marxist analysis. In addition to numerous articles, she has published *Virginia Woolf: Women and Writing* (London: The Women's Press, 1979) and *Women's Oppression Today* (London: New Left/Verso, 1980).

JONATHAN CULLER, Professor of English and Comparative Literature at Cornell University, is the author of many publications on matters of concern to critical theory. His books include *Flaubert: The Uses of Uncertainty* (Ithaca: Cornell University Press, 1974); *Structuralist Poetics: Structuralism, Linguistics, and the Study of Literature* (Ithaca: Cornell University Press, 1975), which won the James Russell Lowell Prize in 1976; *The Pursuit of Signs: Semiotics, Literature, Deconstruction* (Ithaca: Cornell University Press, 1981); and most recently *On Deconstruction: Theory and Criticism after Structuralism* (Ithaca: Cornell University Press, 1982).

MYRIAM DÍAZ-DIOCARETZ, Chilean poet, critic and translator, currently resides in the Netherlands and is a researcher at the Faculty of Letters, University of Utrecht. She has published work on translation studies, American literature, Black American women poets, as well as translations of American poetry. Her books include *The Transforming Power of Language: The Poetry of Adrienne Rich* (Utrecht: HES, 1984) and *Translating Poetic Discourse: Questions on Feminist Strategies in Adrienne Rich* (Amsterdam/Philadelphia: John Benjamins, 1985). She co-edited, with Iris M. Zavala, the first book in this series, *Women, Feminist Identity and Society in the 1980's: Selected Papers* (Amsterdam/Philadelphia: John Benjamins, 1985).

JANE MARCUS, Professor of English and Women's Studies at the CUNY Graduate Center and the City College of New York, has published widely and edited three collections of essays on Virginia Woolf: *New Feminist Essays on Virginia Woolf* (Lincoln: University of Nebraska, 1981) and *Virginia Woolf: A Feminist Slant* (Lincoln: University of Nebraska, 1983); and *Virginia Woolf and Bloomsbury: A Centenary Celebration* (Macmillan/Indiana, 1987). She also edited *The Young Rebecca West, 1911-1917* (1982). Her most recent books are *Virginia Woolf and the Languages of Patriarchy* (Bloomington and Indianapolis: Indiana University Press, 1987) and *Art and Anger: Reading Like a Woman* (Ohio State University Press, 1988).

ELIZABETH MEESE, Professor of English and Adjunct Professor of Women's Studies, The University of Alabama, has published on American writers of the nineteenth and twentieth centuries, Southern women writers, and feminist criticism. Her most recent publication work is *Crossing the Double-Cross: The Practice of Feminist Criticism* (Chapel Hill: University of North Carolina Press, 1986).

ALICE PARKER, Associate Professor of French, The University of Alabama, has published research on eighteenth century French women writers and the *philosophes*, Francophone writers of the American South, and French and Canadian contemporary lesbian writers.

R. RADHAKRISHNAN, Assistant Professor of English, the University of Massachusetts, has published numerous articles on the question of marginalization, politics and deconstruction. His articles includes "Ethnic Identity and Post-Structuralist Differance" in *Cultural Critique*, as well as others in *boundary 2*, *Works and Days*, and others forthcoming in *Poetics Today*, *MELUS* and various collections.

HORTENSE J. SPILLERS, Professor of English and African-American Literature at Cornell University, teaches literature and criticism. She is co-editor, with Marjorie Pryse, of *Conjuring: Black Women, Fiction, and Literary Tradition* (Bloomington: Indiana UP, 1985), and her stories and articles have appeared widely. In 1976, she received the National Award for excellence in Fiction and Belles Lettres for one of her short stories.

GAYATRI CHAKRAVORTY SPIVAK, Andrew W. Mellon Professor of English at the University of Pittsburgh, is the translator of the English edition of Jacques Derrida's *Of Grammatology* (Baltimore and London: The Johns Hopkins University Press, 1976) and author of *In Other Worlds: Essays in Cultural Politics* (New York: Methuen, 1987). Her essays have appeared in such journals as *Critical Inquiry*, *Yale French Studies*, *Social Text*, and *Diacritics*.

CATHARINE STIMPSON, Professor and Dean of the Graduate School at Rutgers University, was the founding editor of the feminist journal *SIGNS*. She is the author of a novel, *Class Notes* (1979), the editor of six books, and chair of the *Ms. Magazine* Board of Scholars and the National Council for Research on Women. Her collected essays, published widely in journals and reviews, are forthcoming in a volume entitled *Nancy Reagan Wears a Hat* (New York: Methuen, 1988).

"Grins . . . without the cat":
Introductory remarks on "The difference within"

Elizabeth Meese and Alice Parker
The University of Alabama

> Every woman I have ever loved has left her print on me, where I loved some invaluable piece of myself apart from me — so different that I had to stretch and grow in order to recognize her. And in that growing, we came to separation, that place where work begins. Another meeting.
>
> — Audre Lorde, "Epilogue," *Zami: A New Spelling of My Name*, p. 255.

> Difference is a form of *work* to the extent that it *plays* beyond the control of any subject: it is, in fact, that without which no subject could ever be constituted.
>
> — Barbara Johnson, *The Critical Difference*, p. xi

> The only thing that is different from one time to another is what is seen and what is seen depends upon how everybody is doing everything. This makes the thing we are looking at very different and this makes what those who describe it make of it, it makes a composition, it confuses, it shows, it is, it looks, it likes it as it is, and this makes what is seen as it is seen. Nothing changes from generation to generation except the thing seen and that makes a composition.
>
> — Gertrude Stein, "Composition as Explanation"

How do we articulate "the difference within," knowing full well the shifting ground on which we/you stand? Certainly we must abandon the dream of an outside or an inside that would provide firm footing, whether we call it "reality," "experience" or "consciousness." Things seen, as Stein observed, are not immutable, nor are words innocent (of earlier con-texts). Subject and object pronouns, the I and the You, however we may try to historicize or fix them, have a protean potential to change before our eyes, implicated in the act of reading, in the exchange between reader and writer, between lovers, the "separation where work begins." The symbolic contract or cultural codes into which we are inserted when we begin to speak and to read engage us in continuous acts of interpretation. The world offers us plots — events raveling and unraveling, conspiracies, moments to mark on a grid — which we spend our lives trying to assemble and read. Instead of providing the key, by means of and about which we might make comforting determinations, language as the arena of our work and play is a repertory of difference. Because determination depends upon identity, the notion of difference is one of the most vexing problems we confront in our efforts to make sense. It inheres in the fabric of language, identity, interpretation, texts, global politics, from the body to the body politic — South Africa, the Middle East, Latin America, the broken cities of the United States where bag ladies wander. Besides the differences we do not hear, there are those we do not have the courage to see.

Reality is stranger than fiction: the master narratives of history are written by politicians and ideologues rather than by poets who understand the ambiguities or literariness of verbal texts. Feminists have worked on methods of displacing hierarchical structures that are a functional correlative of the Name (*Nom/non*) of the Father. They have initiated practices of active listening to undermine hegemonic myths of homo-geneity. Deconstruction added a critique of logocentrism, bipolar reasoning and the metaphysics of presence. Other post-structuralisms helped us revise our understanding of the production of discourse, the constitution of the subject and subject position, and the political implications of the production and consumption of knowledge and texts. Has all of this permitted our thinking to become truly polysemic and multivalent or seriously altered the dialectical bent of most argument? In other words how do we revalue difference?

We can begin with the body. Its polymorphism, traditionally read as dimorphism, provokes in the context of difference rather curious claims —

Barbara Johnson comments in *The Critical Difference*: "If human beings were not divided into two biological sexes, there would probably be no need for literature. And if literature could truly say what the relations between the sexes are, we would doubtless not need much of it then, either" (13); and Robert Scholes observes in *Structuralism in Literature*: "But I believe (with the Marxists) that any method implies its ideology, and structuralism is no exception. Furthermore, it is precisely the ideology of structuralism that we need most desperately today. And this is where love comes in. It is in the differentiation of the sexes that we learn our earliest and deepest lessons about sameness and difference. Sexual differentiation is the basis, not only of our social systems, but of our logic as well. If there were three sexes, our computers would not have begun to think in terms of binary oppositions" (197). So we begin with the body, "his" body and "her" body, anatomically different, the difference "empirically" verifiable and demonstrable — male or female, rarely both. This is clear enough, logical even. But there are doubts — misidentifications, the occasionally veiled signifier that obscures decidability and produces the most unsettling misreadings of the anatomical dimorphism that is supposed to determine identity — for ourselves and others. Perception can be so inaccurate that black can "pass" for white. Or is the mis-nom-er in the category itself? Is the apprehension of any body free of semiotic coding? We wonder further if the male/female paradigm, as Scholes suggests, is the "necessary reason" that we structure our propositions logically and develop our arguments using rhetorical devices that reinforce causality and opposition? Or, in our search for origins, can we find an even more primal duality that served as a model for gender?

Questions of this kind are difficult to engage. Derrida, in remarking on this problem in *L'Oreille de l'autre*, finds himself mis-represented. As an epigraph for her part of the *Diacritics* dialogue with Peggy Kamuf, Nancy Miller offers the following translation of a passage from Derrida: "I will even risk affirming this hypothesis, that the very sex of the addresser receives its determination from the other. I mean that it is the other who will perhaps decide who I am, man or woman. And is it not the case [*Et cela ne se décide pas une fois*] that it is decided once and for all; but it can be decided like that some other time" (48) — the translator/critic or typographer converting his "*cela ne se decide pas*," it is *not* the case, to the more comforting "And is it not the case that it is decided once and for all" (Miller 48). Later, in the English edition of *The Ear of the Other*, Peggy Kamuf, serving this time as translator, continues the dialogue concerning the role of sexual difference and the signature within feminism by offering the following translation: "I will go so far as to risk this hypothesis: The sex of the addresser awaits its determination by or from the other. It is the other who will perhaps decide who I am — man or woman. Nor is this decided once and for all. It may go one way one time and another way another time. What is more, if there is a multitude of sexes (because there are perhaps more than two) which sign differently, then I will have to assume (*I* — or rather whoever says *I* — will have to assume) this polysexuality" (52). The speaker risks what the other will choose to assign, what designation this presumably uncontrollable addressee will elect, thereby placing the speaker's identity, his or her sense of self as subject, at risk, in the realm of the indeterminate or never finally decided. In this simple sequence lurks a mystery.

We experience a particular unease at confusion on the boundaries of gender — women with hair on their breasts and faces, and men without any; men who have breasts and women who don't. Such categorical transgressions go against the grain, producing discomfort that may modulate into horror. They violate the cultural imperatives that direct thought. Thus Derrida notes in "The Law of Genre," "As soon as genre [gender] announces itself, one must respect a norm, not cross a line of demarcation, one must not risk impurity, anomaly, or monstrosity" (203-4). Perhaps of all the monstrously "impure," the hermaphrodite is the most rarely mythologized, unlike the racially indeterminate "mulatta," constructed and romanticized by the white male. It takes the camera of a Brassai or a Diane Arbus to locate beauty in the transvestite or hermaphrodite.

Michel Foucault directs our attention to just such a problematic in the story of *Herculine Barbin, Being the Recently Discovered Memoirs of a Nineteenth-Century French Hermaphrodite*. The materials he assembles illuminate the compulsion of modern Western civilization to ascertain and attribute "a sex — a single, a true sex" (vii), even (and especially) in the ambiguous and complex case of the hermaphrodite. After the mid-nineteenth century, positivism and logocentrism combined to force a status on individuals who appeared to escape the binary logic of acceptable gender. Male family members, clerics, doctors and lawyers worked together to clarify the gender identity of the "pseudo" hermaphrodite: indeterminate or multiple gender would no longer be tolerated. Thus, a nineteenth-century doctor, following the elaborate chronicle of his patients' anatomical irregularities, collects this nugget of "truth" from his observations concerning specific cases of hermaphrodites: "This collection of observations would also show clearly — if it was still necessary to demonstrate it — the fact that hermaphroditism does not exist in man and the higher animals" (139). To secure certainty as to the one "true" identity and corresponding place in society, a sex was assigned at birth and could then be changed once at adulthood, before marriage. The hermaphrodite risked severe punishment, even execution, in the failure to stay put, to embrace the reduction of his or her two sexes (at least) to one and to forestall disruption in the discourse on sexuality and gender.

Such is the story of Herculine Barbin — sexed female at birth (1838), changing to male in 1860 in response to increasing awareness of her "difference" and her illicit love for another woman, committing suicide at thirty (1868). The collective aim of social institutions, as Foucault explains it, was to limit "the free choice of indeterminate individuals. Henceforth, everybody was to have one and only one sex. Everybody was to have his or her primary, profound, determined and determining sexual identity; as for the elements of the other sex that might appear, they could only be accidental, superficial, or even quite simply illusory" (viii). Foucault is quick to point out that, while we recognize the grim humor in such archaic and inhumane practices, we fail to see how these authorizing principles extend to current attitudes and practices. In our own way, we insist on an equally limited and limiting connection between sexual identity and truth: "We are certainly more tolerant in regard to practices that break the law. But we continue to think that some of these are insulting to 'the truth': we may be prepared to admit that a 'passive' man, a 'virile' woman, people of the same sex who love one another, do not seriously impair the established order; but we are ready enough to believe that there is something like an 'error' involved in what they do. An 'error' as understood in the most traditionally philosophical sense: a manner of acting that is not adequate to reality" (x). Herculine Barbin does im-pair the sacred order. Her assigned sex, given her position as a student in a girls' school, occasions the monumental blindness of nuns, teachers and schoolmates to "this puny Achilles hidden in their boarding school. One has the impression, at least if one gives credence to Alexina's story, that everything took place in a world of feelings — enthusiasm, pleasure, sorrow, warmth, sweetness, bitterness — where the identity of the partners and above all the enigmatic character around whom everything centered, had no importance. It was a world in which grins hung about without the cat" (xii). The memoir affirms society's stubborn insistence that gender ambiguity violates the truth. It likewise illustrates the persistence of the secret of sex as a mysterious enigma that escapes the viewer and the viewed, subject and object. The notion of a "true sex" operates at such a fundamental level that only by positioning one's self on the margins through violent removal, are we able to see and attack the pervasive encoding of sexuality through ideologies of gender, heterosexism, the family, the state and the church.

The relationship between sex (biological) and gender (cultural) was upstaged beginning in the seventeenth century by a growing concern with the rapport between gender and sexuality. Early medical research laid the groundwork for the construction of "woman" on the basis of bio-logical essentialism. The radical materialists of the eighteenth century, sensing the categorical limitations of such a system, insisted that reason had no sex. Still, bodies could not be permitted free ascription of gender or unbounded pleasure. As Foucault has shown, the discourse on sexuality emerged from the closed, confidential space of the confessional, whence it passed into the private space of the doctor's office and then into the consulting rooms of psychologist and psychoanalyst. Psychoanalysis actually invented a whole secret space, the unconscious, to contain the male libido and a "dark continent" which, surprise of surprises, was gendered female. What is the relationship between gender and sexuality, the unnamed term always festering below the surface, secreted away but with the power to displace any of the terms to which we come when we come to terms with the problem of gender? Here again the ideologies of heterosexism and the family would convince us that oppositional constructions of gender represent "nature."

Certainly there are other troublesome oppositions as well: white/black, rich/poor, center/margin, self/other, heterosexual/ homosexual. In fact, the homosexual, whose behavior cannot be accounted for in terms of anatomical irregularities (although even now genetic peculiarities have not been ruled out), and must therefore be understood entirely in legal and moral terms, exceeds the threat posed by the hermaphrodite who, in nineteenth-century France, was punished mainly when taken for a homosexual. The analysis of a term like gender demonstrates how easily the descriptive category, understood oppositionally, turns into the normative (right/wrong, normal/abnormal) and the evaluative (good/evil). With the force of a powerful magnetic field, the features of the positive pole coalesce — rich, white, male, normal, center, burying the opposition like some rebellious angel in a textual nether land.

The problematics of difference addressed in this volume represent the papers of The Thirteenth Annual University of Alabama Symposium on Literature and Language (1986). This work or play can be taken as part of an extended conversation within contemporary feminist criticism, formalized several years before in the Barnard conference (1979) and volume entitled *The Future of Difference* (1980), edited by Hester Eisenstein and Alice Jardine. The writers in the Barnard volume all appear to be female, which the preceding remarks would suggest matter little, and the conference occurs in a series designed to examine the issues and problems raised at the boundary of the women's movement and the academy — a paradigm of the outside in contest or relationship with the inside (ix). Eisenstein's introduction contains a useful account of how the concept of difference has functioned in various sites at different times. In the background of this exploration lay the need "to establish the validity of seeing women's experience as a generic phenomenon," the "liberating" move "toward a woman-centered perspective," permitting the view of difference within the category of woman as well as a view of "male experience as different, or even deviant" (xx). In her "Prelude" to the volume, Alice Jardine, the other editor/coordinator, observes, "At this point it seems impossible to think different without thinking it aggressively or defensively" (xxvi).

In assessing our position(s) the first consideration, as Gayatri Spivak reminds us, is that they bear the sign (stigma?) of the institution. What seems to be different between our difference and theirs, reflecting a decision we could make because the Barnard conference work enabled it, is that we purposefully chose to hear the other (Afro-American, Jew, WASP, Indian, male, female, Chilean exile, British Marxist, poet, critic, United States citizen, home owner, renter). We wanted to explore the productive capacity of what Jonathan Culler calls "the power of division" to create or mirror analytically and theoretically complex difference. Elaborating Eisenstein's overview, Michèle Barrett attends to the very instability of the concept of "difference" as an organizing principle; "difference" is shown to encompass sexual and experiential difference as well as textual and positional difference — and often the difference between and among these deployments of the term goes unspecified. Myriam Díaz-Diocaretz traces the elaborate web that forms the matrix of differences within which language and language users exist, exposing how the sign, its designations and attributions never neutral, is always already historically bounded and overdetermined, too ready for us as women who are both subject and object of the social text. Further, it is our sense now, almost ten years after the Barnard conference, that "the future of difference" is to think differences playfully and most of all productively, as an agenda for work and explosive discovery.

The critique of gender from whatever position instills terror in the powerful. Stimpson, citing a recent case in Tennessee, suggests that "policing" the boundaries between men and women is not an abstract, theoretical issue of limited interest to scholars; rather, concern over such regulation encompasses parents, first-graders, citizens' organizations and the courts. At stake are sacred cultural discourses (e.g. heterosexism), institutions (e.g. marriage) and epistemological assumptions that underpin gender boundaries. As Monique Wittig notes, if gender goes so does most of the research generated by the social science truth-producing machines (53). Perhaps the most incomprehensible crossover is that from masculine to feminine; at risk are erasure and invisibility, the election of silence. Who will choose to be the one without the phallus, without signifying capacity? Johnson claims in her introduction to *A World of Difference*, "To say, for instance, that the difference *between* man and woman is an illusion created by the repression of differences *within* each may to some extent be true, but it does not account for the historical exclusion of women from the canon. Jacques Derrida may sometimes see himself as *philosophically* positioned as a woman, but he is not *politically* positioned as a woman. Being positioned as a woman is not something that is entirely voluntary" (2). But what does it mean to be philosophically or politically positioned as a woman? What woman? Who is she and where is the position in which she stands? As soon as identity is sought the law of "difference" comes into play. These questions are the most vexing ones, perhaps because they demand the general answer, but this is precisely the kind of answer that cannot be given responsibly.

To further complicate our inquiry, as Derrida observes in the passage above, his sex is projected by (an)other. Indeed, in her response to the conference, Spivak reiterates Foucault's caution: one's subject position is not chosen; rather, it is assigned — one becomes a sign to be read by another. In an analysis of the "mulatto/a," which can be extended to the issue of gender as well as to the relationship between feminism and critical theory or Marxism and feminism and/or criticism, Hortense Spillers illustrates the limits of attribution: "The 'mulatto/a,' just as the 'nigger,' tells us little or nothing about the subject buried beneath them, but quite a good deal more concerning the psychic and cultural reflexes that invent and invoke them. . . . that in the *stillness* of time and space eventuated by the 'mulatto/a' — its apparent sameness of fictional, historical, and auto/biographical content — we gain insight into the *theft* of the dynamic principle of the living that distinguishes the subject from his/her subjectification." This transformation of the fluid, changing human being into the alienated stillness of the reified, historically bounded identity is, in itself, a process of subjugation and colonization. Such is the work of language and logic in the constitution of the subject: the positionality of the subject hides itself in synchronic opposition. And in another step-around, however provisional one's subject position may appear, this assignation, desired or not, carries with it, as Adrienne Rich has insisted, full political responsibility for one's location in the global scheme of things.

Pursuing a similar line of argument with regard to historiography, R. Radhakrishnan insists on feminism's need to tap "the Utopian radicality of post-structuralist difference and alterity," but at the same time to historicize the radicality through ideologically transformative action in specific moments in order to be politically effective. But the process of historicization that the marginal subject seems always to desire is not without danger. Historical narratives — even our own personal or collective history — conceal political maneuvers beneath their bland, neutral surface. One that is not hard to read is the ideology of masculinity embodied in the multinational military-industrial complex, which produces and polices a clear separation, where men are men and women are women. In her work on the glorification of the feminine by the World War I propaganda machines Jane Marcus exposes the plots authorizing (and recording as history) the production of motherhood and war. If interlocking cultural codes normalize the various positions that make up subjectivity, including gender, the political significance of dismantling such a discourse and of de-fusing (diffusing) its power should be evident.

In the interest of temporary alliances and coalitions, feminism and deconstruction, or perhaps more appropriately, deconstructions and feminisms, need to consider productive points of intersection and translation. The project of consensus building is difficult enough to "figure," as Catharine Stimpson demonstrates, and may indeed be a lost hope, when the notions of organic wholeness and representation, their production and value, are under attack. What kind of relationship is this which the speakers here figure, with an inevitable insistence, as "the marriage" of the two terms. What are they to one another? Do they need each other? Do their families approve? Are they a good couple? Will this "marriage" last? While these are important questions to ask, it is perhaps more pressing to inquire how it is that we have come to conceive of the relationship in these terms. In his attempt to rescue Toni Morrison's *Sula* from reductive readings by previous critics, Houston Baker helps us to rethink heterosexual coupling, marriage and motherhood according to Morrison's rendering of black village life. He reminds us that the most radical reading is not necessarily the most polyvalent, and encourages us to reconsider the categorical imperatives, boundaries and gaps which come into play when terms such as heterosexuality, lesbianism and motherhood are enlisted to define experience monolithically.

The dilemma feminists and deconstructors share is the problem of how to value the infinite play of difference even when it means both dislodging comforting boundaries and demarcating painful separations. A willingness to move from the center to unsettled and improvised subject positions in order to afford maximum freedom to other people(s) leaves us without the protectionism of boundaries that fix subjectivity on the one hand, and articulate our solidarity on the other. Monique Wittig's work on pronouns, notably the barred j/e in *The Lesbian Body*, is a useful model for uncovering the ideological assumptions concealed in subjectivity. Woman, like other colonized people, is wrapped in the master's gaze, the masquerade of femininity that covers "her" nakedness, in post-Freudian terms her "lack." In the monosexual discourse that inscribes this alterity, difference can have only a negative valence, cast out of the master's house into a mythic time/space, categorized as monsters, de-formed into sameness. The radically other will thence return only as a tres-passer, undercover, using the cover of femininity to slip (back) into the master's house, of gentility to slide into his bed, of virginity-virtue to gain admission into his church (where she will cluster, with her "kind," on the other side, in the back, in the balcony). Barred from active participation in the production of meaning, the mul(e)atta, as Spillers argues, is sterile, the fe-male does not en-gender, but simply carries the surrogate phallus to *term*, whence it will be inserted into the Name (*Nom/non*) of the Father. According to the system of ownership (property/propriety) in which the (male) subject sticks (his) phallus in the center, objects (women, children, colonized peoples) circulate by virtue of the exchange value assigned to them. The system depends on a philosophical idealism in the form of the mind-body split that informs Western metaphysics from Plato through Descartes in which the second term (body/desire) must be repressed in order to accord full signifying power to the first. Only a violent and consistent refusal of this totalizing power can decenter it. Let us not fool ourselves: we live in a continuous war zone; the profit motive of late capitalism respects no species nor indeed is the earth itself spared. The cat has long since evaporated into thin air, leaving only the grin.

As long as the mark of gender can be invoked to justify an obsessive preoccupation with same and other, the grins will continue to mock us. Thus the white South African male and his young son can use "colored" girls bathing in the river for rifle practice (Lelyveld, 208), not to mention the activities of the "security" police in Chile, and the Ku Klux Klan's justification of its racism and anti-semitism as protective of white womanhood. Why prefer the homogeneity of the melting pot to the rich and varied tones of the mosaic? The "unease" Spivak invoked when she was obliged to abandon her song and "say" what was "on her mind," is where we may draw a provisional boundary, where we may begin to read the differences within as they are written in that social contract which is nonetheless powerful for our never having signed it (Derrida 1984: 86-89). This collection is offered in the spirit of risky pursuits, tracing some of the obscure tracks of the elusive cat recalled in the grin.

REFERENCES

Derrida, Jacques. 1982. *L'Oreille de l'autre*. Montreal: V1b Editeur.

———. 1984. "voice ii." *boundary 2* (12): 76-93.

———. 1985. *The Ear of the Other: Otobiography, Transference, Translation*. Ed. Christie V. McDonald. Trans. Peggy Kamuf. New York: Schocken Books.

Foucault, Michel. 1980. Intro. to *Herculine Barbin, Being the Recently Discovered Memoirs of a Nineteenth-Century French Hermaphrodite*. Trans. Richard McDougall. New York: Pantheon Books.

The Future of Difference. 1980. Ed. Hester Eisenstein and Alice Jardine. Boston: G.K. Hall & Co.

Johnson, Barbara. 1980. *The Critical Difference: Essays in the Contemporary Rhetoric of Reading*. Baltimore and London: Johns Hopkins University Press.

———. 1987. *A World of Difference*. Baltimore and London: Johns Hopkins University Press.

Lelyveld, Joseph. 1985. *Move Your Shadow: South Africa, Black and White*. New York: Viking Penguin.

Lorde, Audre. 1982. *Zami: A New Spelling of My Name*. Trumansburg: The Crossing Press.

Miller, Nancy. 1982. "The Text's Heroine: A Feminist Critic and Her Fictions." *Diacritics* 12: 48-53.

Rich, Adrienne. 1986. "Notes Toward a Politics of Location." *Blood, Bread, and Poetry: Selected Prose, 1979-1985*, 210-31. New York: W.W. Norton.

Scholes, Robert. 1974. *Structuralism in Literature: An Introduction*. New Haven and London: Yale University Press.

Stein, Gertrude. 1962. *Selected Writings of Gertrude Stein*. Ed. Carl Van Vechten. New York: Vintage.

Wittig, Monique. 1975. *The Lesbian Body*. Trans. David Le Vay. New York: William Morrow.

———. 1981. "One is Not Born a Woman." *Feminist Issues* 1: 47-54.

Nancy Reagan wears a hat: Feminism and its cultural consensus

Catharine R. Stimson
Rutgers University

Like every great word, "representation/s" is a mess. A scrambled menu, it serves up several meanings at once. For a representation can be an image — be it visual, verbal, or aural. Think of a picture of a hat. A representation can also be a narrative, a sequence of images and ideas. Think of the sentence, "Nancy Reagan wore a hat when she visited a detoxification clinic in Florida." Or, a representation can be the product of ideology, that vast scheme for showing forth the world and justifying its dealings. Think of the sentence, "Nancy Reagan, in her hat, is a proper woman." In the past twenty years, feminist thinking about representation has broken apart, a fracture that reflects the larger collapse of a feminist cultural consensus. Some of the rifts have been thematic. What is to be represented? Others have been theoretical. What is the nature of representation itself? I wish to map these rifts, especially those in the United States, and to sight a new cultural consensus.

In the late 1960s, feminists began to share a cultural consensus about the representation of women and gender. Few who built up in that consensus were village idiots. Even without being semioticians, everyone more or less knew that the marriages between the signifier and the signified in that odd couple, the sign, were ones of convenience. Everyone more or less knew that the marriages between the sign and the referent, that hubbub out there, were also ones of convenience. Some survived; others were obsolete, cold, hostile, ending in separation or divorce. Everyone more or less knew that when I exclaimed, "Nancy Reagan wears a hat," it was easier for a fellow citizen of my linguistic community to understand me than for a stranger to do so. Nevertheless, the consensus also offered a rough, general theory of representation that extolled the possibility of a fit between "reality" and its "description" or "image".

Such a general theory framed the five terms of thc feminist cultural consensus. In brief, they were:

1. The dominant, and dominating, representations of women are misrepresentations. Often viciously misogynistic, such misrepresentations shoot and pop up in literature, the media, and the arts; history; philosophy; psychology and sociology; science; law; medicine; myth and religion; and everyday speech. These bad pictures of women are acts of both commission and omission. They both overtly lie, fabricate, and simply erase great realities, such as the presence of women in color. One great reason for the existence of misrepresentations is the fact that men have created and maintained them on the wholesale/holesale and retail/retale level. Having done so, men, like voyeuristic gods, like to gaze at their handiwork. Women then have a limited repertoire of responses. They can believe that they live in order to be gazed upon, in order to be an appearance, in life or in art. Femmes may arrange their chapeaus, for a walk or for a painting. At the same time, women gaze upon themselves in order to make sure they are keeping up appearances. As John Berger, the art critic, wrote in 1972, women must come to consider themselves both "...the surveyor and the surveyed" (46).

2. One of the great tasks of feminism — at once ethical, aesthetic, and educational — is to confront these misrepresentations. As the emotions of confrontation raced back and forth between cool disdain and hot anger, feminists were to engage in lots of activities:

a. *Expose* the mechanisms of misrepresentation. One of the reasons for the appeal of *The Second Sex* was the power of deBeauvoir's explanation of this machinery: men's desire for the Female Other.

b. *Restore* the past, write an accurate history of work, play, homes, arts, crafts, costumes. As the Sears Roebuck case was so painfully to prove, a new history was no mere "academic matter." Feminist historians could disagree, and a trial judge, in a court of law, could use the word of one, and not the other, in his decision.

c. *Generate* accurate representations for the present. Secular feminists would rewrite the body, self, intimacy, and communities. More theological feminists would re-represent the divine, using the materials of either traditional monotheisms or of unorthodox religions: witches, saints, spirits, or the black goddesses that Audre Lorde was to evoke in her poetry.

d. *Project* the future. Through science fiction, Utopias, and dystopias, feminists would render visible the invisibilities of time that might come.

Samuel R. Delaney, for example, in *Stars in My Pocket Like Grains of Sand* (1984), imagines a universe of galaxies that contain about 6,200 inhabited worlds. Despite a vast competition between kinship and sign systems, some of the worlds are domains of congenial diversity. Marq Dyeth, a homosexual space traveller, is the product of a rich "nurture stream." His genetic ancestry, which includes both humans and aliens, reconciles differences.

3. The representation of women had to become far, far more representative if it was to be real.[1] Slowly, grudgingly, a picture of woman gave way to pictures of differences among women that the body, sexuality, age, race, class, ethnicity, tribalities and nationalities had forged. These pictures did more than provide a rich variety of perspectives, of points of view. Far more painfully, they revealed women dominating other women; women using women as The Other; women finding other women revolting. Moreover, agreement about feminist issues did not insure agreement about other public issues. In 1970, Audre Lorde frankly, ruefully, sardonically, articulated that combination of unity and division. Her poem, "Who Said It Was Simple," was about a black feminist, in Nedicks, listening to the white feminists with whom she was to march talk about race. Later, in Alaska, a Tlingit woman, devoted to subsistence culture, wrote, in "Genocide," about another woman devoted to *her* ecological vision:

> Picketing the Eskimo
> Whaling Commission
> an over-fed English girl
> stands with a sign
> "Let the Whales Live."[2]

4. Feminists had a way of judging the legitimacy, accuracy, and cogency of the representations of women. Did they seem true to a woman's experience? Could a woman, would a woman, serve as a witness to that truth? If she could, the representation was acceptable; if not, not. Significantly, the title of an early, influential collection of literary essays was *The Authority of Experience: Essays in Feminist Criticism*. The trust in women's experience has been as common and as pervasive as city noise. To cite but one recent example. In January, 1986, PEN held an international congress in New York City on the theme of "The Writer and the State." The PEN president was that vortex of brilliance, adrenalin, and daffiness: Norman Mailer, never a man to duck out of his masculinity. During the course of the Congress, women protested the lack of women on its panels: only 2 of

24 panelists on a Monday; 6 of 28 panelists on a Tuesday. A seasoned group, the protesters included Margaret Atwood, Betty Friedan, Elizabeth Janeway, Cynthia Macdonald, and Grace Paley. Reporting on the event, Miriam Schneir commented: "There is no substitute for experience, and most of us had gone through all-too-similar experiences, all-too-many times before" (82).[3] Inseparable from such powerful strains in American culture as Protestantism and pragmatism, this term of feminism's cultural consensus praised the narratives of the personal event (the diary, letters, autobiography, self-portraiture, confession, biography) in writing, film-making, and art. Experience generated more than art; it was a source of political engagement as well. By 1972, the "roots of gender politics" were planted. Both men and women were to water them, but experience meant that those roots were stronger for women than for men. Ethel Klein, the political scientist, has concluded: "For women, feminism is part of their personal identity or consciousness. For men, feminism is an abstract issue of rights and obligations. Since both men and women come to feminism from different paths — personal experience in one case and ideology in the other — feminist views are likely to have a greater influence on women's political views than on men" (104).

5. As feminists were to insist upon the connections between the private and the public, the domestic and the political, the reproductive and the productive, so they were to see the buzzing inseparability of culture and politics. To be sure, the powerful tended to get the culture they wanted. A Mailer was the president of PEN. However, powerlessness need be no synonym for passivity. The powerless have a culture of resistance, which works through code; through the direct statement of polemic; and through the indirection of irony and parody. An "Unofficial White House Photograph," which several feminists like to send each other, shows Nancy and Ronald Reagan standing in front of a window with thick, blue curtains. Facing the camera directly, the First Couple smiles eagerly, ingratiatingly. Beyond the window looms the Washington Monument, a pointed phallic column. However, the column looks foggy, misty. Nancy's head (hatless) is placed on Ronnie's torso, clad in a business suit. Ronnie's head (hatless) is placed on Nancy's body, in beruffled blouse and skirt. Decapitation and transposition drain gender of their power — as a guillotine drains a head of blood and oxygen.

Happily, cultural work can change politics, particularly political attitudes, even if that change seems marginal and unpredictable. A recent study by Jones and Jacklin found that college students in an introductory course in Women's and Men's Studies (in California) "scored . . . lower in sexist attitudes towards women . . . at the end of the course" in comparison to a control group and in comparison to their own sexism at the beginning of the semester (13). The victory may seem small, but no victory is too small to dismiss.

In the late 1960s, United States feminists were developing a political as well as a cultural consensus. The political definition of "representation" differs from its cultural use. In politics, the word "representation" tends to mean, not a picture of the world, but a person who can legitimately picture the world of one group for and to another. Such a "representative" speaks for his or her constituency and acts on its behalf. Despite this wee semantic shift, the terms of the political consensus were often similar in kind to those of the cultural consensus. First, feminists believed in the possibility of just representations of "reality," even though political theory since Aristotle and political practice since Adam had unjustly misrepresented women through mistreating and excluding them. Moreover, women could and should be political participants. So doing, they could and should represent themselves and others. A woman could cast exemplary and surrogate votes. Finally, there was a cluster of women's issues that politics had to handle; that politics had to get a handle on. Feminism spoke for a set of legitimate political concerns. The National Women's Conference, in Houston, in November, 1977, articulated them. Months of raw politicking preceded the Conference, between social conservatives and feminists and among feminists. Only that politicking wrote a statement in support of women's studies. Only that politicking produced feminist unity in support of lesbianism. Still, the pressure cooker of the Conference did end with an agenda for feminist politics.[4] Moreover, the state, the federal government, supported the Conference. Washington and Houston served each other.

Like a contract, a consensus manages agreements. Of course, any consensus leaves some opinions out. The United States feminist political consensus omitted or feared certain ideological stances: Marxism and socialism, those demons of American politics; anarchism; the wilder poetries of radical cultural feminism, including the wimmyn's lyrics of lesbian separatism; and the explicit enemy of social conservatism. In Houston, *its* few believers in some state delegations stolidly refused to rise in support of even the blandest measures, such as equal access to credit. Since these excluded non-middles were mutually contradictory, they could not reach, or even imagine, an oppositional consensus, an agreement among outsiders. Moreover, since the feminist political consensus was incomplete, feminist strategies, within and outside of that consensus, were mutually inconsistent. No single representation of feminism could emerge. Media images of feminism boiled up the representational turmoil even more prettily. Contrast two images of feminists who care about peace. One is of the Committee on National Security. Formed in 1982, it has a large Advisory Board of prominent women. It organizes conferences, with female and male speakers, in hotels in Washington, D.C. on defense issues. The second is of a demonstration in March, 1980. A group, the "Spinsters," weaves a symbolic web, "with thousands of yards of colored yarns, threads and strings," around the Vermont Yankee Nuclear Power Plant in Vernon, Vermont (Reid 291-4).

The feminist cultural consensus was more spacious than the political one; more receptive to Marxism, socialism, and lesbianism. For the shapers of that cultural consensus could afford to be more aloof from the inhibitions of electoral politics, freer from the discipline of electoral politics, than the shapers of the political consensus. However, that very looseness helped to render the cultural consensus more vulnerable, more volatile. During the 1970s, five forces ripped and pulled at its fabric: (1) A revivified feminist interest in the specifically female; (2) A rambunctious radical conservatism; (3) Neo-conservatism (the N-Cs); (4) Neo-liberalism (the N-Ls); and, (5) In the mid and late-1970s, feminist post-modernism. Without appearing to think much about it at all, the first four agreed with the feminist consensus about the relationship of representation to reality. In its own way, each also burnished the idea that the maternal was special. "Motherhood" was a natural gift; source of identity; social role; and category of analysis. Together the first four forces endorsed a doubled set of traditional beliefs: in the mimetic power of languages to reproduce the world and in the mimetic power of the female to reproduce the species.

The fifth challenge, feminist post-modernism, had a sweeping theoretical interest in the presence and/or absence of the maternal in phallocentric discourse. However, post-modernism was also skeptical about the possibility of any reality beyond representation. Here the fun began. Among the provocative critics of the theory that representations could give us a picture of reality, could be "realistic," were feminist film critics and film-makers. They subverted the belief that film documentaries could ever tell us the truth (whatever *that* word meant) about women, even if other feminists directed those documentaries. For the very promise of the documentary — that it was a window on reality, that it showed us "real people" — was a lie. The job, then, of the film-maker was to produce avant-garde films that would reveal both the lies of the patriarchy and of the realistic, representational genres that both patriarchs and women had practiced (Kaplan 125-41).

Let me foreground, in turn, each of these five forces:

1. The feminist cultural consensus had tended to play down sex and gender differences, naturalized binary oppositions between female and male. Ethically, the consensus asked its practitioners to stop playing them out. The recognition of the amazing maze of differences among women, of the endless diversity of women's experience as historical agent and as signifier, helped to deconstruct the idea of a single and singular femaleness. If the woman reader was not the English daughter of the British Empire, Jane Eyre was far less apt to be the Exemplary Female Subject.

However, that wilder poetry of radical cultural feminism, spinning away in be/witching campsites at the margins of the consensus, sang of the female. Such music could appeal to lesbian and to heterosexual women alike. For the lesbian, the "female" was an erotic and psychological necessity; for the heterosexual woman, the "female" was a psychological core that might sustain her in a patriarchal society that constantly threatened to ream out real women. The most responsible for the theoreticians of the female insisted that a political will accompany sexual and psychological freedom. In 1977, in "Natural Resources," Adrienne Rich rewrote one of her earlier poems, "Diving Into the Wreck." Mourning the loss of the dream of man as brother; attacking the reality of man as killer, as "blood-compelled exemplar..."; celebrating women and their capacity to transform scraps into patchwork, Rich ends:

> I have cast my lot with those
> who age after age, perversely,
>
> with no extraordinary power,
> reconstitute the world. (67)

A focus on the female, then, could spread out luxuriously. It prepared the non-feminist public for Carol Gilligan's *In a Different Voice* in 1982. After Gerda Lerner and her adaptations of Mary Beard (*Black Women in White America*, 1972; *The Female Experience*, 1977); after Alice Walker

("In Search of Our Mothers' Gardens," 1974), people could ask about a woman's historical tradition. After Jean Baker Miller (*Toward a New Psychology of Women*, 1976), people could ask if women had not developed a different, and precious, set of values. After Jessie Bernard (*The Future of Motherhood*. 1974), Adrienne Rich (*Of Woman Born*. 1976), or Nancy Chodorow (*The Reproduction of Mothering*. 1978), people could ask about the place and representation of the mother. They helped to supplement the obsession of psychoanalysis with mothers and sons with an interest in mothers and daughters.[5] After Hélène Cixous and other French writers, people could ask about a female language, that notable "écriture féminine." French theory helped, too, to conjoin the female with pleasure. It replaced the image of the well-dressed lady with that of the laughing Medusa of Cixous. A woman no longer hid her hair beneath her hat and clothes. Her hair flowed out, like stars strewn across the sky. A woman's lips were no longer pinned shut. They were open; the cries that poured forth were joyous, bliss-ridden. Cixous, however, was tricky. For she inscribed two possibilities. For she apparently promised both a "female" language, from the body, that only women might write, in the white ink of the mother's milk, and a "feminine" language, from a place in the symbolic contract, that both men and women might exude.

2. Radical conservatism was inseparable from the career of Phyllis Schlafley. Women were wives and mothers; men were their husbands and benign rulers. In 1972, she formed STOP-ERA, one of several groups like Happiness of Motherhood Eternal (or HOME) or Humanitarians Opposed to Degrading Our Girls (HOTDOG). Radical conservatism was potent because it could summon up, separately or together, a number of forces. It could call on the institutional power and psychological authority of monotheistic religions, particularly Christianity. Conservative Christianity proclaimed both that the family man's word was law and that the Word was Law. Reassuringly connecting language and moral absolutes, it provided an iron, but never ironic, stability. Unfortunately, the general secularism of the feminist cultural consensus prevented it from sufficiently offering feminist theology as a counter-practice, as a counter-weight, to patriarchal beliefs. Radical conservatism could also appeal to fears: to the fears of women that they would be vulnerable and helpless if men did not protect them economically; to the fears of men that they would be vulnerable and helpless if women did not submit to them; and to the fears of both men and women that the world would be wholly cruel, wholly pitiless, if it had nei-

ther havening homes nor nurturing mother figures. Finally, radical conservatism benefited from defense mechanisms against any unconventional or impermissible sexual desires, including a severing of femininity and maternity.

3. In 1972, too, Midge Decter published a feisty, but yet sniveling, little polemic: *The New Chastity and Other Arguments Against Women's Liberation*, a founding text of neo-conservative thinking about women (the N-Cs). Decter likes some women. She dedicates her book to her mother, "who made being a woman seem such a worthy adventure"; to Sherry, who made the best jokes; and to Jacqueline, "who scatters blessings," an unwitting prophet of post-modernism. For Decter, these women are all that feminists are not: familial; happy and cheerful; giving and generous. *The New Chastity* begins with a sarcastic paraphrase of *The Feminine Mystique*. Intellectually, Decter's feminists, symptoms of the parlous condition of the American Mind, refuse to see several truths: the truth that nature wants women to be heterosexual mothers; the truth that sex is harder for men than for women; the truth that women already have equality and justice; the truth that marriage is not misery and "shitwork," but women's desire. Decter states firmly, "...the plain unvarnished fact is that every woman wants to marry." (p. 142) Emotionally, Decter's feminists are timid boobies, fearful of the struggle that public success entails, self-pitying and self-hating. Feminists are "little girls." Thank no heavens for little girls.

Decter has been the Grand Mummy for a corps of junior female N-Cs. Unlike the social conservatives, Decter's Daughters accept the fact that women, even wives, can work. They can even do intellectual work. They can publish in *Public Interest*, *Commentary* and *The New Criterion*. However, Decter's Daughters have three, interlocking disagreements with feminists. First, these N-Cs trust the market far more than feminism usually does. They distrust any shaking of the market's invisible hand, a shaking that they believe advocates of comparable worth dangerously desire. As a result, N-Cs attribute women's economic position to a historical, and legitimate, alliance between market forces and women's choices, not to discriminatory practices. Second, N-Cs are suspicious of any analysis that speaks of the "patriarchy," "male hegemony," "male dominance," or "gender inequity." Often bland and casual about men's power over women, the N-Cs find feminism grim and paranoid about the social relations of the sexes. Finally, the N-Cs believe that the word "family" applies only to those clusters of intimacy that blood or law creates. Far less cordial to different forms of the family and of intimacy than the feminist cultural consensus was, N-Cs valorise bourgeois family forms and their construction of the maternal role.

Vigorously, Decter's Daughters scrub away at Decter's Feminists. In an article about comparative worth, Rachel Flick admits that those tiresome feminists have at last recognized that sexual differences do exist. But guess what they want now? They want the market to be "nice," to conform to feminine values. They are incapable of accepting the reality that the market has to be "efficient," to act on masculine values.[6] In a review of an edition of essays of feminist criticism by Elaine Showalter, Carol Iannone excoriates her subject. Feminists, obsessed with women's weakness, have "...an extraordinarily withered view of feminine history." They are too perverse even to realize that literature can transcend "...the ordinary life of their times" and address that Mr. Chips of metaphysics: "universal truths." Feminists violate "common sense and scholarly standards." Why, then, have their representations of women become a part of the academy? Because weak-kneed, weak-willed administrators have "capitulated" to feminist critics. In effect, feminist critics have, yes, castrated our educators.[7]

4. In 1983, Judith Stacey incisively isolated a complicated class of ideas that she called "conservative feminism."[8] She located its origins in the late 1970s in the work of Alice Rossi, Betty Friedan, and Jean Bethke Elshtain. Although Stacey praised "conservative feminism" for forcing feminists to think again about intimacy, equality, child development, and heterosexuality, she found the turn towards timidity dangerous. For "conservative feminism" repudiates the sexual politics of the 1960s and 1970s that called for the reconstruction of both sex and gender. Instead, "conservative feminism" celebrates the family and biological motherhood. It scolds feminists for struggling against male domination and deflecting our attention from other questions.

Neo-liberal thinking about women (the N-Ls) are the partners and descendants of such conservative feminists. The N-Ls attempt to mediate among all feminists, radical conservatives, and the N-Cs. Frightened by the difficulties of the feminist political consensus, such as the 1982 defeat of the ERA, the N-Ls position themselves in what they hope will be a new political center. Unlike the N-Cs, the N-Ls do not sneer at feminism. Instead, their responses are ambivalent. On the one hand, the N-Ls can call themselves feminists; can associate themselves with the movement; can announce feminist credentials. They are far more supportive of abortion rights than radical or neo-conservatives. I have more in common with them than I would with a Decter Daughter. On the other hand, the N-Ls disapprove of much of the movement to which they give some loyalty. Although they dislike radical conservatism, the N-Ls tend to attribute its rise, in part, to the strategic errors of feminism.

The N-Ls now have at least two tactics for distancing themselves. First, they proclaim their sorrow that feminism has gone astray. If women of color had to correct an obvious racism in the feminist cultural and political consensus, the N-Ls point to a far less obvious indifference to ordinary women, especially to heterosexual mothers. If women of color want feminism to be more progressive, the N-Ls want it to be more "realistic" about the "average woman's" daily life. This means realizing that the average woman (that sturdy fiction) wants to belong to a "conventional" family — even if she is a part of the public labor force. To help her, the N-Ls call for "protective legislation" for mothers and (heterosexual) families.

The second N-L strategy is to ignore much of what feminism has actually done. Seeking both originality and the publicity that feeds on originality, the N-Ls erase the complexities and accomplishments of the movement they half-embrace. They act as if they were among the first to discover the values of pay equity, or decent child-care policies, or that old war horse, flexi-time. Calling for realism, the N-Ls deal in half-truths.[9]

5. In 1974, Juliet Mitchell, in *Psychoanalysis and Feminism*, signaled the redemption of psychoanalysis as, at the very least, a tool for the exploration of the unconscious and as an explanation of the construction of subjectivity and of a subject's sense of sex and gender. Could we, for example, see Nancy Reagan, in her hat, as a phallic mother? During the 1970s, too, European thinking about ideology, language, and interpretation began to intersect with strains of United States feminist theorizing. It became a matter for meaning that Roland Barthes had published "The Death of the Author" and Mary Ellmann *Thinking About Women* in the same year (1968). In 1979, the Barnard College Scholar and the Feminist Conference, "The Future of Difference," brilliantly presented this swirling confluence of revisionary psychoanalysis, European post-structuralism, and feminism: feminist post-modernism.

Like the feminist cultural consensus, feminist post-modernism tended to watch for the differences among women that history had created rather than for a female difference that history washes over. Indeed, far more radically than the consensus, feminist post-modernism doubted the "naturalness" of any sex differences. Sex and gender were a linguistic affair. Like the consensus, feminist post-modernism asked what politics its theories might entail? If a particular theory seemed persuasive, what practice would it demand? In brief, what might an idea mean for feminism? For an end to social, cultural, psychological and sexual structures of domination?[10]

Despite these virtues, the feminist post-modernists have stirred and troubled the feminist cultural consensus. Adding to the discomfort were the difficulties of the feminist political consensus: the vitriol and viciousness of anti-abortion forces; the loss of the support of the presidency; the defeat of the Equal Rights Amendment; the inability to stop the obscene increase in the pauperization of women and children. To a member of the feminist cultural consensus, post-modernists liked really strange, far-out cultural events. They preferred Gertrude Stein to Charlotte Brontë; Mary Kelly to Georgia O'Keeffe. More important, though in a feedback loop with this aesthetic preference, were the questions the post-modernists were asking about representational codes; their often abstract interrogations of signifying practices as the matrix of meaning and subjecthood; and their fascination with that old boy network, the phallus. Describing her project, Lisa Tickner writes: "It was psychoanalysis that permitted an understanding of the psycho-social constructions of sexual difference in the conscious/unconscious subject. The result was a shift in emphasis from equal rights struggles in the sexual division of labor and a cultural feminism founded on the reevaluation of an existing biological or social femininity to a recognition of the processes of sexual *differentiation*, the instability of gender positions, and the hopelessness of excavating a free or original femininity beneath the layers of patriarchal oppression." (19)

The theory that representational machineries were reality's synonyms, not a window (often cracked) onto reality, eroded the immediate security of another lovely gift of Western humanism: the notion of a conscious self that generates texts, meaning, and a substantial identity; a notion that a recent Koren cartoon wistfully parodies. The scene is a birthday party. Like all of Koren's people, the party-goers have pop eyes, armadillo noses, and spiky hair (except for men going bald). Balloons litter the ceiling, presents the floor. Around the table sit eight little girls, some in paper hats, staring at a happy Birthday Girl and at her cake with six candles. Smiling watchfully and sweetly, Mother holds the back of Birthday Girl's chair. Holding a tray full of glasses and bowls of ice cream, Dad stands at attention. Ah, sighs the Birthday Princess, "I'm able to experience the totality of who I am!" (20)

Poor Birthday Princess! For what if her identity were not such a piece of cake? What is Western humanistic notions of the self were a snaring delusion? What if we are inextricably caught under the net of our own concepts? What if we thrash within the "hermeneutic circle?" As a result, we may never be aware enough of our own perspectives to use them to interpret anything reliably. Moreover, what if the unconscious writes our scripts? If so, is it not vain and silly to think that we know what the "self" is? And why do we insist on an integrated self that is the center of the world? What if we are fragmented, decentered? Can we not be post-modern enough to accept, even to enjoy, this?

One example of the move from the feminist cultural consensus to post-modernism. In Western thought, the metaphor of the "cave" in Plato's *Republic* (Book VII) is an influential trope for the ascent to reason. In the cave, we see only shadows. Freed from the prison of the cave, we can stagger outside and see the sun of truth. However, an alternative myth of the cave also exists, that of the crevice in which the Cumaen Sybil dwells and exhales prophetic speech.

In the Romantic period, in 1818, Mary Shelley visited Italy with Percy Shelley. They visited Naples and the landscape of the Sybil. In 1826, a widow, Mary Shelley wrote her novel, *The Last Man*. In an "Introduction," her narrator elaborates on that autobiographical fact. She tells of going to Naples in 1818 on a beautiful December day with a companion. They enter the Sybil's cave. They go deeper and deeper until they grope their way into a room with a stone bench. Its floor is strewn with leaves and bits of bark. The narrator's companion sees that writing, ancient and modern, covers them. From time to time, the two return to the cave to read the inscriptions. After her companion's death, the narrator forms her story from those inscriptions. She adds to, adapts, and translates them.

Next, in the New Feminist period, in 1979, the critics Sandra M. Gilbert and Susan Gubar took on the metaphor of the cave. Powerful shapers of the feminist cultural consensus, they saw the cave as a representation of women in patriarchy. Her "cave-shaped anatomy is her destiny." However, women can alter that destiny. Sadly, Mary Shelley only partly realizes the power that might have been hers. Anxious about entering culture, she lets her male companion identify the writing on the leaves. Yet, to her glory, she stitches together the "dismembered, dis-remembered, disintegrated" pieces of her "precursor's art" (94-99).

Then, in 1985, a poststructuralist critic, Toril Moi, approached Gilbert and Gubar, among others. Moi is a smart, hard-edged intellect. Why, she asks sardonically, do Gilbert and Gubar insist that the woman artist *gather up* the Sibyl's leaves? Why do they want a "whole text"? An organic representation? Is this, ironically, not a phallic desire? Why can't Gilbert and Gubar approve of disconnections? The post-structuralist adds: "Parallel to the wholeness of the text is the wholeness of the woman's self: the integrated humanist individual is the essence of all creativity. A fragmented conception of self or consciousness would seem to Gilbert and Gubar the same as a sick or dis-eased self" (66).

Heel, feminist physicians, and heal thyselves.

The feminist cultural consensus, that contract about opinions, is beyond restoration. Its practitioners are too numerous, too diverse, and too varied for one agreement to accommodate all the theories, ideas, and perceptions by and about women in the post-modern world. The question is not how to paste and staple a consensus together again, but rather, how to live culturally and politically with fragmentation. Happily, United States public opinion routinely, if casually, supports feminist issues. For example, a recent profile of college undergraduates claimed that about 92% presented themselves as liberal, middle of the road, or only moderately conservative. Over 75% thought a woman should have "freedom of choice" about abortion. A majority of men, about 60%, but a minority of women, 40%, thought that "pornographic materials should be legally available to adults." Such agreement gives feminists a chance, despite radical and neo-conservative rantings, despite neo-liberal pressures, to think things through. (Sadly, the number of undergraduates who wanted to go on to graduate or professional education in women's studies, like the number who wished to do so in botany, geography, and the foundations of education, was too small to be measured.)[11]

At and in this moment, two responses to fragmentation are unacceptable. The first is to imitate the great male modernists and lament fragmentation; to speak, as Hardy did, of the "ache of modernism"; to grieve, as Yeats did, that the "center will not hold"; to picture, as Eliot did, the world as a wasteland, as heaps of filthy shards, chips with neither fish nor mister. The second unacceptable response is to howl, not at the fathers, but at the daughters, at the feminist post-modernists; to accuse them of burrowing up to male intellectual masters, of betraying their political commitments, of writing obscurely, of being ungrateful.

For the feminist post-modernists have gifts for the feminist cultural consensus. Even if they prove to be theoretically inadequate or incomplete, their writing helps everyone cultivate open, subversive spaces within cultures, including feminist cultures. Those acts of cultivation help weed out conformity; repetitions of outworn ideas; jejune, if seemingly satisfactory, assumptions about the reflectiveness of our representations of the world; and presumptions about the value of monolithic generalizations about the female.

A shot of post-modernism might have alerted feminists to some of the dangerous complexities in two contemporary fights in which a cultural consensus broke down, and did so in the realm of politics, in legislatures and courts. There, people had to choose among and about representations of women. Often, these legislators, judges, and juries were not accountable to, and for, feminism. One struggle, the more serious, has been over pornography and over laws that would enable women to declare a pornographic image a violation of her civil rights. In this, I have opposed such laws and supported the Feminist Anti-Censorship Task Force (FACT). I signed on to the April 8, 1985 "Amici Curiae" brief in the Indianapolis case (American Booksellers Association, Inc. v. William H. Hudnut III).[12] Like other FACTionalists, I have abhorred both the representations of violence against women and a struggle within feminism about pornography that has distracted our attention from the issues of: "...real equality, real power — strengthened civil rights legislation, affirmative action to achieve economic parity, improved education, access to public office, better services for victims of violence and abuse" (Duggan and Snitow 65).

In part, this struggle within feminism has been about the nature of the representation of female sexuality. Should feminists picture women's bodies as exploited, at risk, at danger, or should feminists "put forward a politics that resists deprivation and supports pleasure"? (Vance 23)[13] Simultaneously, are women to be pictured as wholly exploitable, delicate, wholly at danger, or are they capable of resistance and strength? In part, the struggle has been about the relationship of the state to the production of images. When can the state, whether an individual citizen sets it in motion or not, control that production? In part, the struggle has been about the ways in which we read, in which we interpret imagery. Can the law spot a representation of "sexual subordination"? Can one image be extracted from a narrative as a whole? A tag from a syntagmatic process? In part, the struggle has been the relationship of images to behavior and about the ability of a positivist social science to graph that relationship? Does an image directly influence behavior? If so, how? Or, as the "Amici Curiae" brief stated, correctly: "Sexual imagery is not so simple to assess. In the sexual realm, perhaps more so than any other, messages and their impact on the viewer or reader are often multiple, contradictory, layered and highly contextual" (9).

Finally, in part, the struggle has been about the ability of one woman to speak for all women; for one woman to become a common voice; for the deep structure of one throat. On January 2, 1986, Andrea Dworkin testified at the New York City Hearings of the Attorney General's Commission on Pornography. Like Catharine A. MacKinnon, Dworkin has defined and passionately supported anti-pornography legislation. Dworkin's speech was well-crafted and rhetorically shrewd. Identifying herself with all women; picturing women as tortured and men as torturers and rapists, she summoned the Commission to listen to women, to believe them, and to relieve them of their gags and bonds. She was, as well, a voice for other victims who could not be heard.[14] Other commissioners, accepting the truth of that self-representation, then expressed a debt to her for inspiring them to battle, as if her voice, at once individual and collective, had caused them to march out, like French soldiers behind St. Joan.

My second case is the Ginny Foat trial. Let me admit that I wrote a skeptical review of *Never Guilty. Never Free*, her autobiography.[15] Born into an Italian, working-class family, Foat ultimately became president of California NOW. In 1983, she was charged with murder. Apparently, another NOW member helped to arouse the charging legal authorities. The only evidence was the "word" of a brutal, alcoholic ex-husband, Jack Sidote. Reasonably, a jury found her innocent. For feminists, the Foat case involved the survivability of two Utopian representations of women: that they are essentially innocent, essentially good, and that they are, like the women in violent pornography, essentially victims, an image that the image of innocence makes logically necessary.

In the media, in court, and in her autobiography, Foat incorporates these representations into her self-dramatization. Submerging her will, willfulness, and strength, she asks other feminists to believe her because life and Sidote have battered her. Yet, the gaps in her narrative are holes into which doubt must flow. Nevertheless, like Dworkin, she claims the right to speak for all women. The jurors who freed her apparently did so, not because she had suffered under patriarchy, but because they found "reasonable doubt" about her guilt, a patriarchal legal standard. Yet, after her trial, Foat declared the verdict a victory for all women. "Well," a female juror said, "I didn't elect her to speak for me" (Hawkes, 363).

Another gift of the feminist post-modernists is the urgency of their desire to construct sophisticated new ways of thinking about the subject and her society. Unfortunately, feminism lacks any organization (a sweetly old-fashioned word) within which to test, refine, and revise those new ways. Instead, feminism has a number of cultural committees, organizations, caucuses, and disciplines. Even within them, feminists struggle to consider issues of gender, race, and class together. In the same way, although feminisms together represent a national movement, they have no national party. A consensus emerges haphazardly.

We badly need a group that would call together members of these committees, organizations, caucuses, and disciplines. I am aware of at least three weaknesses in such a proposal: the Utopianism of my faith in the ability of people to deal with the mutual suspicions that swirl around any meeting room, any gymnasium and symposium, be it spatial or electronic; next, the inadequacy of any cultural theory that fails to ask how it might influence television, the most powerful machinery of representation in the West; and finally, the limit of any cultural theory that has no accompanying social theory, no real connections between culture and society. Weak though it is, my proposal imagines how players (of all genders) might juxtapose perspectives to lace together a new, perpetually provisional feminist cultural consensus.

As Donna Haraway suggests, such a group, chary of any theory of a group's essential unity, would set up coalitions. It would search for affinities, not for a common identity (73). Equally chary of a dominant discourse, such a group would trust oppositional viewpoints, like those of women of color. Adapting the legacy of the post-modernist Virginia Woolf of *Three Guineas* and her Society of Outsiders, Haraway fictionalizes a Sister Outsider. With her other sisters, she speaks an "infidel heteroglossia" (101). Given its multiplicity of oppositional voices, such a group would, I suggest, have to develop an ethics of correction; an ethics that delights, not in the imposition of "right," but in charity of response, clarity of speech, and self-consciousness about principle and practices.

With such an ethics, my group might dwell within theoretical questions that affect our daily lives, as quantum waves do space. If we cannot represent women as total victims, how do we represent pain without blaming the victim? If post-modernism has erased the humanistic picture of the coherent, individual self, what will justify an ethics of respect for the individual person? Without believing in totalities again, can we have communal ties other than a joy in opposition? Can an ethics of correction permit both feminists and radical conservatives to speak together? The last such experiment, between some radical feminists and some social conservatives, did end up with that anti-pornography legislation.

Despite that coalition, feminists might have a special aptitude for such an "infidel heteroglossia." This is not because of some "female" talent for balancing marginality and affiliation, but because of the moral and strategic necessities that have forced feminists to practice what I call "herterogeneity." Feminists have begun with the obvious acknowledgement of some sexual difference between female and male, of some difference between the penis and the vagina. They have recognized gender differences between feminine and masculine.[16] However, with the corrections of feminist post-modernism, they have begun to graph how pervasively the structures of discourse have boxed up sexual difference and jockeyed to create gender difference. Because, too, feminists are dwelling with differences among women, among the many interpretations of "her," they have instructed themselves in living among differences, among many genes and genera. Such lessons have warned feminists of both monolithic and dualistic thinking; of too great a trust in the article "the" and the conjunctions "either" and "or." Herterogeneous thinking prefers the article "a" and the conjunctions "both/and."

The need even to imagine such a conference center for the practice of a new feminist cultural consensus, of herterogeneity, marks a movement in which boundaries are dissolving. The turmoil over the older feminist cultural consensus is a synecdoche as well for a larger cultural moment in which old, often dear borders are going, going, but not quite gone. Indeed, the radical conservatives, the N-Cs, and, to a degree, the N-Ls, are hammering in supports for the shaky fence posts and stakes. Contradictions about the "appropriate" representations of gender, that boundary between female and male, abound. A county in Tennessee adopts a first-grade textbook. It shows a girl named Pat and a boy named Jim reading and cooking raisin pudding, ham, and tomato on toast. Jim cooks before Pat, earlier than Pat *and* in front of Pat. Appalled, Robert B. Mozert, Jr., and his colleagues in COBS (Citizens Organized for Better Schools) sue the schools.

The image of Jim cooking before Pat shows first-graders an absence of God-given roles for the two sexes. Mozert, Jr., and COBS feel the schools are promoting a religion: secular humanism. So doing,they are violating constitutional provision after constitutional provision.[17]

Contradictions among representations of gender also tumble over each other. On the front page of the *New York Times* during a week in March, 1986, are three photos: (1) To the upper left are two married couples in evening dress: Ronald and Nancy Reagan (hatless) of the United States; Brian and Mila Mulroney of Canada. A president and a First Lady, a Prime Minister and a First Lady, are being ceremonial, which now entails being cordial. (2) To the upper right are two men in business suits. A representative of the Phillipine Commission investigating the Marcos billions is getting documents from a representative of the United States government. There is no immediate image of President Cory Aquino. (3) Down the page, in the center, so that the three pictures form a female "V," is Sarah Ferguson, then betrothed to Prince Andrew of England. Male photographers with cameras surround her. Embodying Berger's thesis, they are looking at her, fixing her. Then, in Section C, on the first page, on the bottom left, is a headline, "Women Now the Majority in the Professions." The story runs over to another page (C-10). It reports that although an earnings gap still exists between men and women, women have just become the majority, overall, in the professions. With the story is a mock engraving. Four women, in Victorian dress, are doing modern and post-modern jobs: architect, scientist, computer specialist, doctor. Holding newspaper is an isolated man. He might be shy. He might be patronizing. Furtively, he watches them.

Such a landscape of contradictions demonstrates the "Cagney and Lacey" syndrome. In the TV show, Cagney and Lacey are friends. They work in that citadel of masculinity: the police station. However, both women are white. Moreover, they work among men. Other than Cagney and Lacey, the show has very few women.[18] A synecdoche of this contradiction is the fact that Cagney is single; Lacey is married. Between them, the working couple practice domestic alternatives.[19]

As the mass media seek to contain this tumult, feminists both profit from and deconstruct it. They push and prod at the picture. What, a feminist might ask, would Cagney and Lacey be like if they were active lesbians? If only one of them were an active lesbian? What if she were to leave the precinct and drop by what was once the Duchess Bar in Sheridan

Square for a beer? However, simply because such explosive feminist activity can happen, it neither exempts feminisms, nor renders them immune, from internalizing the contradictions that pulsate around us. Nor does such explosive activity keep feminists like me from having to manage still another contradiction: internalizing a belief in the worth of the hurly-burly competitive marketplace of ideas even while calling for representative groups that would soothe that competition through a conversation that would button up the homicidal thrusts of competition.

Eventually, conversations must end in action; remonstration in demonstrations, and not simply the demonstrations of logical proof, even if we believe that our remonstrations have been in parts and partial. We need, too, a consensus about what a feminist switching point might be, a switching point when we must move through theory to practice. I believe that we reach such a switching point when we confront survival issues for women and children, for almost any woman, and certainly for any child. Survival issues are food, water, shelter, health, education, and protection from any domestic or state violence. In *The Brothers Karamazov*, Ivan declares that he cannot believe in God because he sees children being beaten on earth; because he has watched parents force a 5-year-old girl to eat shit. (Book V, Chapter IV, "Rebellion.") Both cultural and political feminism began in the refusal to accept women's pain, the sound of "hurt" in "herterogeneity." Now, a refashioned cultural and political feminist consensus might see a switching point between speech and act in the arduous toil for survival of women and children.

Would Nancy Reagan doff her hat in the direction of this representation of rectitude?

NOTES

I gave earlier versions of this paper at the Barnard College Scholar and the Feminist Conference, March 22, 1986, and the Seminar on Sex, Gender, and Consumerism, New York University Institute for the Humanities, October, 1986. A companion essay, "Woolf's *Room*, Our Project: Feminist Criticism Today," is in preparation for publication.

1. An irrefutable analysis of the intellectual price feminism has paid for forgetting women of color is Maxine Baca Zinn, Lynn Weber Cannon, Elizabeth Higginbotham, and Bonnie Thornton Dill, "The Costs of Exclusionary Practices in Women's Studies," *Signs: Journal of Women in Culture and Society* 11(1986): 290-303.

2. Nora Dauenhauer, "Genocide." *That's What She Said: Contemporary Poetry and Fiction by Native American Women* ed. Rayna Green (Bloomington, Indiana: Indiana University Press, 1984), 69.

3. See, too, PEN American Center, *Newsletter*, No. 58 (Spring 1986).

4. Agenda items were: arts and humanities; battered women; business; child abuse; child care; credit; disabled women; education; elective and appointive office; employment; Equal Rights Amendment; health; homemakers; insurance; international affairs; media; minority women; offenders; older women; rape; reproductive freedom; rural women; sexual preference; statistics (the need to have information); women, welfare, and poverty. See National Commission on the Observance of International Women's Year, *The Spirit of Houston: An Official Report to the President, the Congress and the People of the United States* (Washington, D.C.: March, 1978).

5. Marianne Hirsch, "Review Essay: Mothers and Daughters," *Signs* 7(1981): 200-22, remains a solid survey of this 1970s development. The academic interest in mothering in the 1970s anticipated an increased practice of mothering in the 1980s. In 1976, only 58.3% of the women in the cohort then in their 20s had at least one child. In 1986, 78.2% of the women in that same cohort had at least one child.

6. See, too, Rachel M. Flick. "When Do Parents Grow Up?". *Public Interest* (1982): 68. 115-120.

7. Carol Iannone, "Feminism and Literature". *The New Criterion* 4 (1982): 83-87; Elizabeth Lilla, in "Who's Afraid of Women's Studies?" *Commentary* 81 (1986): 2, is more generous. She admits that women's studies comes in many forms, "...from serious works of social history to overtly political ideology"(53). But her story about attempts at Kenyon College to incorporate the new scholarship about women's studies into its curriculum tells the familiar N-C story about morally feeble administrators and intellectually feeble feminists who are still tough enough to want to indoctrinate the academy.

8. Although I am more sanguine about contemporary feminism than she; although I am more grateful to Jean Elshtain's warnings about the state than she, I am in debt to Stacey. For my own response to Friedan, *The Second Stage*, see my review in *Ms.*, "From Feminine to Feminist Mystique," (December 1981), 16, 18, 21.

9. I owe the phrase "neo-liberal thinking about women" to Sara Lennox, during a seminar I conducted at the University of Massachusetts/Amherst, November, 1985. Sylvia Hewlett. *A Lesser Life: The Myth of Women's Liberation in America* (New York: William Morrow and Co., 1985) exemplifies ambitious, somewhat historically suspect, N-L thought. See, too, Jan Rosenberg, "Hard Times for the Women's Movement," *Dissent* (Fall 1986), 401-405.

10. Conference papers are in *The Future of Difference*, ed. Hester Eisenstein and Alice Jardine (Boston: G.K. Hall, 1980; New Brunswick, New Jersey: Rutgers University Press, paperback, 1985). Some of feminist post-modernism's most suggestive thinkers were there. I will not give a comprehensive bibliography of feminist post-modernism, but among its vital texts are: Teresa deLauretis, *Alice Doesn't: Feminism Semiotics Cinema* (Bloomington: Indiana University Press, 1984); Teresa deLauretis, ed., *Feminist Studies/ Critical Studies* (Bloomington: Indiana University Press, 1986); Jane Flax, forthcoming book on feminism, psychoanalysis, and post-modernism; Sandra Harding, *The Science Question in Feminism* (Ithaca, New York: Cornell University Press, 1986); Donna Hara-

way, "A Manifesto for Cyborgs: Science, Technology, and Socialist Feminism in the 1980s," *Socialist Review*, 80 (1985): 65-107; the poetry and theory of the HOW(ever) group, 554 Jersey Street, San Francisco, CA 94114; Alice A. Jardine, *Gynesis* (Ithaca: Cornell University Press, 1985); Kate Linker, guest curator, *Catalogue* for *Difference: On Representation and Sexuality*, (New York: New Museum of Contemporary Art, 1984); Elizabeth A. Meese, *Crossing the Double-Cross: The Practice of Feminist Criticism* (Chapel Hill: University of North Carolina Press, 1986); Hortense Spillers, forthcoming work on black women and culture; the various essays of Gayatri C. Spivak. The name Alice returns again and again among the post-modernist feminists: Alice Jardine, Alice-in-Wonderland, Alice B. Toklas.

11. "Fact-File," *Chronicle of Higher Education* (February 5, 1986): 27-30.

12. No. 84-3147 in the United States Court of Appeals for the Seventh Circuit. On February 24, 1986, the Supreme Court struck down the Indianapolis anti-pornography legislation, which the Amici Curiae brief had opposed.

13. The book originated in the 1982 Barnard Scholar and the Feminist Conference, an explosive conflict among various theories about the representation of female sexuality. The debate about pornography entered the mainstream feminist press in the April, 1985, *Ms.* On a red cover, white letters read, "Is One Woman's Sexuality Another Woman's Pornography?"

14. Attorney General's Commission on Pornography, *Final Report, July 1986* (Washington, D.C.: U.S. Department of Justice, 1986), Vol. I: 769-772. I am writing a longer paper on the representation of women and gender in the Meese Commission report.

15. *Never Guilty. Never Free: The Ginny Foat Story*, with Laura Foreman (New York: Random House, 1985). My review, "Coming to Grief," is in *Nation* (October 12, 1985), 347-352. Ellen Hawkes, *Feminism on Trial: The Ginny Foat Case and Its Meaning for the Future of the Women's Movement* (New York: William Morrow and Co., 1986), unravels Foat's self-defense persuasively.

16. Sandra Lipsitz Bem, "Gender Schema Theory and Its Implications for Child Development: Raising Gender-aschematic Children in a Gender-schematic Society," *Signs: Journal of Women in Culture and Society* 8(1983): 598-616, has influenced my thinking here.

17. "See Jim and Pat Cook. Jim Cooks First," *New York Times* (March 13, 1986), A-26.

18. I wish to thank Marilyn B. Young and Gaye Tuchman for their years of instruction about the meaning of Cagney and Lacey.

19. Leslie W. Rabine, in her fascinating "Romance in the Age of Electronics: Harlequin Enterprises," *Feminist Studies* 11(1985): 39-60, suggests that the popularity of Harlequins may lie in their dramatization of the "juncture between ...(women's) sexual, emotional needs on the one hand and their needs concerning work relations on the other. . . " (39).

REFERENCES

The Authority of Experience. 1977. Ed. Arlyn Diamond and Lee R. Edwards. Amherst: University of Massachusetts Press.

Berger, John. 1977. *Ways of Seeing*. New York: Penguin Books.

Decter, Midge. 1972. *The New Chastity*. New York: Coward, McCann & Geoghegan, 1972; Berkely Medallion, 1973.

Duggan, Lisa and Snitow, Ann. 1984. "Porn Law Is About Images, Not Power", *Newsday* (September 26, 1984): 65.

Flick, Rachel M. 1983. "The New Feminism and the World of Work." *Public Interest*: 71, 33-44.

Gilbert, Sandra M. and Gubar, Susan. 1979. *The Madwoman in the Attic*. New Haven: Yale University Press.

Haraway, Donna. 1985. "A Manifesto for Cyborgs: Science, Technology, and Socialist Feminism in the 1980s". *Socialist Review* 80: 65-107.

Hawkes, Ellen. 1986. *Feminism on Trial: The Ginny Foat Case and Its Meaning for the Future of the Women's Movement*. New York: William Morrow.

Jones, Gerald P. and Jacklin, Carol Nagy. 1986. "Changes in Sexist Attitudes Towards Women During Introductory Women's and Men's Studies Courses". Unpublished ms.: 13.

Kaplan, E. Ann. 1983. *Women and Film: Both Sides of the Camera*. New York and London: Methuen.

Klein, Ethel. 1984. *Gender Politics*. Cambridge: Harvard University Press.

Koren. 1986. *New Yorker* (October 20): 20.

Moi, Toril. 1985. *Sexual/Textual Politics*. London and New York: Methuen.

Reid, Catherine. 1982. "Reweaving the Web of Life". *Reweaving the Web of Life: Feminism and Nonviolence* ed. Pam McAllister, 291-294. Philadelphia: New Society Publishers.

Rich, Adrienne. 1978. *The Dream of a Common Language: Poems 1974-77*. New York: W.W. Norton and Co.

Schneir, Miriam. 1986. "The Prisoner of Sexism: Mailer Meets His Match". *Ms*. (April 1986): 82.

Shelley, Mary. 1826. *The Last Man*. London: Henry Colburn.

Stacey, Judith. 1983. "The New Conservative Feminism". *Feminist Studies* 9: 559-83.

Tickner, Lisa. 1984. "Sexuality And/In Representation: Five British Artists". *Catalogue* for *Difference: On Representation and Sexuality*. New York: New Museum of Contemporary Art.

Vance, Carole S. 1984. "Pleasure and Danger: Toward a Politics of Sexuality". *Pleasure and Danger*. Boston: Routledge and Kegan Paul.

Some different meanings of the concept of "difference": Feminist theory and the concept of ideology

Michèle Barrett
City University, London

This paper arises from a double inquiry about recent work using the notion of "difference." Increasingly I have been surprised by what can be fitted into this capacious hold-all of a concept, and unclear as to the meaning of the term in different contexts. Feminism's historic tension between "difference and equality" is fully recognized in a contemporary movement whose politics and theory are deeply divided about whether to prioritize that which defines the category "women" today, or whether to look to the eradication of the sexual difference on which such a politics is inevitably based. This traditional feminist definition of "difference" underpins many debates of both a strategic and a theoretical nature, from welfare policy to the psychic condition of femininity. It is based, however, to use the motif of the conference title, on a conception of difference *between* women and men, who are themselves seen as relatively unproblematic categories. In this sense the traditional feminist understanding of "difference" is necessarily likely to resist any move to deconstruct the gendered subject on which that feminist politics was based. So a new politics, recognizing "the difference within" the idea of woman, is radically challenging to conventional feminist arguments. We have, you could say, two conceptions of "difference" at work in these feminist debates: the one an essentialist model drawing on the "difference between" women and men and the other a deconstructive model, pointing to the "difference within" woman as a category and women as a group. These two models are, I suggest, in competition rather than complementary. In the course of the paper I hope to explore other meanings of "difference" that have generated comparable contradictions.

My second inquiry is more specific and concerns the concept of ideology. In the course of recent work on this topic I became interested not in why the concept of ideology had been so extensively criticized recently, but in why criticisms from sharply varying, indeed contradictory, positions had been collapsed into a consensually critical attitude towards the idea of a theory of ideology. This I intend to illustrate in the course of looking at the different ways in which "difference" has been constituted and deployed in feminist debates.

"Difference" I

The first version of difference that I want to consider briefly is the straightforward "sexual difference" position, but in the form of recent work within psychoanalytic theory. The feminist historian Sally Alexander, for example, has used Lacanian theory in order "to place subjectivity and sexual difference" firmly at the center of her research. The characteristic concerns of this approach are indicated in the following passage, whose general emphasis on instability and discontinuity serves only to highlight the given nature of the sexual difference that explodes its absolute certainties into the text:

> Subjectivity, and with it sexual identity, is constructed through a process of differentiation, division and splitting, and is best understood as a process which is always in the making, is never finished or complete. In this sense, the unified coherent subject presented in language is always a fiction, and so susceptible to disruption by the unconscious (or in collision with an alternative concept of the self in language). Everyday speech with its discontinuities, hesitations, contradictions, indicates on the one hand the process itself, and on the other, the difficulty the individual subject has in aligning her or himself within the linguistic order, since there are as many different orders as there are discourses to structure them and always the possibility of more. *A difficulty which is underlined for the little girl/woman by the impossibility for her of taking up a positive or powerful place in a culture which privileges masculinity and therefore men.* Subjectivity and sexual identity are always achieved with difficulty, and the achievement is always precarious. The unpredictable effects of that achievement remain inaccessible to conscious thought in the repressed wishes to be one with the other, to belong to the other sex, as well as envy and desire for the

> other sex. Both subjectivity and sexual identity are therefore unstable and involve antagonism and conflict in their very construction. Antagonism and instability are lived out not only within the individual psyche and its history, *they mediate all social relations between women and men*; they prefigure and cohabit with class antagonisms, and, as the history of feminism demonstrates, may well disrupt class solidarities (133; my italics).

We might note that in this account the elemental force of sexual difference is not restricted to abstractions of language, culture or the symbolic order: it applies specifically to women and men as social historical actors. As a generalizing theory about the differences between women and men it of necessity cannot and does not address itself seriously to the question of differences within those categories. The resulting psychic reductionism and essentialism is, of course, a recurrent issue in various arenas of debate about psychoanalysis. The important exception here is Nancy Chodorow's attempt to tie up object-relations theory with, on the one hand a sociological backdrop to the society at large and the place of the family within it (not too successful, as the model is so rigidly Parsonian), and on the other a consideration of historically gendered parenting. Chodorow's work, interestingly, has motivated and complemented, and been integrated into, a wide variety of feminist studies in the USA and elsewhere. In Britain at least, however, it is viewed with some suspicion by a far more purist feminist psychoanalytic tendency.[1] This is largely because of an increasingly clear polarization between those who still believe a theory of subjectivity could or should be aligned with some broader perspective that encompasses the non-psychic.[2]

Juliet Mitchell's path-breaking recuperation of Freud, in *Psychoanalysis and Feminism*, is still popularly regarded as the benchmark text of psychoanalytic feminism. Yet it is worth remarking that over a period of years many of the adherents of this approach have been divesting themselves of the theory of ideology in which Mitchell's work was originally set. In 1974 Juliet Mitchell wrote "The patriarchal law speaks to and through each person in his unconscious; the reproduction of the ideology of human society is thus assured in the acquisition of the law by each individual. The unconscious that Freud analyzed could thus be described as the domain of the reproduction of culture or ideology" (413). Mitchell's Althusserian formulation might be complemented by the emphasis in works by Lacan and Kristeva that found a similar popularity in the mid 1970's.[3] Much of the optimism in that period that some synthesis between Marxism and psychoanalysis might be found was attributable (in retrospect) to the stress put, by both Lacan and Kristeva, on the notion of a "symbolic order" in which the individual subject is positioned.

This concept of the "symbolic," counterposed by Lacan to the "imaginary" pre-Oedipal world and by Kristeva to the perversely-defined "semiotic" sphere whose psychic content was also pre-social, can be seen as an inheritor of the concept of ideology. The symbolic order was, certainly, defined in such a way as to make it more like "culture" than "ideology," but nevertheless a clear distinction was drawn between interior psychic content and the external social world in which the individual subject must take its place.[4] The "law of the father," the patriarchal social order and symbolic system, in these presentations of psychoanalytic theory, is a clearly social concept and the mechanisms through which subjectivities are constructed and positioned within it are not dissimilar from those popularized in the Althusserian view of ideology.

This "social" perspective has now decisively declined in favor of a version of psychoanalytic theory that sees emphasis on the operations of the unconsciousness as in some sense *in competition* with a social theory of ideology. Jacqueline Rose, in an article that clarifies this development in a particularly sharp way, believes that the concept of the unconscious was in danger of being lost in these appropriations of psychoanalytic theory. She writes: "For while it is indeed correct that psychoanalysis was introduced into feminism as a theory which could rectify the inability of Marxism to address questions of sexuality, and that this move was complementary to the demand within certain areas of Marxism for increasing attention to the ideological determinants of our social being, it is also true that undue concentration on this aspect of the theory has served to cut off the concept of the unconscious, or at least to displace it from the center of the debate"(89).[5]

In practice, much recent work — in Britain at least — has tended simply to slough off any concern with social, cultural or ideological questions in favor of a much more technical discussion couched resolutely and exclusively within not merely psychoanalytic discourse but even the assumptions associated with clinical practice. This, as it happens, has gone hand in hand with a more general interest in applications of psychoanalytic theory that might be thought of as "essentialist," a drift whose manifestations might be noted, to take two rather varied examples, in the renewed interest in Melanie Klein as well as in the popularity of Luce Irigaray, the most overtly essentialist of the "new French" school.

So I make two observations about "sexual difference" in this context. Although the strict Lacanian approach is concerned to interrogate assumptions about gender identity, there is nonetheless a sense in which "difference," as widely used in psychoanalytic discussions of sexual difference, invokes an essentialist conception of gender identity and gendered subjectivity. It is no accident that the sex/gender distinction, for a number of years a crucial point of reference for feminism's project, is in this discourse explicitly refused. The "sexual difference" perspective is one based necessarily in the paradigm of difference-between rather than difference-within. Psychic fragmentation, for example, is considered as a specific feature *of* femininity — indeed counterposed to a less fissured masculine subjectivity — rather than as a tool for deconstructing femininity as a category.

"Difference" II

A second meaning to "difference" can best be located in the fundamental insight of Saussurian linguistics, that meaning is constructed through linguistic opposition rather than through absolute reference. In the context of this volume there is scarcely any need for me to spell out the Derridian elaboration of *differance* and the deconstructive critical practice that accompanies it. "Difference," in this sense, is a shorthand for a theory of meaning as positional or relational: an approach that offers a fundamental challenge to the "realist" epistemological certainties of much Western social thought as well as to what we could call, "classical theories of representation." Although it is obviously unsatisfactory to collapse this sense of difference into a broader category of "post-structuralist" thought as a whole, there are some general issues that seem to me to be brought into play when considering the implications of these arguments.

In the first place there is the question of epistemology and the status of the social world. Many varieties of post-structuralist thought share an antipathy towards any theory of knowledge presupposing a sharp distinction between a world of objects on the one hand and concepts on the other. Epistemology, and the entire question of what might constitute "knowledge," are either rejected or held in suspension in what has come to be termed "anti-foundationalist" discourse. More specifically directed towards Marxism is the critique of *totality* or the assumption that we can speak of an ensemble of social relations. Terry Lovell's description of these positions as philosophical "conventionalisms", in which the world is understood as "in effect constructed in and by theory" emphasizes the distance that has been travelled from analyses that are either historical or materialist (15). The rejection of "grand narrative" (whether seen in terms of the world, the text or the critic), characteristic of post-modernist thought, is the counterpart or sequel to the rejection of epistemology. And, I may add, equally difficult to achieve: covert epistemology and meta-narrative being common signs of the difficulty of banishing these traditional foundations of intellectual work.[6]

The question of whether these theoretical positions are compatible with feminism as a historical political movement, raises interesting issues. Certainly it can be pointed out that the politics generated from these perspectives tend towards the textual and the local, although I do not say this in a disparaging spirit. It can be stated that the apprehension of difference is necessarily a project that cuts across the idea of a common feminist political purpose for women. It can be seen that the "micro-politics" stemming from Foucault's work are, whilst obviously in harmony with feminism's convictions about the inter-relatedness of personal and political life, scarcely likely to transform any major social institutions overnight. It does not need remarking that the post-modernist project is explicitly hostile to any political project beyond the ephemeral. All these are widely rehearsed in the general debates of contemporary social theory. The category of "post-structuralist" thought is, however, a very problematic one to impose upon a broad set of positions. That there are important differences within this loose category is highlighted by the contrast between Derrida and Foucault on the organizing concepts of difference and power.

I could illustrate this by quoting from the program of the conference on which this volume is based: "Organized around gender, race and class as sites of difference, the symposium will explore the intersections of these terms as they present themselves in different texts, strategies and preoccupations." Of course gender, race and class *are* sites of difference, but they are also sites of the operation of power. They often involve relations of exploitation. We do not have to sink to the vulgarity of mentioning lynchings, wife-murder or asbestosis to point to the agnosticism inherent in the idea of "difference," when considering racism, gender or class: there is a vocabulary and an analysis of domination, servility, subordination, oppression and marginalization that has already spoken of the power dimensions of these differences. I could illustrate this at my own expense, too. Mary

McIntosh and I recently published, in response to Black feminist critiques of various white socialist-feminists, a critical reflection on the ethnocentrism of our arguments about family/state/work connection. Much of the critical response to that article focused, I now think with some justification, on the political implications of our focusing on ethnocentrism — the ethnic specificity of our previous arguments — at the expense of a proper consideration of racism.[7] Difference, rather than power, had been our focus and our political weakness.

Two further matters seem to me to be of relevance to the relationship of feminist theory to "the difference within": the role of women in the subject matter of these debates and the question of the subject. A number of feminist have argued, and even more assumed, that because women were so marginalized in the theoretical organization of, for example, Marxism that any new body of theory would offer a greater space and flexibility. A contemporary equivalent to this in British debate is the question of what post-modernism offers women. Angela McRobbie is relatively optimistic that the urban anonymity of the modern/post-modern city offers women a way out from the rigid expectations of closed communities; Janet Wolff points out that the culture of modernity is nonetheless historically masculine. At the least, the question remains open.

That of the subject, however, is much less open. One of the major achievements of the "difference"(II) approach has been to criticize and deconstruct the "unified subject," whose appearance of universality disguised a constitution structured specifically around the subjectivity characteristic of the white, bourgeois man. The critique of humanism goes back, of course, to Althusser and beyond and is now quite hegemonic in modern theory. There is, however, a conflation in this literature between humanism in general and liberal as a specific historical ideology, which I find unhelpful. The problem is neatly illustrated by the index entry on humanism in Terry Eagleton's *Literary Theory*, which baldly announces "humanism, see liberal humanism" (236). I will confine myself here to two brief comments on this conflation. The assumption that the deconstructed and the fragmented subject of contemporary theory is politically progressive, let alone politically powerful, remains unproven. Secondly, the honorable tradition of "humanism" as a secularizing force is done scant justice by the current historically-myopic use of humanism as a straightforwardly pejorative term.

In moving on, I should summarize the grounds on which the concept of ideology is rejected from the difference-within position. It is inherently "epistemological," having to propose knowledge or truth claims against which ideology is counterposed; it makes no sense without a conception of society as some form of totality — however disjunctive; it presupposes a human subject, even if the constitutive role of ideology in the development of subjectivity is recognized.

"Difference" III

A third sense of "difference" offered in current feminist debate is effectively a recognition of diversity. Historically, in modern feminism, this had its first strong appearance in the divisions arising from class difference between women and from the contending political projects of feminism and the left. In Britain, the process of the waning of this contradiction was begun by a dawning consciousness among white feminists of what was being said about the nationalism and imperialism. Soon the issue of racism, and the rise of an autonomous Black feminist movement, began to take on its present political significance. The specious claims of feminism to represent equally all women, to speak with one voice, were rapidly demolished. Although the two issues of racism and class are established as major axes of difference between women, the claims of nation, region and ethnicity, as well as age, sexual orientation, health and religion are also pressing.

Where "difference" II tends towards theoreticism in its treatment of the theory/politics tension, "difference" III goes to the pragmatic end of the spectrum, relying on experience as a guide to both theory and politics. Here I want to try and sketch out a group of related ideas and methodologies which combine, in my view, to make this pragmatic definition of difference extremely influential and popular in feminist circles in general, if not necessarily so in modern critical theory. The dominant voices of contemporary white anglophone feminism are Mary Daly, Adrienne Rich, Andrea Dworkin and Dale Spender. As both Hester Eisenstein and Lynne Segal have argued, a common thread running through their writings is essentialism: "a feminist version of the eternal female" (Eisenstein 106). Although this is not the essentialism based on an assumption of women's language, culture and personality, it is rooted in psychic, social and cultural "separate spheres." This essentialism goes hand in hand with intellectual separatism. In British sociology, for example, this has taken the form of claims to stake out a "feminist methodology" whose characteristic is subjectivism and the restriction of knowledge to experience (Stanley and Wise). This keys into a well-trodden debate about women's studies and the academic marginalization (sometimes a self-imposed exile on the part of its practitioners) of work on women. The case made by Elaine Showalter against the political neutralities of "gender studies," and for a committed intellectual orientation towards women, seems to me to be still in contention. For it can just as readily be argued that feminist academic separatism provides the most convenient basis to leave untouched the dominant theoretical and methodological assumptions in the academic disciplines; thus gender can be seen as potentially more subversive from a feminist point of view than a substantive focus on women.

The inordinate value attached to experience in popular feminism is aligned to an excess of both relativism and pluralism. Dale Spender claims that "at the core of feminist ideas is the crucial insight that there is no one truth, no one authority, no one objective method which leads to the production of pure knowledge" (5). Adrienne Rich's aphorism "objectivity is male subjectivity" summarizes the claims of this valorization of experience. It is not, I think, a "performative statement"; it is a statement with a clear, if over-stated, cognitive content and truth claim. It leads inevitably to pluralism. And pluralism, indeed, *is* the lowest common denominator of contemporary feminism. Pluralism, as Gayatri Chakravorty Spivak has rightly remarked, "is the method employed by the *central* authorities to neutralize opposition by seeming to accept it. The gesture of pluralism on the part of the *marginal* can only mean capitulation to the center" (218).

The category of experience is an extremely problematic one for contemporary feminism. Perhaps some of the most interesting work now being done on issues of methodology and science is that associated with the "feminist standpoint" school of Sandra Harding, Nancy Hartsock and Evelyn Fox Keller. For many feminist writers, however, the category of experience is transparent, and indeed precisely the objection to theories of ideology is that they claim to offer a reading of experience as a text rather than accepting it as a political truth. In this sense the notion of ideology registers a significant challenge to the taken-for-granted nature of experience in these discourses. It is worth emphasizing that these new versions of experience-based feminism, like the nineteenth century "separate spheres" models they follow, can never seek to problematize the idea of the human subject. They are firmly locked within an empirical, humanist framework.

Discussion

Three uses of the notion of "difference" have been aired — no doubt the distinctions are in some ways artificial and there is certainly overlap between them. But I would want to stress too, that there are not merely *differences* between these three deployments of the concept, there are disagreements and outright contradictions. Difference I emphasizes difference between women and men, while Differences II and III emphasize difference "within" the category of women. Difference II rejects the human subject on which Difference III is predicated. Difference III is also predicated upon the apprehension of an unproblematic ontological reality — the historical and institutional organization of social division — that is explicitly refused by Difference II. Differences I and III incline towards essentialism; Difference II is deconstructive in its approach to gendered subjectivity.

The question as to whether these perspectives can be reconciled is clearly an important one. For the moment, the common use of "difference" for such a variety of meanings is confusing. Sexual difference, positional or textual difference and experiential diversity are best identified separately.

NOTES

1. Jacqueline Rose, for example, in *Sexuality in the Field of Vision* (London: Verso, 1986) characterizes Chodorow's book as one that "displaces" the unconscious in favor of a more sociological conception of gender imprinting, thereby failing to problematize the acquisition of sexual identity.
2. The work of, for example, Cora Kaplan and Rosiland Coward reflects this broader project. See Coward's *Female Desire: Women's Sexuality Today* (London: Paladin, 1984), and Kaplan's *Sea Changes: Culture and Feminism* (London: Verso, 1986).
3. See particularly Jacques Lacan, *The Language of the Self*, trans. Anthony Wilden (New York: Delta, 1968); Julia Kristeva's work of the period is usefully collected in *The Kristeva Reader*, ed. by Toril Moi (Oxford: Blackwell, 1986).
4. J. Laplanche and J-B. Pontalis, in *The Language of Psychoanalysis* (London: The Hogarth Press, 1973), state that one of Lacan's two aims in his use of the concept of the Symbolic was "To show how the human subject is inserted into a pre-established order which is itself symbolic in nature in Lacan's sense" (440).
5. Rose goes on to suggest that my discussion of psychoanalysis, under the general heading of ideology, in *Women's Oppression Today*, "graphically illustrated" this general displacement of the concept of the unconscious. Whilst this may be true, it seems more relevant to point to the emphasis that Mitchell laid on the concept of ideology as the

framework of her analysis in 1974, and the extent to which this has now been rejected by exponents of a psychoanalytic sexual difference position.

6. Alex Callinicos has argued that the "meta-narrative" that informs Derrida's work is the project to dethrone philosophy in favor of a textualist literary criticism, rather than the ostensible aim of recognizing the heterogeneity of discourses: see "Postmodernism, Post-Structuralism and Post-Marxism?", *Theory, Culture and Society* 2 (No 3): 85-101. Similarly Paul Hirst and those associated with the rejection of epistemology are shown, by both John Thompson and Jorge Larrain, to be themselves engaged in epistemological discourse: see John B. Thompson, 1984, *Studies in the Theory of Ideology* (Cambridge: Polity Press), 97; Jorge Larrain, 1983, *Marxism and Ideology* (London: Macmillan), 191.

7. Replies are carried in *Feminist Review* Nos 22 and 23 (1986).

REFERENCES

Alexander, Sally. 1982. "Women, Class and Sexual Differences in the 1830s and 1840s: Some Reflections on the Writing of a Feminist History." *History Workshop Journal* 17: 133.

Barrett, Michèle and McIntosh, Mary. 1985. "Ethnocentrism and Socialist-Feminist Theory." *Feminist Review* 20: 23-48.

Chodorow, Nancy. 1978. *The Reproduction of Mothering: Psychoanalysis and the Sociology of Gender*. Berkeley: University of California Press.

Eagleton, Terry. 1983. *Literary Theory*. Oxford: Blackwell.

Eisenstein, Hester. 1984. *Contemporary Feminist Thought*. London: Unwin.

Harding, Sandra. 1986. *The Science Question in Feminism*. Ithaca: Cornell University Press.

———, and Hintikka, Merrill, eds. 1983. *Discovering Reality: Feminist Perspectives on Metaphysics, Methodology, and Philosophy of Science*. Dordrecht: Reidel, 1983.

Lovell, Terry. 1980. *Pictures of Reality: Aesthetics, Politics, Pleasure*. London: British Film Institute.

MacRobie, Angela. 1984. Review of Marshall Berman's *All That Is Solid Melts Into Air*. *Feminist Review* 18.

Mitchell, Juliet. 1974. *Psychoanalysis and Feminism*. Harmondsworth: Penguin.

Rose, Jacqueline. 1986. *Sexuality in the Field of Vision*. London: Verso.

Segal, Lynne. 1987. *Is the Future Female? Troubled Thoughts on Contemporary Feminism*. London: Virago.

Showalter, Elaine. 1986. "Shooting the Rapids: Feminist Criticism in the Mainstream." *Oxford Literary Review* 8: 218-24.

Spender, Dale. 1985. *For the Record: The Making and Meaning of Feminist Knowledge*. London: Women's Press.

Spivak, Gayatri Chakravorty. 1980. "A Response to Annette Kolodny" (unpublished). Cited by Marcus, Jane. "Storming the Toolshed." In *Feminist Theory: A Critique of Ideology*, ed. Nannerl O. Keohane, Michelle Z. Rosaldo, and Barbara C. Gelpi, 217-35. Chicago: University of Chicago Press.

Stanley, Liz and Wise, Sue. 1983. *Breaking Out: Feminist Consciousness and Feminist Research*. London: Routledge.

Woolf, Janet. 1985. "The Invisible Flâneuse: Women and the Literature of Modernity". *Theory, Culture and Society* 2: 37-48.

The asylums of Antaeus
Women, war and madness: Is there a feminist fetishism?

Jane Marcus
City College of New York

1. Helen's plot

If all history (or at least historiography) is a fiction, as contemporary theorists tell us, an interesting question for literary critics is whether all fiction is history. It is easy for the literary to accept the new narrativity of historians and, since Foucault, the study of history as a discourse. Can historians, accustomed to raiding the literature of an age for examples, accept an equal revelatory force in fiction as in events as evidence of lived reality? Does a battle lie the way a poem lies, to get at "the truth"?[1] Certainly Elsa Morante's devastating *History: A Novel*, recording as it does the personal experience of politics, anti-semitism and fascism, the Nazi occupation of Rome and the aftermath of World War II from the point of view of a frightened widow schoolteacher, her epileptic child,'Useppe, born from her rape by a German soldier, and two extraordinary dogs, is a straightforward answer to the literary question.[2] The historical question is increasingly vexed by the work of the "new historicists." And even radical critics like Gayatri Spivak in *In Other Worlds* would suspend postmodern suspicion of "truth-value" in special cases like the Subaltern Studies Group's work on Indian history, but would not extend this to the history of women. Like Rebecca West's brilliant two-volume documentary novel of Yugoslavia in the same period, *Black Lamb and Grey Falcon*, which focuses on a Jewish poet and his domination by Gerda, his German wife (read Goethe, German patriarchal culture), this text questions its own status as fiction by asserting that when it writes the experience of the victimized, it writes "real" history.[3] In the same sense, Poulenc's opera of the early fifties, *Dialogues of the Carmelites*, uses the "abjection" of a frightened girl in a convent during the Terror to contemplate the victims of the Holocaust.

The writing of history is all a matter of the construction of more or less plausible plots. When women read traditional male history, like Virginia Woolf in *Three Guineas*, they throw up their hands at its bias and prejudice — she claims that for truth, authenticity and authority, one is forced to use biography, autobiography and fiction as the true histories of women's lives and interpreters of political events. As Isa Oliver in *Between the Acts* cries, "Is there another plot? Will the author come out of the bushes?"[4] Foucault, like Woolf, has taught us to read the two rhetorics together, the high drama's discourse against the conversation going on between the lines and between the acts, and to see the author/ historian's controlling ego like Miss LaTrobe's blood-filled shoes, trampling on the grapes of wrath so that his or her particular truth may go marching on.

How can feminist criticism construct the *other plot* by reading the fictions of history and history in fictions differently? In the marriage of the two disciplines history has often used literature as a handmaiden to provide comic or tragic relief, human interest as a distraction from an unrelenting procession of facts. And for many literary critics those facts have been used as "masculine" proof or support for literary readings. Will New Historicism function any differently for feminists than Old Historicism? Can this marriage be saved? Can the two work together as partners?[5] Can the plotters recognize that there are other plots as well?

The purpose of the present essay is to destabilize the standard plot of the literature of World War I and its relation to history through a supposedly feminist history by Sandra Gilbert, to demonstrate that history and literature deserve equal narrative force in a cultural text. I find a "double voice" in her text, a reaffirmation of the traditional male plot. I propose a theory of the *feminist fetish*, collating and adapting recent work of Naomi Schor on female fetishism and Tom Mitchell on iconography and commodity fetishism to discuss the poster art and political dress of British Suffragettes.

At first our plots as feminist critics were very simple. In our righteousness we assumed that our heroines were always fighting the good fight and our writers plotting the good plot. Post-structuralism and deconstruction, murdering father-authors and paternal texts, asked us to de-authorize women's lives and words before they had even entered in to any canonical share in literary authority. Confused but determined, we found we were writing the materialist sub-plot of contemporary criticism.[6] Find a lost woman writer, drag her, kicking and screaming, from the limbo of obscurity, reprint her works, write her life, compare her to her peers, discuss her relationship to her mother, her father, her daughter. Watch her ascend into the heavenly canon of the *Norton Anthology of Women's Literature*. Simultaneously the feminist historian has rescued the stranded ghosts of reformers and working women, peasants and nuns, and re-evaluated their movements. Sometimes fiction has come to her aid in recreating their lives. But the feminist critic has learned that history as it is written and taught by men is often too fictional for our purposes and patriarchal plots are too rigid. Like Miss LaTrobe in the bushes, the authors of History insist that the audience see it *their* way, in the same old boring and repetitious plot. We have had to do our history from scratch. Some of our heroines stubbornly insist on staying in limbo and refuse to be moved by our missionary zeal. Tragic plots become comic and farces turn into melodrama. Just when we thought that Djuna Barnes was seduced by her father, it turns out that she was in love with her grandmother. Now we have a new plot with a vengeance — a grandmother incest plot.[7]

What does this plot have to do with the primary patriarchal historical plot, the myth of Antaeus? "Civilization," according to the myth, consists of the story of the giant who builds a temple to his father with the skulls of his enemies. What do we do with the woman writer's dream of her dead grandmother in drag? Can the feminist plot include the plots of race and imperialism?

Early in Virginia Woolf's anti-war novel *Between the Acts*, Lucy Swithin finds in the story of the giant Antaeus in Lempriere's classical dictionary the origin of the superstition to "knock on wood," to ward off evil (the particular evil here is World War II). The wood is the tree of the earth mother, archetypal nurse. Antaeus is the archetype of the patriarchal ethos of war, heroism and death, calling itself civilization. Because the mother goddess revives him whenever his body falls to earth or touches wood, he is invincible. Ironically this plot depicts death and destruction as protected and perpetrated by the maternal life force. (Antaeus is eventually killed by being crushed in the air with his body separated from mother earth.) Woolf's novel is about what the state does to women when it makes war. *Between the Acts* argues, like *Three Guineas*, that the militaristic patriarchal state needs the collaboration of women to make war and casts her in two crucial and needed roles of mother and nurse. Women workers, of course, always work. The state and its servant soldiers need her physical presence as war-nurse or mother in a fetishization of her force as healer. Throughout history, woman has responded to the needs of patriarchal war-making and enforced fetishization with varying degrees of enthusiasm for producing the next generation of cannon fodder, by nursing the wounded, maintaining culture and producing food in the absence of men and suppressing her own desire for political autonomy or social freedom in the interest of the community at large.[8]

Whether she collaborates or not, the patriarchy's poet will still claim that the Trojan War was fought over Helen whatever its real economic or imperialistic motives may have been. The "Asylums of Antaeus" may be seen as the real and imagined places where the contradictions of her state-enforced roles drive woman mad (where she fights fetishization and fails). She speaks out of the confusion and fear derived from this condition in a double voice. Isa, in *Between the Acts*, cannot bond with her "sister," gang raped by soldiers in a newspapar account she reads. Her art is sentimental scraps of poetry hidden in her account books, for she is a prisoner in the patriarchal family, forced to play the dutiful wife and mother despite her husband's infidelities and aggressions and her father-in-law's rule over her children's upbringing. Pointz Hall is her prison and madhouse, while it is also the center of English culture and history teaching her to fetishize herself as wife and mother (Mary on the Flight into Egypt) and she is perceived by readers as an incarnation of Isis restoring the body of Osirus ("He is the father of my children."). Deconstructing my own plot with Celeste Schenck's powerful new genre critique, one may read Isa's romantic love lyrics in their conservative theme and form as a product of her love/hate heterosexual condition, the poem about an aeroplane's flight enacting her own desire to flee with a lover from the maternal grounding role war casts for her as woman writer. Isa sees her unfinished poems as "abortive," failing in the maternal birth plot assigned to her by war. She interrupts her own escape narrative to order soles for lunch. Since self-interruption is the valorized trope of *A Room of One's Own*, Isa takes her place in Woolf's history of victimized Judith Shakespeares.

Studying the rise of Italian fascism, Maria Macchiocci has brilliantly analyzed the state's projection of the roles of mother and nurse on to women, depriving them of other identities while investing the myths of sacred motherhood and war nurse with mysterious powers symbolized in blood. One sees how "She gives life and heals wounds" becomes "men die for her; she caused the wounds," in a deliberate confusion of signs and signifiers.[9] Like Rosselini's film, *The White Ship*, the propaganda posters of the British War Office contained this double message and it is repeated in the misogynous poems of D. H. Lawrence and Wilfred Owen and in Hemingway's *The Sun Also Rises*. Virginia Woolf protested against the state's distorting propaganda about war nurses in the scene in *The Years* where Peggy and Eleanor pass the statue of the martyred war heroine, Nurse Cavell, shot by the Germans in Belgium. Eleanor thinks that the only sensible words uttered in the Great War were Cavell's "Patriotism is not enough." Though these words are inscribed in small letters at the base of the statue, the state has erased its enemy by bannering the opposite sentiment "For King and Country" in large letters at the top, denying Cavell's radical pacifism and imaging her for their own ends.[10] Peggy sees the figure as like "an advertisement for sanitary napkins," linking menstrual blood and soldiers' wounds precisely as the war propagandists wished its observers to do.

The *double voice* of the statue of Nurse Cavell, its feminist pacifism overlaid by the patriarchal state's jingoistic "For King and Country," like Isa's confusion about "what we must remember, what we must forget" in *Between the Acts*, is a text for studying women in war-time. Sandra Gilbert in *The Madwoman in the Attic*, (written with Susan Gubar) already a classic in feminist criticism, has taught us to hear another intonation of the double voice in women's texts. Consequently, it is disheartening and confusing for readers to make sense of her "Soldier's Heart: Literary Men, Literary Women and the Great War."[11] My problem with reading the essay suggests that we need to understand the implications of our methodologies and to analyze the plots of our own essays. Publication in *SIGNS* constitutes instant canonization, and no historian or critic of the period can ignore this essay. So, it seems necessary to understand it to proceed further and to build on its premises in order to continue our collaborative practice of making a feminist revision of modernism, not to mention using literature for and as history. In replacing the double message of "soldier's heart" with Nurse Cavell's bandage, the image of "No Man's Land" with the image of the "asylums of Antaeus," one is offering another plot. Ideologically, the essay reassures man that certain forms of feminism will not foil their ancient plot or attempt to topple the temple. Gilbert speaks a plot as double-voiced as the writers whose subtexts she so brilliantly explored in *The Madwoman in the Attic*. The reader of "Soldier's Heart" is in an awkward and uncomfortable position. Now that the statements that affirm that women were sexually excited by the dead bodies of men on the battlefield when this essay was delivered as a lecture, have been formulated as a series of rhetorical questions which undermine the authority of women's experience as well as her own words, one's discomfort increases. The double voice is first evidenced in the problem of simultaneously writing literary criticism and social history. This is a coupling one applauds — like the strategy of writing with Susan Gubar, the critic is attacking Western notions of individual genius. But the voices don't speak together. The over-voice is critical; the undervoice raids history for real examples of male fantasies about women, neglecting the recent works of feminist historians to re-place women in the period, e.g. Martha Vicinus' *Independent Women*. Gilbert's essay also confirms the status of the male canon of war literature from Lawrence to Hemingway to Wilfred Owen. It argues that their vision of women as bloodthirsty vampires who gloat over men's death and derive pleasure and profit from war is correct. The essay is addressed to the male reader to confirm the arguments made in Paul Fussell's *The Great War and Modern Memory* and Eric Leed's *No Man's Land: Combat and Identity in World War I*, which are called "brilliant" in the text and "major texts" in the footnotes. Those who have worked long in the primary documents of this period will be shocked by the plot of Gilbert's essay, its misuse of historical "facts". It is factually incorrect as well as distorted. Women's works are quoted in support of these readings by male writers and historians, but not when they present their own plots. The sensationalistic tone of the essay suggests that it was somehow perverse and neurotic of women to enjoy their work as nurses or ambulance drivers, a vision enforced by rhetorically opposing "No Man's Land" to Charlotte Perkins Gilman's *Herland*. The women who suffered through World War I are characterized as unbalanced amazons, as if, because a few young women were convinced by the Tory Party that it was their patriotic duty to distribute white feathers to conscientious objectors, women were the cause of war and not its helpless victims, the cause of male sexual impotence, not its puzzled observers (like Rezia in *Mrs. Dalloway* or Antonia White's heroines, or the three women who nurse the shell-shocked soldier in Rebecca West's *Return of the Soldier*.)

Had the essay centered itself on women's war writing rather than men's, had it been addressed to women readers instead of confusing and "othering" us, "Soldier's Heart" might have critiqued the patriarchy. World War I in fact wiped out women's culture, one might argue instead. At the height of the suffrage movement in 1911 there were 21 regular feminist periodicals in England, a women's press, a feminist bookshop, the Fawcett Library and a bank run by and for women. What is most disturbing about Gilbert's declaration that women had no history, ignoring the enormous bibliography of women's early feminist scholarship as well as memoirs, poems, plays, fiction and feminist pamphlets, is that it inspires fear that our own present decades' work will be equally "lost" in fifty years. Judith Kazantzis' and Catherine Rielly's anthology of women's war poetry, *Scars Upon My Heart* shows women choosing war as a theme before Owen and Sassoon, and writing from every conceivable ideological position from the patriotic to the pacifist. Rose Macaulay's "Many Sisters to Many Brothers," "Oh it's you that have the luck, out there in blood and muck," reflects women's envy of action but poets like S. Gertrude Ford blamed the war-lords and profiteers.[12] To valorize the writing of men who blamed women for the war is a deep distortion of literature and history.

Gilbert's essay is illustrated with several posters from the Imperial War Museum, but it does not examine the ideological propaganda machine which produced these mythic mothers, nurses and young jingoes who demand that men go and fight. It assumes uncritically that women created these images or approved them, a subject I will discuss more fully later. It agrees with male writers that war "suggests female conquest" (424) and that during wartime women became "even more powerful," a contradiction of her previous argument (423) that women were "powerless." Each of these statements is directed to a different audience. Gilbert states that the war dispossessed men of "patriarchal primacy" while it gave women votes and jobs. In actual fact, British women did not get the vote until 1928; in 1918 only women over 30 with the property qualifications got votes.[13] Gilbert's characterization of women's "sexual glee" at men's death as well as guilt at surviving the war seems to me utterly wrong. The heroine of Norah James' *Sleeveless Errand* commits suicide as a superfluous woman, reflecting a post-war reality which historians have not wished to deal with.[14] Elizabeth Robins records her rage in *Ancilla's Share* that women workers were dispossessed of their jobs when the men returned and thinks the suffragettes were mistaken in suspending their activities, since they were worse off economically after the war. Over 66,000 enlisted women and 1,200 officers lost their jobs, as well as thousands of W.A.A.C.'s, W.R.A.F.'s, W.R.E.N.'s, V.A.D.'s and women police, not to mention the wholesale turnout of women in Civil Service and the new rule against marriage for teachers and civil servants.[15]

What does Gilbert mean when she says that women had "no sense of inherited history to lose"? The suffrage movement had produced, just as our own movement today has done, a spate of histories of women; "The Pageant of Great Women" was regularly produced on stage and every reader of the weekly *Votes for Women* knew by heart the fifty-year history of the struggle for the vote, for education, for jobs and professional training. The state asked women to forget that newly acquired "history" and to sacrifice yet again their own desire for social freedom and political equality.[16] Many of them did not. The women's movement provided its own plot and for the first time women did have a "sense of inherited history."

A strong pacifist feminism emerged during and after the war (it is a great dis-service to women's history to describe Vera Brittain, the great Pacifist, as simply an ignorant girl who learned about men's anatomy by serving as a VAD nurse) and Sylvia Pankhurst gave the Communist Party a big boost by bringing left-wing feminists to help in the Dock Strike and turning her newspaper, *The Women's Dreadnought* into *The Workers' Dreadnought*.[17] Gilbert might have compared the figures in the government posters to the figures designed by women themselves. Not nurses or mothers, the suffragettes' icon was Joan of Arc, the militant maiden out for vengeance. Armed and chaste, she symbolized struggle, a *real* battle of the sexes for ownership of women's sexuality, and a conscious feminist fetishization. That she was armed, and neither maternal nor a nurse, was part of her power. The state's posters were a direct response to the suffragettes' images of themselves as virgin warriors. The splendid Lolly Willowes in Sylvia Townsend Warmer's brilliant novel feels oppressed by one of these horrible posters as she does volunteer work during the war and frees herself from the image of woman as nurturer with great relief after the war.

One of the most serious problems the woman reader of Gilbert's essay faces is the lack of references to women historians of the period. And one is appalled at the uncritical use of the work of the sensationalistic journalist, David Mitchell, whose vile and disgusting misogyny in *Women on the Warpath* is only equalled by his filthy mud-slinging attack on suffrage and its supporters in *Queen Christabel*. No reputable historian would use this material as if it were "history." When Gilbert asks "Does male death turn women nurses on?" (436) and "Was the war a festival of female misrule . . . ?" (437) one can only reply that she is asking the wrong questions. When she moves on to homoerotic relations she does not see that the men had power and the women did not. Homosexuals and lesbians are not equal as "others." There is a real difference in class and power between elite homosexual officers and Radclyffe Hall's ambulance drivers.[18] Worst of all, Gilbert ends her piece by declaring that Virginia Woolf's muse was war, and by calling *Three Guineas* a "violent antipatriarchal fantasy" only expressive of "hostility to men" (445) " . . . a number of women writers besides Woolf felt that not only their society but also their art had been subtly strengthened, or at least strangely inspired, by the deaths and defeats of male contemporaries." (446) This slander is followed by the statement: "many women *returned* (emphasis added) into embittered unemployment or guilt-stricken domesticity after World War I"(449).[19] To describe as a self-chosen "retreat" the governmental, institutional and social pressure to get out of the work force is a regrettable misreading of history (by which I do not mean that "history" written by the unbalanced David Mitchells of this world). In the "war of the images" which Gilbert declares is our heritage from this war, she has declared her partisanship with the images created by the state propaganda machine, with Owen and Lawrence, and male establishment historians. Women workers, writers and political thinkers deserve more than the lower half of a double discourse. Critical fetishization of these familiar female figures is not inscribed in a feminist plot. If she writes in a double voice, the critic can no longer expect the reader to puzzle over a text which claims women were empowered by a war which devastated their lives and their movement.

An essay in which the critic speaks in two voices is like the statue of Nurse Cavell. Beneath the body of the nurse with the bandage is woman's message as subtext, while the superscript proclaims allegiance to the patriarchal plot. But double discourse will no longer do. The feminist critic is no longer in the position of the Victorian novelist, writing in patriarchy, providing a subersive undertext which is open to misreadings by women. Women readers want their own plot or plots. The plot of Gilbert's history is prophetically overturned by a fiction of Antonia White called "Surprise Visit" in which the heroine, a publisher's assistant in London, revisits Bedlam, the madhouse, where she, like so many other women who were not "empowered" by World War I, was incarcerated. The plot of this fiction proposes another history. The women's asylum has become the Imperial War Museum. Among the tanks and guns and uniformed figures, Julia Tye is driven mad again by a statue of a nurse, the figure the propaganda machine created to keep women in line, as well as men: "Then she saw the figure standing deceptively still . . . a uniformed nurse, staring fixedly at her and coldly smiling. Now she knew for certain where she was and who she was. She sagged down on her knees, whimpering: 'No . . . Oh, no! . . . Not there . . . Not in the pads . . . Don't put me back in the pads! I'll be good, Nurse Roberts, I'll be good.'"[20]

The pads may be read as the patriarchal strait jacket, and Julia Tye's voice as the feminist who is intimidated by a powerful restraining woman's voice insisting that women be read as men see them. Gilbert does not see what a critical strait jacket the limited paradigm of "the battle of the sexes" provides. In the "surprise visit" to her own past and the horrible connection between men's war and women's madness expressed vividly in the spatial metaphor of institutional enclosure, the hospital for madwomen turned into the museum of war and death, Antonia White treats the unspoken and unwritten history of the suffering of her own generation of war widows. When she sees the church-like dome of the old Wren Building her mind reverts to its sepia image stamped on the asylum's plates — from inside the patients see the outside, the image a reward for having cleaned their plates, suggesting an anorexic subtext to the script of women's madness in which the matriarchs enforce patriarchal prescriptions. The story reaches far beyond its autobiographical subject, the madness treated in *Beyond the Glass*. Written late in White's life, in 1965, this story expresses the "*abjection*" Kristeva defines as that which is excluded from phallocentric discourse, a gesture of the feminist "political unconscious" against the kind of male history which buries women's madness in the war museum. It is an effective antidote to Gilbert's treatment of the "sexual glee" of women in wartime Britain. The horrors of Bedlam are erased, as women's history always is, by aeroplane propellors and gas-masks. The ideology of male valor remains a powerful force so that women are still ashamed to claim their mental suffering as equal to that of crippling or death on the battlefield. White's fiction *is* women's history, as Gilbert's history is a fiction.

In her autobiography, Antonia White vividly recalled her first clear memory of her father, the classics master, standing at the hearth under "the gilt and marble clock in the shape of the Parthenon," with the black marble fireplace framing her in memory forever in woman's place in a Mausoleum of Classical Patriarchy. Daddy's Girl under the middleclass mantel/mantle is like Sylvia Townsend Warner's young Osbert's lost mate in "Cottage Mantleshelf." White's father taught her to recite, at age three, in Greek, the first line of the *Iliad*: "Sing, oh Goddess, the wrath of Achilles . . ." He taught her "to give things their right names" and would not tolerate "baby talk," initiating her into the "symbolic" order of language very early.

Women, goddesses or not, have been singing the wrath of Achilles for far too long (228).[21] Yet, Antonia White eventually sang her own wrath, the missing song in men's war memorials, refusing to be "good" for the patriarchal nurse. Bedlam become the Imperial War Museum is the "asylum of Antaeus," the site of convergence of the female with war and madness, the heart of one of the unsung *other* plots.

If fighting men suffered "soldier's heart" and shell-shock, it is well to remember that women on the domestic front were also driven mad by war and death and loss. Tough women like Vera Brittain served as VAD's but cracked up afterward. And women writers, though no one has yet written that chapter in literary history, later went to Spain to fight fascism, like the poets Sylvia Townsend Warner and Valentine Ackland. The lesbian communist couple boldly and politically published a volume called *Whether a Dove or a Seagull*, in which their individual poems were not identified, as a protest against the literary polities of reputation.[22]

Aside from its radical critique of the discourse of Western dualism, Sylvia Townsend Warner's poem "Cottage Mantleshelf" critiques the patriarchal heterosexual *copula* as nicely as Derrida.[23] A woman's narrative of war, like Woolf's portrait of Septimus Smith, and using the same figures of roses to represent Englishness, it sings the unsung homosexual non-hero of the wrong class as an Art Deco portrait in pink and black of the blasted hearth of the "Home Front." Unhinged and uncoupled, the "nancy boy" is one of the unnamed skulls in Antaeus' temple. Even patriarchal time rejects him as a partner:

Cottage Mantleshelf

On the mantleshelf love and beauty are housed together.
There are two black vases painted with pink roses,
And the two dogs carrying baskets of flowers in their jaws.
There are the two fans stencilled with characters from Japan,
And ruby glass urns each holding a sprig of heather,
And the two black velvet cats with bead eyes, pink noses,
    and white cotton claws.
All these things on the mantleshelf are beautiful and are
    married:
The two black vases throb with their sympathetic pink roses,
The puss thinks only of her tom and the dog of his bitch.
On the one fan a girl is coquetting and on the other a man,
Out of the same vein of fancy the urns were quarried,
Even the springs of heather have been dried so long you
    can't tell 'tother from which.

But amid this love and beauty are two uncomely
whose sorrows
Isled in several celibacy can never, never be mated,
One of them being but for use and the other useful
no more.
With a stern voice rocking its way through time
the alarm clock
Confronts with a pallid face the billowing to-morrows
And turns its back on the enlarged photograph of
Young Osbert who died at the war.

Against the crumpled cloth where the photographer's fancy
Has twined with roses the grand balustrade he poses,
His hands hang limp from the khaki sleeves and his
legs are bent.
His enormous ears are pricked and tense as a
startled hare's,
He smiles — and his beseeching swagger is that of a nancy,
And plain to see on the picture is death's indifferent
rubber stamp of assent.
As though through gathering mist he stares out
through the photo's
Discolouring, where the lamp throws its pink-shaded
echo of roses
On the table laid for supper with cheese and pickles and tea.
The rose-light falls on his kin who sit there
with whole skin,
It illumines through England the cottage homes where
just such ex-voto
Are preserved on their mantelshelves by the
living in token that they are not as he.

Uncomely and unespoused amid the espousals of beauty,
The cats with their plighted noses, the vases pledging
their roses.
The scapegoat of the mantleshelf he stands and may not
even cleave
To the other unpaired heart that beats beside him and apart,
For the pale-faced clock has heard, as he did, the voice
of duty
And disowns him whom time has disowned, whom
age cannot succor nor the years reprieve.

(*Collected Poems*, 21-22).

This poem, parodying Laurence Binyon's patriotic "For the Fallen," and also appropriating the Barge Speech from *Antony and Cleopatra* as well as the rose-colored glasses of War Memorials, *is* the history of World War I, as powerfully as Sylvia Pankhurst's *The Home Front* is a fiction. The coupling which I have arranged here between fiction and history as authorities for each other in the narrative of women and war suggests that when the one doesn't speak without the other, the hierarchy of sub- and super-script is dissolved to foreground the woman's text. If we read Townsend Warner and White, rather than Owen and Lawrence, at least we won't be contributing to that pile of skulls, the patriarchal "civilization" of Antaeus. "Patriotism is not enough" is what Nurse Cavell really said. It is her voice we need to hear, not the voice of the propaganda portraits of the nurse as the patriarchy's policewoman. While it is not my purpose to fetishize fact-mongering in literary criticism, Gilbert's misreading of women's experience of war makes clear that Clio and Calliope had better be on speaking terms to avoid further distortions.

It seems to me that the valorization of theory is partly to blame for the shoddiness of contemporary scholarship. If critics believe that the method is all and that they can unlock the meaning of any text, and film or painting — without contextualization, subsequent blunders are bound to happen and little work of enduring value will be produced. On the other hand, scholarship without theory assumes objective "truths" can be captured. We need as well to examine the ideology of our subjects and ourselves. Certainly my own text is not innocent; its bias is openly expressed, though one can never approach full self-disclosure. One would also encourage feminists to be bolder in their reading of women's writing and to resist the premature canonization of particular texts (like *Jane Eyre* and *The Yellow Wallpaper*). This continual re-reading settles the new discipline too soon into patriarchal patterns, recursive (and ultimately conservative) circling around the same texts, when finding *new* ways to read (I firmly believe) is the result of reading new or newly-discovered writing in new ways. I realize that I am merely restating here the politics of my own experience as a critic, that for me theoretical statements have come out of close readings of texts in their ideological and historical settings.

Yet I do not agree with the British empiricists in the debate about the uses of literature as social evidence. The Craig-Egan argument that "the more historically accurate a piece of imaginative writing is, the better it is likely to be. And the better it is aesthetically, the more historically accurate it is likely to be," strikes me as primitive. I have trouble with the meaning of words like "accurate" and "better," which disguise the authoritarianism and hidden canon behind the argument. Who decides? On this principle the war poems of Owen and Sassoon, revalorized for feminism by Gilbert, remain canonical, historically and aesthetically "better" and "accurate" because the accepted social ethic privileges the combatant's version over the non-combatant's. Sylvia Townsend Warner's "Cottage Mantleshelf" remains unquiet on the domestic front, "uncomely and unespoused" like the photograph of "young Osbert." This seems to me to be a very bad coupling of history and literature as partners who will ultimately privilege all realist art over the fantastic or the surreal, as well the history of Achilles' wrath over Julia Tye's breakdown, temporal over spatial art. A more fruitful inquiry might be to translate Fredric Jameson's "political unconscious" so that gender becomes a workable component of the theory.[24] The effect of Gilbert's essay is to affirm male hegemony in action in World War I, male literary hegemony over writing in this period and male cultural hegemony over images of women, to insist that Helen's text must record only Achilles' wrath.

The ideological conjunction of woman, war and madness is expressed even more dramatically by Antonia White's 1928 story, "The House of Clouds." Lyrically surreal, it captures the historical reality of the mental instability of war-widows because it breaks down the stable relation of narrative authority and the text floats in hallucination, forcing the reader to experience Helen's visions as Woolf does with Septimus in *Mrs. Dalloway*. Hints of ambiguous sexuality and transvestism unsettle both texts. Septimus' moment of joy comes in Rezia's hat covered with roses. Helen is whisked off to the madhouse in a nightgown and her husband's army overcoat. "The House of Clouds" details the stages of making a grieving woman into an "Inmate" of an institution, strait jacket, drugs, forcible feeding, cold baths, solitary confinement. These "facts" by which one could put together a precise description of twenties' clinical practice in treating the insane, are the physical setting of "confinement" of Helen's body while her mind is liberated in its vision.

The "femininity" of these texts is expressed in their spatiality, textualizing the place of confinement and eliminating for heroine or reader the sense of time, blurring day and night, confusing minutes with years. In fact the temporal structure of the story is not a mimesis of sick to well, the usual story of gradual recovery into "sanity," but the building of the reader's sense that the doctors and nurses are thieves who rob Helen of her visions, a defeat rather than a recovery: "She gave up. She accepted everything. She was no longer Helen or Veronica, no longer even a fairy horse. She had become an Inmate"(66). For Helen, health is loss of imagination. The cure is experienced as a loss of freedom.

When she is first put in the asylum White's Helen recalls her fear of her father and the doctor: "They were going to take her away to use her as an experiment. Something about the war." (47) This personal "neurosis" seems to me an "accurate" historical account of what happens to women in war-time. "'Morphia, mo-orphia, put an M on my forehead,' she moaned in a man's voice"(47). Her vocal transvestism makes her a female Orpheus, Orphia/Ophelia speaking women's madness and poetry. She is marked as a prisoner of Man, ventriloquist of his mandate that she must not kill herself, marked as war always marks woman, for Motherhood. She hears voices, and she conflates the two oppressive war poster figures of nurse and mother:

> 'You must all dress as nurses,' said the second voice,'then she thinks she is in a hospital. She lives through it again, or rather, they do.'
>
> 'Who . . . the sons?'
>
> 'Yes. The House of Clouds is full of them.'
>
> One by one, women wearing nurses' veils and aprons tiptoed in and sat beside her bed. She knew quite well that they were not nurses; she even recognized faces she had seen in picture papers. These were rich women whose sons had been killed, years ago, in the war. And each time a woman came in, Helen went through a new agony. She became the dead boy. She spoke with his voice. She felt the pain of amputated limbs, of blinded eyes. She coughed up blood from lungs torn to rags by shrapnel. Over and over again, in trenches, in field hospitals, in German camps, she died a lingering death. Between the bouts of torture, the mothers, in their nurses' veils, would kiss her hands and sob out their gratitude.
>
> 'She must never speak of the House of Clouds,' one said to another.
>
> And the other answered:
>
> 'She will forget when she wakes up. She is going to marry a soldier' (50, 51).

White here deconstructs the valorization of valor in the literature of heroism. What can staunch the wounds of vicarious shell-shock or compare these voices to Septimus'? Those militant mothers who willingly sacrifice their sons in war, pictured in the papers opening bazaars with stiff upper lips, also figure in Woolf's portraits of the matriarchal Lady Bruton and Lady Bradshaw in *Mrs. Dalloway*. Virginia Woolf, Antonia White and Sylvia Townsend Warner understood the true obscenity of British official war propaganda in its mobilizing of icons of motherhood and nursing for their destructive patriotic ends. Gilbert reads the enormous abstract *pietà* of nurse-mother, holding a small wounded soldier on a stretcher as proof that women were thrilled at their power over invalid men. The poster is titled "The Greatest Mother in the World," and it may have been constructed by a clever propagandist to appeal to the recruits' fears of the maternal, but the abstraction of the figure and her iconographic relation to the virgin mother also signals that war and motherhood are complicit. (It is an interesting cultural note that French WWI recruitment posters in Les Invalides do not use abstract figures of mothers or nurses to represent France.) It is also perfectly obvious that this poster is an insidious simple reversal of the famous forcible-feeding suffrage poster in which the doctor and nurses appear to "rape" a suffragette victim.

In a recent provocative essay, Nancy Huston argues from archetypal images throughout history that "men make war because women make babies." Like the writers I have cited, Huston's political consciousness sees women as oppressed by this insistent connection which serves the continuation of destruction. The refusal of motherhood (seen in the birth control movement and lesbianism) on the part of women, and pacifism on the part of men, is a refusal to play these ideologically defined roles. Thus the persecution of birth-controllers and pacifists during and after the war and the obscenity trial for *The Well of Loneliness* are a historical continuation in the public mind of the matrix of signs linking the inimical concepts of life and death, motherhood and war. They have no natural affinity but are coupled anew for every war to glamorize destruction and keep women producing cannon fodder for the next. Women were oppressed and manipulated by these powerful images, which mobilized their maternal and nurturing instincts to glamorize killing. Like Lolly Willowes, they were made to feel guilty and unpatriotic if they feared or distrusted these images. Gilbert does not see that the figure of the "grey nurse," imagined by the super-masculine Peter Walsh in *Mrs. Dalloway*, is a powerful critique of his own abstraction and idealization of women into roles of mother, nurse England, the Home Front and the imperialists' excuse. Because he cannot relate to real women, he is susceptible to those abstractions in which the female image is shamelessly used to represent truth, justice, liberty or fate. He fetishizes in a classically Freudian way (his knife) the phallic mother. Peter's sinister "grey nurse" is the British imperialist's (he is an Indian civil servant) Mother Country, a figure of speech first exploited by Virginia Woolf's grandfather, James Stephen, as head of the Colonial Office. The "Mother Country" of British patriarchal Imperialism is a "phallic mother" with a vengeance.

Antonia White's "House of Clouds" is another of the asylums of Antaeus, where the forbidding nurse-mother figure is seen for what she is, the police-woman of patriarchy, the woman who enforces in other woman the continued complicity of motherhood and war. White sings Helen's song, not the wrath of Achilles, but woman as horse in men's war games. Helen sees herself in the mirror as a fairy horse "ridden almost to death" or a stag with antlers, and "dark, stony eyes and nostrils red as blood. She threw up her head and neighed and made a dash for the door"(53). The nurses drag her along iron tracks to her room:

> She came out of this dream suddenly to find herself being tortured as a human being. She was lying on her back with two nurses holding her down. A young man with a signet ring was bending over her, holding a funnel with a long tube attached. He forced the tube down her nose and began to pour some liquid down her throat. There was a searing pain at the back of her nose: she choked and struggled, but they held her down ruthlessly. At last the man drew out the tube and dropped it coiling in a basin. (55)

This scene (Plate 1) of forcible feeding of a woman in a mental hospital after the war recalls with vivid intensity the experiences of the suffragettes who hunger-struck in Holloway Gaol before the war and were forcibly fed on government orders, a particularly violent response to passive resistance as a political strategy by the feminists, a very ugly chapter in British history depicted in a well-known suffrage poster. Women died and were disabled by forcible feeding. Their lungs often filled with liquid. Constance Lytton never recovered. The madwoman and the suffragette are joined in this scene, as they are joined in *women's history*.

This joining sharply indicates the necessity to free women's history from the yoke of male periodization, as Joan Kelly asked "Did Women Have a Renaissance?" and Joan Scott argues in *Behind the Lines*. If Gilbert's study had bean written as women's history, it would have avoided centering on men's war and seeing women only in subordinate relation to it. In women's history, the pre-war cultural achievements of women in politics and art reached a high point from 1906-1914. The War Office's propaganda

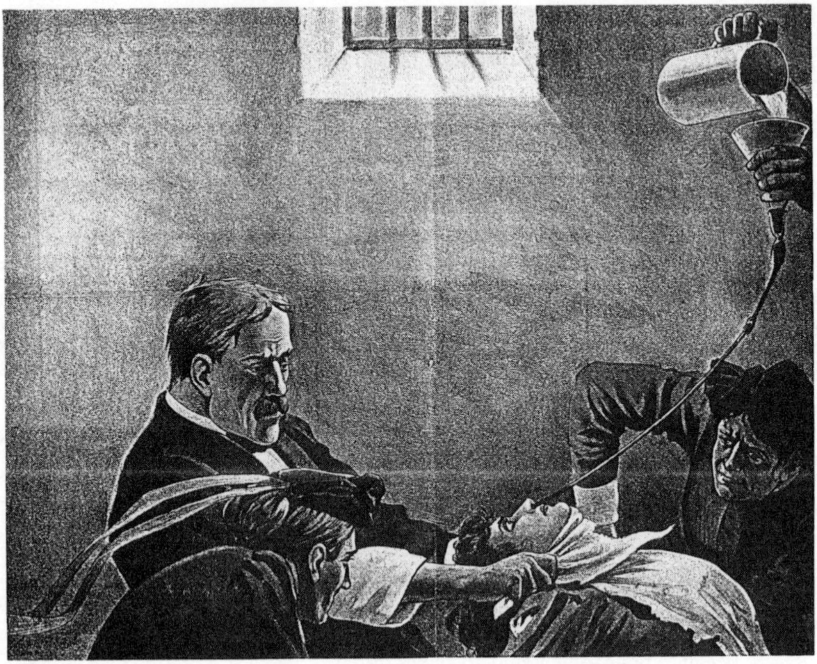

Plate 1.

posters of nurses and mothers, wives sending their men to war — were a *response* to the overwhelming powerful public iconography of the women's suffrage movement, a challenge to the figures of Amazon Joan of Arc, the virgin warrior and the professional single woman drawn as the protector of mothers and children. The image of the powerful single woman at work or as the champion of her sex, the great posters of female victimization, the woman being forcibly fed and the Cat and Mouse Act poster (which dramatized the Liberal Government's release of hunger-strikers only to pounce and re-arrest them when they spoke in public, see Plate 2) had to be wiped out of the public mind by the only images of women allowed by a nation at war, the nurse, the mother, the worker. One could argue that the propagandists had to work particularly hard to erase the powerful new images created by women for women at the height of the movement. Certainly the symbolic purple, white and green colors of the Women's Social and Political Union, their glorious banners, buttons, parades, processions,

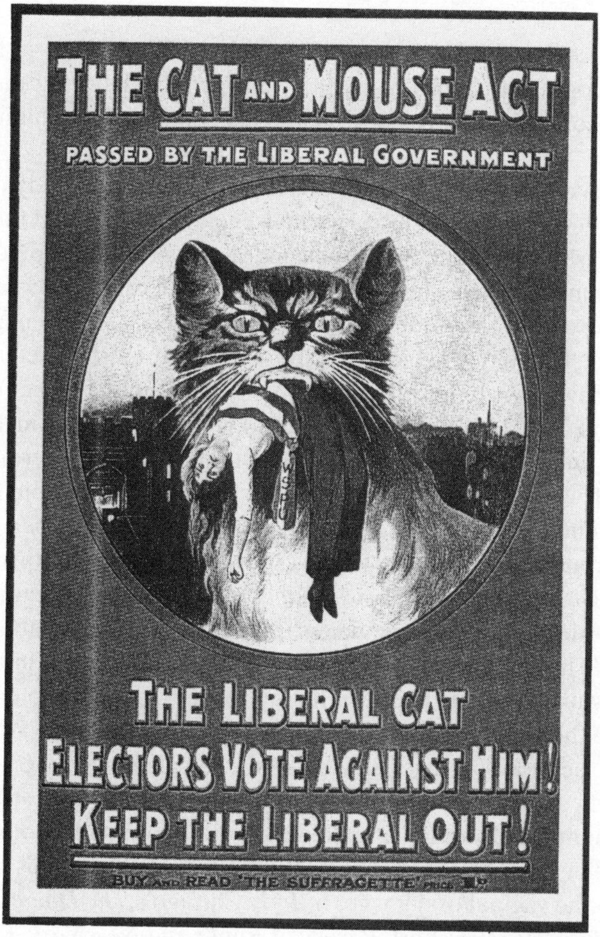

Plate 2.

pageants and public displays, as well as the weekly posters produced by the suffrage atelier and distributed all over the country, were a daunting feminist propaganda machine, whose effects had to be countered by an equally powerful official propaganda.

The enormous matriarchs and fearfully forbidding phallic mothers and stern young wives pointing equally phallic fingers, urging men to go and fight, cannot in any sense be seen as women's images of themselves, but rather as such effective patriarchal projections that ordinary soldiers and university-educated poets could blame the women at home for the deaths of their comrades. Psychologically sophisticated, the War Office "artists" provided the people with a phallic mother fetish which deflected their sexual anxiety and controlled the (natural) fear of castration and wounding in wartime.

If we make a feminist revision of Tom Mitchell's fine study of the history of the rhetoric of iconoclasm, we may begin to understand the process. The idol-smashers historically see the childish pagan and primitive "others" as irrational and obscene, he argues. "The rhetoric of iconoclasm is thus a rhetoric of exclusion and domination, a caricature . . . The images of the idolators are typically phallic . . . and thus they must be emasculated, feminized, have their tongues cut off by denying them the power of expression or eloquence"(113). Of course Mitchell is concerned with male high art and politics and aesthetics in Lessing and Burke. Official government idol-smashing of women's self-images in WWI works on the popular level of taste, and functioned well in Punch cartoons and newspaper drawings, where valorous virgins became hateful spinsters, or comic viragoes. Especially effective were captions in newspaper photos of police beating the suffragettes, which declared that violent revolutionaries were attacking law and order. (The text denied the image.) Well-dressed women in the photos are shown with their hair being pulled by rowdies and the violence is projected on to the victim. Thus the male script of iconoclasm toward women's images may be seen as a masculinizing of the female image, the war posters being a particularly good example of the *exclusion* of figures of happy and successful unmarried women and the substitution of phallic mothers.[25]

Masculine iconoclasm still functions according to this script. In response to the vaginal/oral images of Judy Chicago's *The Dinner Party*, the ordinarily decorous *New York Review of Books* and *New York Times Book Review* printed reviews by two of the most prominent U.S. art critics written in obscene and sexually insulting language, using words seldom used in family newspapers, and the artist herself was masculinized as authoritarian, tough and autocratic. Women's self images are so threatening a rival iconology to patriarchy's traditional control over the image of woman for its own ends, that the suppression of them calls out all the big guns.

Proof of the power of the male iconoclastic script of devaluation of women's self-image is that the suffragettes' extraordinary renaissance of women's political art came to be seen, not only by the public, but by socialist feminist Labour Party leaders, as the suspicious *cause* of fascism. In 1939 in *The New Propaganda* (Left Bookclub), Amber Blanco White, twice a Labour candidate in parliamentary elections, and daughter of Mrs. Pember Reeves, an active Fabian feminist, wrote:

> The actual methods now so widely used were first made use of by the Suffragettes. They introduced the practice of advertising a political movement by deliberate "publicity stunts" as an adjunct to the preaching of its doctrines. Such devices as chaining one woman to the railings in Downing Street and posting another as a parcel addressed to the Prime Minister — their processions, their window-smashing, their self-imposed martyrdoms — would all have commended themselves (if used by his own side) to an up-to-date Minister of Propaganda. The Suffragettes also adopted, for use among their own followers as distinct from the public, the same means for whipping up excitement, the same emotional appeals for sacrifices, the same technique for arousing irrational hostility against their opponents as the Fascist dictators are now employing to keep their followers in order. Theirs was in fact, towards the end, an organization run on Fascist lines and characterized by an authentically Fascist violence and emotionalism and exaggeration. (11)

This chilling analysis, comparing fascism to the violence and emotionalism of women, repeats exactly the Tom Mitchell formula for historical iconoclasm. Fascism, this most patriarchal of political movements is feminized by its left-wing enemy in order to be discredited. Amber Blanco White has been dispossessed of her own history as a woman and has internalized a male moral judgment of her sisters, who did, in fact, win the vote for her as monsters.[26]

2. The semiotics and somatics of woman's suffrage[27]

The somatics and semiotics of Women's Suffrage in England deserves a much more thorough study than I can outline here. A massive feminist iconology was created from 1906-1914, drawing one imagines on traditional symbolism in the purple (suffering or loyalty), white (purity) and green (hope) of the colors of the W.S.P.U. In the first concerted effort of women to create their own self-images after centuries of imprisonment by male images of women, the suffrage artists, including Clemence and Laurence Housman in the Suffrage Atelier in Kensington, and the Artist's Suffrage League in Chelsea, used every conceivable style from Slade School Pre-Raphaelite to the socialist realism of Sylvia Pankhurst's prison sketches. Women also moved into public space in a great body, literally and figuratively. Aware of the dangers, they costumed themselves for each occasion, in their rose-laden hats and best Edwardian lady-like dresses, in academic gowns or clothes and banners symbolizing their work, processions of girls in white dresses flanked by vanguards of Joan of Arcs on horseback. They dressed up as historical heroines in *The Pageant of Great Women*; Annie Kenney was paraded at Christabel Pankhurst's side in the clogs and apron of a mill girl long after she had left Lancashire behind. The leaders were photographed and enshrined on posters in their Holloway Prison uniforms to glamorize their hunger strikes. Photographs of Mrs. Pankhurst and a host of other leaders were as popular as those of actresses, and middle-class married women in the country worked long hours on eloquent silk flags and banners signifying regional, religious or occupational women's organizations, to be carried in mass demonstrations.

The art of the posters, flyers and pamphlets ranged as wide as support for suffrage across classes and varied in intensity, class bias or idealization of women. Some of it draws deliberately on fashion or sentimental ideals, while other posters burst with the cartoon vigor of revolutionary propaganda art. Deliberate fetishism in costume and disguise in the W.S.P.U. loosened rigid ideas about dress. Some young women cropped their hair and wore tailored coats and skirts with Byronic silk shirts and ties, like Cicely Hamilton and Christopher St. John of the Actresses' Franchise League. Ancient Mrs. Wolstenholme-Elmy marched in her beaded black Victorian gown and bonnet. Militant Christabel Pankhurst, who planned the window-smashing demonstration in Bond Street, was photographed for her followers in the most ethereal Paris dresses. Then she would appear on the platform in the academic gown, which symbolized the law degree she had earned but could never use as a woman. The signs changed in the feminist semiotic system. They played on every aspect of public attitudes toward women, sliding the signifiers of powerlessness and inferiority of classical feminine stereotypes into their opposites, exploiting even the most appalling victimization through forcible feeding when they were on hunger strike, or the Cat and Mouse Act, which allowed the suffragettes to go without food until the point of death, then released them to re-arrest them as soon as they spoke in public.

These two posters strike me as particularly important in the semiotic "discourse" of suffrage. The crude "rhetoric" of these posters allowed them to be read as rape scenes, and invested them with a permissable rage on the part of the viewer at male violence, in the government cat who molested the mouse, the doctors and nurses who held down the victim and forced liquid into her nose. The forcible-feeding/rape poster also recalls the famous picture of the French psychiatrist, Charcot, hypnotizing a hysterical patient, conflating the government treatment of women political prisoners who were struggling for the vote with helpless victimized women in insane asylums. (For forcible feeding of pacifists see John Rodker, *Memoirs of Other Fronts*, Putnam, 1930.) I raise this issue of clear expression of male violence in suffrage semiotics, because it is expressly denied by Paula Hays Harper in a misinformed essay on suffrage posters, drawing on an extremely small sample and unaware, apparently, of the enormous collections in the London Museum and the Fawcett Library, as well as their rich variety of artistic styles.[28] Arguing that the posters "have little aesthetic quality," Harper claims that they are all "conventional" and reflect the collusion of women "with the social status quo," and represented an appeal by middle class women to men. Their tremendous range, from conservative to radical aesthetically, as well as in terms of content, actually reflects a much more complex situation. The suffrage agitation represented all classes and many special interest groups of women from right to left politically, from anarchists and socialists to Catholics and members of the Primrose League. Iconography was the field on which they fought out their political differences. Decorative art nouveau frames and borders for idealized Pre-Raphaelite figures were early movement appeals to popular images of women, but the art changed as the movement changed.

It seems to me that women's poster art, and its borderline status between commercial art and painting, should be as important to modern women's history as photography is to Modernism in general. Women naturally drew on commercial fashion art which was aimed at them and transformed it for political purposes — one might say they *translated semiotically the signs of commodity fetishism into a deliberate feminist fetishism*. Their first move was to de-eroticize the common images they stole from the Pre-Raphaelites. Their last move, before they were crushed by atavistic matriarchal martial iconoclasm, was to depict rape and male violence against women, including the "bestiality" of the cat and mouse. Their effectiveness is quite obvious in Amber Pember Reeves' iconophobia of the 'thirties, in which fear of fascist propaganda causes her to remember and blame the suffragettes' posters. She does not remember the pretty Pre-Raphaelites but rather the woman chained to the railings. Harper claims that suffrage posters lack audacity and refuse to attack men and are thus weak both artistically and politically. The innocent reader would be convinced that women didn't deserve the vote, as Gilbert's essay argues that women gained a wicked pleasure from the deaths of men in WWI. Neither essay does justice to women's history, though both may eventually be seen as functioning within criticism as certain wings of the suffrage movement did in reassuring men that feminists mean no harm to the establishment.

Stories of the somatics of the suffrage struggle enliven all the memoirs of its participants. They all take particular pleasure in recounting the ways in which exploitation of their femininity foiled the police or the government. When the beatings of police and rowdies at demonstrations grew severe, they carried hat pins and wore cardboard "armour" *under* their dresses to carry off their lady-like image.[29] Elizabeth Robins, the American actress, contributed her experience of the effect of dress to the policy of the board of the W.S.P.U. She wrote of dressing as a poor woman in London at night and the response of men, convincing upper-class women that the same men who were good husbands and fathers were violent and rude to women of other classes. There was obviously a great deal of play-acting and political "travesty" in cross-class dressing within the movement, which brings out the conjunction of the Freudian concept of fetishism with the Marxist in this instance of what I shall call *feminist fetishism*.

Lady Rhondda, the founder of *Time and Tide* and the Six Point Group, recalls a characteristic experience: "Aunt Janetta, carrying a small and unobtrusive parcel, which was in fact a hammer done up in brown paper, strolled down Oxford Street. She was a beautiful woman . . . with soft curly hair and a very gentle and spiritual face — the face of a saint — and she dressed well. It would have needed a wily policeman to identify her with the popular view of the Shrieking Sisterhood. Opposite the windows of D. H. Evans she stopped, and, murmuring to herself 'Whatsoever thy hand findeth to do, do it with all thy might,' upped with the hammer and splintered the window" (162).[30] After breaking several windows she was arrested. As soon as she was out on bail, Lady Rhondda relates, she went back to D. H. Evans and bought a hat, "for she was a most scrupulous woman." The smashing of the Bond Street windows by women dressed exactly like the mannequins on the other side of the glass is telling example of feminist semiotics in the service of an attack on commodity fetishism. It also doesn't take a Freudian to explain the effect of feminine sexual solidarity in those masses of huge, flower-bedecked Edwardian hats as they marched in the West End, smashing the icons of their oppression while wearing them as emblems of class and gender. One of the funniest moments in Dame Ethel Smyth's *Streaks of Life* is the story of the dignified Mrs.

Pankhurst's determination to overcome her inability to throw rocks and the composer's devotion of a day to teaching and practice before one of their "raids."

The ultra-femininity of the suffragettes, while it may have begun as a strategy to avoid male contempt, circulated within a female libidinal economy which equated desire with political freedom, and which is most powerfully suggestive in Christabel Pankhurst's posing of herself as Joan of Arc reincarnated. The armed virgin on horseback was a feminist fetish, which figured the spirituality of the movement with a subtext of sexuality in the horse and the attractive medieval maleness of the tights, coat of mail and sword. Her self-sufficiency as a pure warrior and her chastity frightened men as much as it excited women, and it epitomized a valorous concept of female chivalry, exploiting all the iconography of lady and knight inside an expanded definition of the female. During the war Christabel was able to translate this figure directly into a phallic and jingoistic Brittania, but at the height of the suffrage movement, she stood for invincibility against male sexuality and a code of honor among women which played on medieval chivalry by role playing on the field of femininity, rewarding with favors and ribbons and celebratory dinners and breakfasts the heroic women who survived the horrors of forcible feeding in jail and those who were molested and beaten in brutal police attacks, like "Black Friday."

This brilliant political use of pageantry and ritual eroticized real danger and the threat of death, honoring wounded veterans of the "sex war" as heroines for their physical courage. It is one of the few recorded historical moments of concerted public physical bravery on the part of women as a sex, and consequently has received little attention from historians except those wishing to discredit the somatics of suffrage chivalry as collective "hysteria." Joan Kelly has pointed out that cross-dressing, the carrying of weapons and chivalric codes existed before the 17th century among European women. Thus Christabel may be seen as the restorer of arms to the woman.

For Edwardian women to expose themselves deliberately to the bullying and brutality which accompanied their demonstrations and to suffer the searing pain of hunger striking and forcible feeding was to make explicit the sexual dimensions of state-condoned misogyny, to point out to the public and to themselves that their common experience as women was unmistakably the experience of rape. In the libidinal economy of suffrage a political rape victim was a heroine, not a social outcast, thus they established their solidarity with poor prostitutes and unwed mothers. The suffrage struggle fetishized female suffering so that women of all classes could identify with its production of a specifically female code of honor, a serious threat to male historical dismissal of women as creatures without a sense of honor, or as Freud would put it, without a superego. Women were outraged by heavily-circulated suffragette photos of frail Mrs. Pankhurst fainting in the arms of a policeman and the staged photos of Emmeline and Christabel in prison uniform, fusing the lady and the criminal.

Another example comes from the recent memoirs of actress Elsa Lanchester. I quote them because they may serve to dispel the myth that the suffrage movement was totally middle class and also because they indicate the use of asylums in political reprisals against feminists. The memoirs are interesting in themselves. The reader who expects to find the story of her marriage to Charles Laughton is instead confronted with Lanchester's lifelong obsession with her radical mother, Edith, known as "Biddy." As one of the first generation of Cambridge-educated upper-class women, Edith joined the S.D.F., became Eleanor Marx's secretary and set up housekeeping with Elsa's father, an Irish working man named Shamus Sullivan. Her father and brothers "kidnapped" her and had her certified as insane. The document committing her listed the "supposed cause" of her madness as "over-education" (2). The incident became an international *cause celebre* on the left and crowds of demonstrators outside the asylum soon won her release to "live in sin" with Shamus. She remained a staunch communist and feminist until her death. Elsa recalls that she went often as a small child with a contingent of leftists to march in suffrage demonstrations, and her mother went to jail:

> Instead of waving red flags and wearing buttons saying S.D.F., we waved green, white and purple flags and wore clothes of those colors, with buttons saying W.S.P.U. There was one awful rally when, encircled by the police in chain formation, the vast crowd became a jellified mass moving as one. Biddy shouted to me, below her waist level, "Keep your arms down!" "Yes!" screamed Shamus, "Keep your arms down, girlie, don't reach up, they might get broken." Another time when I was with Biddy at a suffragette rally I was pushed into a doorway in Scotland Yard. The police all had truncheons and were banging women on the head. I screamed a lot, I think, but the whole thing now is oddly still, *a picture with no sound at all* (17; emphasis added).[31]

Elsa Lanchester's vivid memory, after seventy years, of male violence against woman as a "*picture with no sound at all*" suggests an iconophilia bred by the somatics and semiotics of suffrage, which taught her to see women's bodies as feminist fetish. Their words are erased even in dreams. Exactly the opposite is true of Amber Blanco White's iconophobia, linking feminist fetishization with fascism. Both women were the daughters of active political mothers. Amber Blanco White was actually the mistress of H. G. Wells, and the model for the suffragette in his novel, *Ann Veronica*. What Lanchester and White have in common is an identification of feminism with pictures, not words, with spatial modernism, for the suffrage campaign's visual iconography does indeed anticipate all contemporary political campaigns in its non-verbal rhetoric. In their breaking of the images of male false goddesses and creation of new female forms, the iconoclastic suffragettes were self-subverted by the war posters and the historical accusation of serving fascism. Tom Mitchell quotes Jean Baudrillard on how this rhetoric of fetishism comes back to haunt those who use it (205).

Mitchell argues, however, that Marx's concept of fetishization could be more useful to aesthetic analysis than the concept of ideology. It is clear from the suffragettes' art that commodity fetishism serves more than a bourgeois class function, and equally clear that psychological fetishism rises from the female unconscious as well as the male, and that both are inscribed in cultural texts. They may also be consciously exploited by political artists (see Lillian Robinson's *Sex, Class and Culture*). What I have tried to do in this paper is to use Mitchell's suggestion along with Naomi Schor's work on a revision of Freud's concept of fetishism to extend to the female case. Schor follows Sarah Kofman's argument in *The Enigma of Woman* that fetishism is not a perversion peculiar to men and that female fetishism articulates a paradigm of undecidability, an oscillation between denial and recognition of castration, a strategy which allows a woman to keep her human bisexuality from being anchored to one pole. Schor examines female fetishism in George Sand: "Indeed, I would suggest that ultimately *female travesty*, in the sense of women dressing up as or impersonating other women, constitutes by far the most disruptive form of *bisextuality*: for, whereas there is a long, venerable tradition of naturalized intersexual travesty in fiction, drama and opera, the exchange of *female* identities, the blurring of difference within difference remains a largely marginal and unfamiliar form" (370).

In my extension of Mitchell's Marx to female subversion of commodity fetishism and Schor's Freud from female to feminist fetishism, I am suggesting that the suffrage movement deliberately created multiple new images of women as a political act, unsettling female identity in the process. The fetish was less a maternal phallus (as is clear in the war posters) or an "oscillation between denial and recognition of castration," but an oscillation between denial and recognition of *rape* as the common denominator of female experience. The question for the suffrage propagandists was whether or not to depict (and therefore call down on themselves) representations of their own victimization at the hands of male violence.

Examples of Schor's *bisextuality* may be found, however, in the poster rhetoric and Antonia White's "inmates"; the rejection of firm boundaries between characters in Virginia Woolf's *The Waves* and much women's fiction up to and including Grace Paley, especially Marilyn Robinson's *Housekeeping*. The perfect case of "bisextuality" is in the lesbian costume party in Djuna Barnes' *Nightwood* as well as the tatoos, writing on the body and the merging of costume and flesh in the whole novel. Miss Bruce in Jean Rhys' short story, "Illusion," who collects sensuous dresses but dresses in public in tweeds is another example of female fetishism. Female identity is startlingly unsettled in the recently reprinted novels of Molly Keane (M.J. Farrell) where one character's hare lip becomes an erotic attraction and women characters wear each other's clothes. The phenomenon of female fetishism was only marginal and unfamiliar until Naomi Schor named it. My naming of *feminist fetishism* and the narration of its failure to survive wartime iconoclasm is clearly complicit in a new iconoclasm. It does not answer the question I posed at the beginning of whether all histories are fictions or fictions histories but it suggests that we interrogate our own plots as we generate them.

NOTES

My thanks to Angela Ingram, Catharine Stimpson, Tom Foster, and Blanche Cook for their helpful comments on this paper. The present essay was written for the University of Alabama Conference in October 1986, "The Differences Within: Feminism and Critical Theory." I want to thank Elizabeth Meese and Alice Parker for their editorial comments. It also appears in *Arms and the Woman*, edited by Helen Cooper, Adrienne Munich, and Susan Squier, and in another version in the *New Historicism*, ed. Harold Veeser (Methuen, 1988).

1. For a discussion of these issues see Paul Veyne, *Writing History* (Wesleyan University Press/Harper and Row, 1986), and Dominick La Capra, *History and Criticism* (Ithaca: Cornell University Press, 1986), and Hayden White's review essay, "Between Science and Symbol," *TLS* (Jan. 31, 1986): 109-110.

2. Focusing on the experience of catastrophic events by domestic animals, children and women, this novel trangresses the borders between the two disciplines and questions the unspoken division in western culture between the virility of "history" and the femininity of "art," clearly privileging the latter as truth-bearer.

3. By blurring genres — fiction, poetry, reporting, travelogue, history — this book is not only the epitome of '30's documentary, it goes beyond the "realism" aimed at by left writers in its "untruthful" fictions. See the essay by Clare Colquitt, "A Call to Arms: Rebecca West's Assault on the Limits of Gerda's Empire in *Black Lamb and Grey Falcon*," *South Atlantic Review* (Spring 1986). Many of the details of the plot of *The Years* appear in Francis Iles' 1939 *Malice Aforethought*.

4. The formalist nature of much post-structural exegesis has dismissed biography, autobiography, historical and textual studies as uninteresting literary practice. However, like Woolf, feminists are searching women's autobiographies, debating, as in the 1986 Stanford Conference on Autobiography and Gender and several forthcoming collections of essays edited by Domna Stanton (*N.Y. Literary Forum*), Shari Benstock (*The Private Self*, forthcoming, North Carolina U.P.), and Celeste Schenck and Bella Brodsky (*Life/Lines*, forthcoming Cornell U.P.), their value as "truth" in relation to the concept of the fictionality of all texts. Problematic for feminists is the issue of maintaining skepticism about author-ity in uncanonized and unread texts and the wish to share our reading pleasure with a large audience. We are often unwilling to make that last deconstructive turn of undermining our own readings of these neglected works until they have been recuperated fully into literary history, though critics like Gayatri Spivak, Elizabeth Meese and Shari Benstock are negotiating a plot which unites deconstruction with feminism.

5. For a provocative discussion of disciplines as couples, see Alice Jardine, 1986. "Death Sentences: Writing Couples and Ideology," *The Female Body in Western Culture*, ed. by Susan Suleiman, 84-96 (Cambridge: Harvard University Press).

6. If deconstructive or Lacanian critiques are "the cutting edge" of scholarship, feminist materialism is a grimmer reaper with a dull scythe — if one fills out the whole figure of research as a kind of International Harvester machine, not a particularly suitable metaphor for our work, in any case.

7. See Mary Lynn Broe, ed. 1988. *Silence and Power: Djuna Barnes, A Revaluation* (Carbondale: University of Southern Illinois Press).

8. In "The Matrix of War: Mothers and Heroes," in *The Female Body in Western Culture* (see above), Nancy Huston argues from "myth and historical archetypes" that "men make war *because* women have children" (119). Huston ends by pointing out that pacifism and contraception have become 20th century political responses to the nuclear and demographic explosions which threaten the world, in which men refuse military service and women refuse "maternal service." It would be very interesting to study the ideological connections between birth controllers and pacifists in World War I in England and the interlocking rhetorics of both movements in pamphlets and fiction of the period. It is certainly clear that neo-Malthusians feared feminism because it implied to them an

immediate drop in the birth rate which would make England vulnerable in wartime. An unspoken connection between motherhood and war was made by E. M. Forster, defending *The Well of Loneliness* from censorship, connecting lesbianism with pacifism. For a devastating example of internalization of the mother/hero ethic, see the letter from "A Little Mother" in Robert Graves, 1930, *Goodbye to All That*, pp. 270-275 (New York: Cape & Harrison Smith), and Angela Ingram's analysis in "Un/Reproductions" in *Women Writers in Exile*, ed. Ingram and M. L. Broe (Chapel Hill: U. of North Carolina Press). For the post-war militarization of motherhood, see Enid Bagnold's *The Squire* (1938). Her 1917 *A Diary Without Dates* got her dismissed as a VAD nurse, and the *Happy Foreigner* (1920) studies the aftermath of the war in France.

9. See my discussion of this point in "Liberty, Sorority, Misogyny," in *The Representation of Women in Fiction* ed. by Carolyn Heilbrun and Margaret Higonnet, 1982. (Baltimore: Johns Hopkins University Press). Celeste Schenck's essays "Feminism and Deconstruction: Reconstructing the Elegy," *Tulsa Studies in Women's Literature*, 5 (1986) and "Exiled by Genre: Modernism, Canonicity and the Politics of Exile" forthcoming in Broe and Ingram, *Women's Writing in Exile* are useful here on the valuing of women poets only on the experimental male model. Alex Zwerdling calls Isa's poems the "geriatric pastoral" in "*Between the Acts* and the Coming of War," *Novel*, 10 (1977). See also Elizabeth Abel's reading in "The Lady Vanishes: *Between the Acts* and the Return to Freud," forthcoming in her book on Woolf and Freud (University of Chicago Press).

10. See my essays on *The Years* in *Virginia Woolf and the Languages of Patriarchy* (Bloomington: Indiana University Press, 1987). William Kent's *Encyclopedia of London* reports that "Patriotism is not Enough" was added to the statue by the Labour Government in 1924 (524).

11. Note that Newton and Rosenfelt in the introduction to *Feminist Criticism and Social Change* (New York and London: Methuen, 1986) cite this essay as a sign of a new commitment to history on the part of Gilbert, an improvement on *Madwoman*.

12. In addition the difference between Vera Brittain's *Testament of Youth* and the recently published *Chronicle of Youth*, the original diary from which she wrote that great pacifist classic, is worth study.

13. In "The Indescribable Barrier: English Women and the Effect of the First World War," Laura E. Mayhall argues that Gilbert's thesis is incorrect and proves the case with statistical evidence: "The experience of war itself, however, did not create a barrier between men and women. The division occurred when women who aided the war effort threatened the exclusivity of the male power structure." New work on WW I is being done by Jan Calloway, Claire Culleton, George Ott, Linda Palumbo and Susan Millar Williams.

14. See Angela Ingram's 1986 essay "'Unutterable Putrefaction and Foul Stuff': Two Obscene Novels of the 1920's". *Women's Studies International Forum* 9.

15. Robins joined Lady Rhondda in the founding of *Time and Tide* in May, 1920, along with Rebecca West and Cicely Hamilton. They (all feminists) founded the Six-Point Group, to influence legislation affecting motherhood, health, women's wages, equal pay, pensions, custody of children.

16. See Ellen N. La Motte. 1916. *The Backwash of War: The Human Wreckage of the Battlefield as Witnessed by an American Hospital Nurse*. (G.P. Putnam's) banned for its

pacifism, and Angela Ingram's "Un/Reproductions." Sylvia Pankhurst's *The Home Front* (Hutchinson, 1930) is also valuable. Ingram's discussion of the banned novel *Despised and Rejected* is especially good on the links between the mother/hero theme and homosexuality and pacifism. I am grateful for her help throughout this paper.

17. Over half the members of women's suffrage organizations became pacifists during the war. The Women's International League for Peace and Freedom, founded in 1915, became a forum for feminist pacifists. See Anne Wiltsher, 1985. *Most Dangerous Women: Feminist Peace Campaigners of the Great War* (London: Pandora); Gertrude Bussey and Margaret Tims. 1965, *Pioneers for Peace: Women's International League for Peace and Freedom* (London: Allen and Unwin); and Blanche Wiesen Cook. 1978, *Crystal Eastman on Women and Revolution* (N.Y.: Oxford University Press). See also Sylvia Pankhurst's *The Home Front* and Patricia Romero's *E. Sylvia Pankhurst: Portrait of a Radical* (New Haven: Yale U.P., 1987) and my review of it in *The Women's Review of Books*, May, 1987.

18. For graphic description of the real horrors suffered by women nurses and ambulance drivers during the war, see Helen Zenna Smith's (Evadne Price) 1930-33 trilogy, .*Not So Quiet . . .*, *Women of the Aftermath* and *Shadow Women* (London: Albert Marriott) and Mary Borden's *The Forbidden Zone* (NY: Doubleday, 1930). (I am writing an introduction to a Feminist Press 1988 reprint of *Not So Quiet. . . .*) In view of the horrors preserved here, Radclyffe Hall's view of ambulance drivers is extremely romantic in *The Well of Loneliness*. A much more interesting project for feminist historians is to study the war's effect on the masculinization of lesbianism. This would certainly help to explain the pro-fascism of many lesbian artists before and during the next war. For a stunning critique of the destructiveness of war mentality on women, see Rosemary Manning, 1984, *The Chinese Garden*, first published 1962 (London: Brilliance Books); three ex-V.A.D.'s found a school for girls in 1919 and their masculine militarism ruins the lives of the next generation of lesbians. See also Manning's autobiography *A Time and A Time* (London: Marion Boyars, 1986).

19. Elizabeth Robins points out in *Ancilla's Share* the wholesale removal of women from the labor force in 1919. Aside from several thousand service women and munitions workers who lost their jobs, women bus-conductors were released and the hostility to working women was so great that women jurors were challenged. Cambridge University not only refused to give women degrees but now limited enrollment to 500 women. The medical schools and hospitals refused women students again. In all, three quarters of a million working women had been dismissed from their jobs. Sandra Gilbert's hostility to Virginia Woolf and to feminist pacifism in general is hard to understand; she invests Woolf with her own commitment to the paradigm of "the battle of the sexes," reaffirming all the old arguments of Hynes' *The Edwardian Turn of Mind*, instead of interrogating this paradigm from a feminist perspective.

20. For the treatment of the nurse and women's madness, see a different view in White's friend Emily Coleman's *The Shutter of Snow*, N.Y.: Viking, 1930, now rpt. 1986 Virago/Penguin). In Susan Fromberg Schaeffer's *The Madness of a Seduced Woman*, the nurse is a saviour and friend and the narrative is addressed to her. A horrifying nurse like Antonia White's appears in Virginia Woolf's *The Voyage Out*, frightening Rachel in her dying fever. The transformation of Bedlam to the Imperial War Museum gives one the same uncanny chill as a visit to Les Invalides in Paris, where the ex-hospital now houses Napoleon's Tomb and a vast collection of war memorabilia.

21. In "Surprise Visit" Julia recalls being frightened by her two former nurses at a dance. In "Clara IV," which was to be the fifth novel after the *Frost in May* quartet, Julia (Clara) meets two of the nurses on a channel steamer in 1928. She sees them in the mirror, her recurrent image of female madness. Jones and Smith remain sadistic and kind, each still playing their old roles of good cop and bad cop.

22. The recuperation of Townsend Warner as a political writer has begun with Barbara Brothers' "Writing Against the the Grain: Sylvia Townsend Warner and the Spanish Civil War," forthcoming in Broe and Ingram, eds., *Women Writers in Exile*. See also p. 168 of my *Virginia Woolf and the Languages of Patriarchy*.

23. For Sylvia Townsend Warner as a feminist critic, see my "Still Practice A/Wrested Alphabet: Toward a Feminist Aesthetic" in Shari Benstock, *Feminist Issues in Literary Scholarship* (Bloomington: Indiana University Press, 1987). Mrs. Dalloway is herself a version of the Home Front in her assumption that Septimus died for her and Peter Walsh's imaging of her as England (the Assumption of the Grey Nurse), his excuse for imperialism. Similarly suffused in patriotic English rose-light, Mrs Dalloway is also a nay/saying Penelope/Molly as Woolf responds to Homer and Joyce's war narratives.

24. See my "Laughing at Leviticus," 1988, in *Silence and Power: Djuna Barnes, A Revaluation*, ed. M. L. Broe (Carbondale: University of Southern Illinois Press), for a way to genderize Jameson.

25. This *textual* denial of what the image of state violence against protesters actually shows (and this is true of television newscasting as well) and the projection of violence onto the victim, continues to operate very effectively and actually makes clear that, socially, words may still dominate pictures as vehicles of rationality, though this is obviously changing.

26. Gilbert's affirmation of the standard patriarchal interpretation of women's role in the war is a similar case.

27. I use the word somatics as body-language after the fine essay by Catharine Stimpson, "The Somagrams of Gertrude Stein," in *The Female Body in Western Culture*, ed. Susan Suleiman, cited above.

28. Like Gilbert, Harper accepts the standard valuation of the war posters over the suffrage art, failing to distinguish between the enormous resources of official government propaganda and the art produced by volunteer artists in a movement for social change. She also does not see the war posters as an iconoclastic destruction of the previous self-made images of the women's movement. Harper claims that few suffrage posters survive and that they have been ignored. This is not the case. An enormous selection was mounted on exhibit several times in the 1970's in London. They may be seen in the London Museum or the Fawcett Library, or, far more easily on the library shelves, illustrating all the histories of women's suffrage. A particularly large selection is reproduced in Midge McKenzie. 1975. *Shoulder to Shoulder* (New York: Knopf). For a thorough study of suffrage iconology, see Lisa Tickner's forthcoming *The Spectacle of Women: Imagery of The Women's Suffrage Campaign 1907-1914* (London: Chatto & Windus/Hogarth 1988). Tickner argues the suffragettes' use of the phallic mother image works with the hystericization of women's bodies and also describes the battle over possession of the image of the "womanly woman."

29. For further discussion of the politics of dress, see my "Transatlantic Sisterhood," *SIGNS* 3: 744-55. Elizabeth Robins was fond of pointing out that the French fashion house of

Worth invented the "hobble skirt" which was very tight at the bottom, at the height of the suffrage movement when women were striding through the streets.

30. Other memoirs relate cloak and dagger stories of the Pankhursts' escape from the police in the garb of working women, as widows in heavy black mourning, in wigs and shawls, a whole costume party of political cross-dressing.

31. Lanchester also recalls marching in the great demonstration for Emily Wilding's funeral. A brilliant "new woman" with two university degrees, Emily Wilding was killed by running in front of the king's horse at the Derby. Historians have invariably treated her as a hysteric or a joke, quoting someone who says he felt sorry for the horse. It is perhaps too embarrassing to relate that women actually died for the vote, as British propaganda still denies heroism to hunger-striking martyrs to the Irish cause. Elsa Lanchester's child's eye view of the occasion is a memory, after seventy years, of the colors and the shiny steel nuts, bolts and screws on the road, fallen from cars and horse buses in the funeral parade.

REFERENCES

Barnes, Djuna. 1937. *Nightwood*. New York: Harcourt, Brace & Co.

Brittain, Vera. 1979. *Testament of Youth*. London: Fontana/ Virago.

Broe, M.L. and Ingram, A., eds. 1988. *Women's Writing in Exile*. Chapel Hill: University of North Carolina Press.

Chitty, Susan, ed. 1983. *As Once in May: The Early Autobiography of Antonia White and Other Writings*. London: Virago.

Craig, David and Egan, Michael. 1982. "Historicist Criticism." In *Re-Reading English*, ed. Peter Widdowson, 207-222. London: Methuen.

Harper, Paula Hays. "Votes for Woman? A Graphic Episode in the Battle of the Sexes." *Art and Architecture in the Service of Politics*, ed. Henry A. Millon and Linda Nochlin, 150-161. Cambridge: M.I.T. Press.

Higgoner, Margaret (and Jensen, Michel, Weitz). 1987. *Behind the Lines: Gender and The Two World Wars*. New Haven: Yale U.P.

Huston, Nancy. 1986. "The Matrix of War: Mothers and Heroes." In *The Female Body in Western Culture* ed. Susan Suleiman, 119-136. Cambridge: Harvard University Press.

Iles, Francis. 1939. *Malice Aforethought*

Jameson, Fredric. 1981. *The Political Unconscious: Narrative as a Socially Symbolic Act*. Ithaca: Cornell University Press.

Kazantis, Judith and Reilly, Catherine, ed. 1981. *Scars Upon My Heart: Women's Poetry and Verse of the First World War*. London: Virago.

Kelly-Gadol, Joan. 1977. "Did Women Have a Renaissance?" In *Becoming Visible: Women in European History*, ed. Renate Bridenthal and Claudia Koonz. Boston: Houghton Mifflin.

———. 1984. *Women, History, and Theory: The Essays of Joan Kelly.* Chicago and London: University of Chicago Press.

Kristeva, Julia. 1985. *Powers of Horror.* New York: Columbia University Press.

Lanchester, Elsa. 1983. *Elsa Lanchester, Herself.* New York: St. Martin's Press.

Leed, Eric. 1979. *No Man's Land: Combat and Identity in World War I.* New York: Cambridge University Press.

Macciocchi, Maria. 1979. "Female Sexuality in Fascist Ideology." *Feminist Review* 1: 59-82.

Mackworth, Margaret Haig. Viscountess Rhondda. 1933. *This Was My World.* London.

Mitchell, David. 1966. *Women on the Warpath: The Story of the Women of the First World War.* London: Jonathan Cape.

Mitchell, W. J. T. 1986. *Iconology: Image, Text, Ideology.* Chicago: University of Chicago Press.

Morante, Elsa. 1984. *History, A Novel* (1974). New York: Vintage .

Robins, Elizabeth. 1924, London. *Ancilla's Share: An Indictment of Sex-Antagonism.* rpt. Westport, Conn.: Hyperion Press, 1976.

Robinson, Lillian. 1978. *Sex Class, and Culture.* Bloomington: Indiana University Press.

Robinson, Marilynne. 1982. *Housekeeping.* New York: Bantam.

Schenck, Celeste. 1986. "Feminism and Deconstruction: Re-Constructing the Elegy." *Tulsa Studies in Women's Literature* 5(1986): 13-27.

Schor, Naomi. 1986. "Female Fetishism: The Case of George Sand". *The Female Body in Western Culture* ed. Susan Suleiman, 363- 372. Cambridge: Harvard University Press.

Spivak, Gayatri Chakravorty. 1987. *In Other Worlds.* New York: Methuen.

Vicinus, Martha. 1985. *Independent Women.* Chicago: University of Chicago Press.

Warner, Sylvia Townsend and Ackland, Valentine. 1933. *Whether a Dove or a Seagull.* N.Y.: Viking.

Warner, Sylvia Townsend. 1982. *Collected Poems*, ed. Claire Harman. New York: Viking.

West, Rebecca. 1941. *Black Lamb and Grey Falcon.* London: Macmillan.

White, Amber Blanco. 1939. *The New Propaganda.* London: Gollancz, Left Book Club.

White, Antonia. 1928. "The House of Clouds" and "Surprise Visit." In *Strangers*, 45-66. London: Virago, 1981.
Woolf, Virginia. 1925. *Mrs. Dalloway*. New York: Harcourt, Brace & Co.
———. 1929. *A Room of One's Own*. New York: Harcourt Brace & Co.
———. 1931. *The Waves*. New York: Harcourt Brace & Co.
———. 1937. *The Years*. New York: Harcourt, Brace & Co.
———. 1938. *Three Guineas*. New York: Harcourt, Brace & Co.
———. 1941. *Between the Acts*. New York: Harcourt Brace & Co.

When Lindbergh sleeps with Bessie Smith: The writing of place in Toni Morrison's *Sula*

Houston A. Baker, Jr.
University of Pennsylvania

> If a woman has always functioned "within" the discourse of man, a signifier that has always referred back to the opposite signifier which annihilates its specific energy and diminishes or stifles its very different sounds, it is time for her to dislocate this "within," to explode it, turn it around, and seize it; to make it hers, containing it, taking it in her own mouth, biting that tongue with her very own teeth to invent for herself a language to get inside of.
>
> Hélène Cixous, "The Laugh of the Medusa"

I

In an interview conducted by the Afro-American literary critic Robert Stepto, Toni Morrison describes her relationship to space and place as follows:

> I felt a very strong sense of place, not in terms of the country or the state, but in terms of the details, the feeling, the mood of the community . . . .I think some of it is just a woman's strong sense of being in a room, a place, or in a house. Sometimes my relationship to things in a house would be a little different from, say my brother's or my father's or my sons'. I clean them and I move them and I do very intimate things "in place." I am sort of rooted in it, so that writing about being in a room looking out, or being in a world looking out, or living in a small definite place, is probably very common among most women anyway (1979: 213).

In so far as black domestic labor makes a narrow circuit from kitchenettes to white folk's kitchens, it may be considered beyond the reaches of conscious history by Richard Wright and others.[1] But insofar as it becomes — in the inscription of Morrison's writing of "intimacy" — a production of order, it is at the ritual foundation of the black community's systematic definitions of itself. In fact, as avatars of those who were accessible and unshackled between the above deck worlds of white sailing machines and their suffocating holes, the domestic marks the boundaries of communal space.[2]

Interiority and the frontier of violation coalesce in the accessible body of the African woman. The question of propriety, a "normal" place query, is conflated or confused with one of "intimacy." The body's male owner and violator (the European slavetrader) is in an altogether different relationship to it from its intimate occupant. And the nature of the intimacy achieved by the occupant as domesticator is quintessential to definitions of Afro-American community. The occupant marks the "boundary case" of ownership.

In Morrison's description this marking, or systemization of interiority, is a function of *cleaning*. And it is the anthropologist Mary Douglas who most persuasively coalesces ideas of order and danger, cleaning and violation in her discussions of dirt in *Purity and Danger*.[4] She writes: "Dirt is the by-product of a systematic ordering and classification of matter, in so far as ordering involves rejecting inappropriate elements . . . We can recognize in our own notions of dirt that we are using a kind of omnibus compendium which includes all the rejected elements of ordered systems. It is a relative idea. Shoes are not dirty in themselves, but it is dirty to place them on the dining-table"(35).

Douglas's definition of dirt as "matter out of place," is suggestive for the purifying negotiation of matters mandated by the above deck world of the slaveship. A rejection of the assumptions, if not the conditions, of violation — an obstinate insistence on a deeper intimacy, as it were, provided conditions of possibility for the very existence of Afro-American system. The unmediated, above deck world reduces the scope of concern from a desire for possession of the Western machine, to a psychic quest for achieved and ordering intimacy. The shift is something like that between world historic forces and embedded ancestral energies of survival.

Continuing her conversation with Stepto, Morrison notes that when she wrote her novel *Sula*, she "was interested in making the town, the community, the neighborhood, as strong a character as I could. . . . My tendency is to focus on neighborhoods and communities. And the community, the black community. . . it had seemed to me . . . was always there, only we called it the "neighborhood" (214). What Morrison ultimately seeks in her coding of Afro-American PLACE is a writing of intimate, systematizing, and ordering black village values. For in "City Limits, Village Values," she suggests that black writers retain always a respect for "community values," for "village values." (38). And chief among these values, in her view, is the "advising, benevolent, protective, wise black ancestor . . . imagined as surviving in the village but not in the city." (39). Morrison, thus, pulls away from what has been considered the standard Afro-American story of a willed and unvarying progress of blacks from rural hamlets to passionate endorsement of modern, urban technological arrangements of life. Her notions of Afro-American making as they are told in *Sula*, therefore, seem almost to emanate from an altogether different expressive tradition. For Sula begins not in the manner of Richard Wright's *Native Son*, with airplanes over the city, but with the definition of an "intimate" black neighborhood at the moment of its negation: "In that place, where they tore the nightshade and blackberry patches from their roots to make room for the Medallion City Golf Course, there was once a neighborhood. . . It is called the suburbs now, but when black people lived there it was called the Bottom." (3). This is Morrison's "village" or "community" or "ancestral" home of the folk in their ritual confrontation with stark daily and yearly necessities occasioned by what the narrator of *Sula* calls "A joke. A nigger joke" (4).

The "nigger joke" in *Sula* is offered as an explanation for the name of "that place." It is called "the Bottom" because it originated in the tricky economics of Afro-American slavery. Having promised a slave both freedom and a piece of "bottom land" if he performed some very difficult chores, a white master reneges, granting freedom easily enough but constructing a ruse to convince the slave that barren hill land buffeted by wind and eroded by rain is "rich and fertile" *bottom land* (5). Explaining to the skeptical slave that from God's perspective, the barren hill is the very bottom of heaven, the white master succeeds in his deception.

This etiological tale of place naming inscribes the fact and fantasy of capitalism in *Sula*. It is the writing of an American betrayal that can be read as follows in the words of W. E. B. DuBois: "But the vision of 'forty acres and a mule' — the righteous and reasonable ambition to become a landholder, which the nation had all but categorically promised the freedmen —

was destined in most cases to biter disappointment" (233-34). The joke within the Bottom is the deprivation of the "means of production" that characterized America's relationship to former slaves. This betrayal, broken promise and sublation, are determinative in the world of *Sula*. For life in the Botton is exalted neither through agricultural production nor productive industrial labor associated with construction and running of a "modern" world. Instead, the Bottom's character is a redaction of the folk's innovative survival of a "joke."

The joke, in fact, comes to stand as the signifying difference within the whole of the novel's discourse. It mocks the Bottom's rocky autonomy like the repressed content of preconscious thought.[3] Drawn down into a collective white and black unconscious, the denial of black advantage re-emerges as an acceptable discursive form whose displacements and distortions allow its scandalous content to escape censure. Blacks and whites alike tell the joke to secure the meager comforts of self-esteem and self-justification. The "nigger joke," then, not only names "that place," but also provides the unconscious of Medallion and the Bottom with a slightly pleasurable rationale for the average person's powerlessness in the face of an exclusive, capitalistic control of the world. Working-class white men tell the joke when they are out of work. Immigrant men and boys tell it in order to bond with racist whites. Blacks tell it to achieve self-exoneration. All who tell it laugh to keep from crying at their powerlessness.

A community veritably created as the function of a "joke" requires special rituals for survival. The return of the repressed signalled by the "nigger joke" represents a general absence of control, an antecedent and exterior determination of, at least, the space in which a community can set life in motion. Since the denial represented is general, or global, as I have suggested by noting the variety of groups it subsumes, it seems fitting that capitalism's most indisputable moment of global/technological "modernism" should produce the preeminent ritualist of *Sula*.

Who can deny that the most awesome mobilization of capitalism's prowess the world had ever witnessed until 1914 was World War I? And who, after reading *Sula*, fails to apprehend Shadrack, the handsome young black man bathed in the terrifying fires of that global conflagration, as a blasted sign of capitalism's maddening control of man's fate?

Upon his discharge from a veterans facility, Shadrack makes his way back to the Bottom and institutes an annual ritual — National Suicide Day, scheduled for the third of January. He is the first character we encounter in

Sula, and the chapter in which his story is recounted is entitled "1919." The format of the narrator's tale is, thus, a chronicle.

Shadrack has seen a fellow private destroyed by war. The boy's face is blown off in the very first moment of the very first battle in which Shad participates. This carnage drives Shad insane. The picture of brains sliding down the back of the soldier's body which "ran on, with energy and grace, ignoring the drip and slide of brains" (8) is an image of dismembered humanity, of the absurd horror produced by exploitative workings of power. Upon his return to the Bottom, Shadrack says, "No," in madness and in thunder, to such terrifyingly unstable conditions of existence. His National Suicide Day is intended as a prophylaxis against such disorder. Through a manipulation of images and instruments of death it is meant affectively to reduce death to a "residual" category.[4]As the guardian of spaces of sudden and unpredictable death, Shadrack becomes a latter day Charon, an antinomian figure of matted hair, obscene language, and exposed genitals who provides reassuring grounds of "abnormality" for the Bottom's traditional rites of birth, harvest, and matrimony. Shadrack, one might say, is an unequivocal, public wrong against which the Bottom defines its right. "Once the people understood the boundaries and nature of his madness,they could fit him, so to speak, into the scheme of things" (15). Shadrack is scarcely a mere eccentric. He appears, in fact, as a gigantic, Blakean inscription on the landscape of *Sula*. His most distinctive signature is that of the existentialist. Reversing the Bible's characterization of Shadrack[5] as a man whose faith enabled him to escape the commands of authority and the fiery furnace of the State, Morrison's mad ritualist is a consciousness blasted and terrified into non-sense by the awesome workings of Statepower. God is decisively dead in Shadrack's universe; the initiative belongs to madmen alone. Like the Bottom community itself, Morrison sets this wrongman in distinctive contrast to Mrs. Helene Wright, the second character encountered as the chronicle moves to "1920."

Helene Wright (nee, Sabat) has evolved in a way that directly counterpoints Shadrack's emergence. From the outlawed dominion of the Sundown House of prostitution in New Orleans where she was born and an association with witches marked by her surname "Sabat," she has moved to the sheltering Ohio matrimony that makes her "Wright." The Bottom unwittingly cooperates in the woman's obsessive flight from her mother's sexuality by domesticating her name; they call her, simply, Helen. Without sketching her history in great detail, one can surely read Helene as a descendant of the women described in Morrison's *The Bluest Eye*, black women who have tamed both their hair and their passions in order to be rid of "the funkiness. . . . The dreadful funkiness of passion, the funkiness of nature, the funkiness of the wide range of human emotions" (68). Helene is, likewise, a precursor of that community of Dead women in *Song of Soloman* who spend their days inside the house, making artificial roses.[6] Her privileged project in *Sula* is the thinning of both her daughter's nose and her imagination.

She succeeds mightily in dimming Nel's imagination until it is but a faint remnant of the luminescent energy displayed on the daughter's return from her greatgrandmother Cecile's funeral in New Orleans. On the night of her return, having glimpsed possibilities of life beyond the Bottom and having witnessed her mother's sad reversion to a coquette under the "mate eyes" of a white train conductor, Nel declares her difference. Her mirror stage revery reads: "I'm me. I'm not their daughter. I'm not Nel. I'm me" (28). The narrator comments: "Each time she said the word *me* there was a gathering in her like power, like joy, like fear" (28). But the "me" dreamed by the daughter is effectively erased by her churchgoing, compulsively orderly, and communally respected mother. For Helene's house is one of oppressive neatness, providing a marked contrast to the *Peace* residence at number seven Carpenter Road.

Again, Morrison's subtle delight in nominalism, a delight that competes in *Sula* with an ironic essentialism, surfaces in the name "Peace." For surely a more cacophonous household than Eva Peace's would be difficult to discover outside of Morrison's own corpus, or, the provinces of Latin American fiction. Eva, the one-legged grandmother of Sula, lives in her house with assorted boarders, a white hillbilly whom she derisively calls "Tar Baby," her daughter Hannah who will "fuck practically anything" and requires "some touching every day," her son Ralph (called "Plum") for a brief time, and three four-foot tall grotesques collectively named by Eva "the Deweys."

The very construction of her dwelling, described in a subtle rephrasing of Christian scripture as "a house of many rooms," testifies to a kind of antinomian disorder (30). Eva's place has "been built over a period of five years to the specifications of its owner, who kept on adding things: more stairways — there were three sets to the second floor — more rooms, doors and stoops. There were rooms that had three doors, others that opened out on the porch only and were inaccessible from any other part of the house;

others that you could get to only by going through somebody's bedroom" (30). The depiction reminds one of surreal constructs in the paintings of Escher. The house's ceaseless increase is a testimony to its owner's desire for expanded dominion. In a curious way, in fact, it attests the very "manlove" that we are told is the ruling creed of the Peaces. The endless stairways, for example, are a delight for the Freudian dream analyst.[7]

The multiplication of structure at Eva's, however, is finally closer to the antinomian increase of Shadrack's inversive inventories[8] than to conspicuous, capitalistic display. The ceaseless expansion is a compensatory gesture by a woman who has suffered dismemberment in the office of survival. When her husband BoyBoy (who is not unlike "the Deweys" in either his name or his infantile and abusive behavior) deserts her in the dead of winter, Eva is hardpressed to find means of survival. After her infant son "Plum" almost dies of constipation and she is forced to, literally, extract the rock-like waste from his anus in a bitterly cold outhouse, she resolves to take action. She leaves her children with a neighbor and disappears for eighteen months, returning with her left-leg severed and enough money in hand to depart her one-room cabin and build Number Seven Carpenter Road as a Boardinghouse.

What one might say is that Eva, in Morrison's rewriting of the Biblical first woman Eve, is scarcely a chaste, whole, helpmeet for Patriarchy. She is a dismembered black woman who refuses to expire in the backwash of any man's history. Like Shadrack, she says "Uh uh. Nooo." to the given arrangement of things (34). In order to defeat the dreadful course of capitalism's "joke," she subjects herself to dismemberment, sacrificing a leg for the sake of insurance premiums, or, so the myth of her loss is told.

She converts her very body into a dismembered instrument of defiance — and finance. Her act is as much an utterance of the *Non Serviam* as that of her slave precursor described by a Works Project Administration interviewee as follows: "I knew a woman who could not be conquered by her mistress, and so her master threatened to sell her to New Orleans Negro traders. She took her right hand, laid it down on a meat block and cut off three fingers, and thus made the sale impossible" (Sterling 57)

Similarly, Eva refuses to become a will-less object of exchange left to die in barren, one-room arrangements of the Bottom. She becomes, instead, one in the Party of Shadrack, advocating an inversive "manlove" that makes both her and her daughter "sooty" in the estimation of Helene Wright. In addition, she absolutely refuses to be bound by traditional, middle-class definitions of motherhood and responds to her daughter Hannah's query "Mamma, did you ever love us?" with the following tirade: "'No time [to play or engage in affectionate gestures]. They wasn't no time. Not none. Soon as I got one day done here come a night. With you all coughin' and me watchin' so TB wouldn't take you off and if you was sleepin' quiet I thought, O Lord, they dead and put my hand over your mouth to feel if the breath was comin' what you talkin' 'bout did I love you girl I stayed alive for you can't you get that through your thick head or what is that between your ears, heifer?'"(69)

In the bleak world of 1895 (the year of Booker T. Washington's Atlanta Compromise Speech and the one before the infamous *Plessy* v. *Ferguson* decision that made "separate but equal" the Jim Crow law of the land), there was no time for black women to engage in playful nonsense. There was but one incumbency: a dismembering sacrifice of the body to ensure survival and life for the children. The refusal of maternal non-sense is terrifyingly displayed, however, not in Eva's mere tirades against traditional behaviors, but in her fiery execution of her own son.

When Plum finally returns to the Bottom after his service in World War I, he is a heroin addict. Refusing to allow him to regress to infancy and, as she graphically states it, "crawl back in my womb" (71), Eva pours kerosene over him and sets him on fire. She is pictured in her homicidal scene as a giant heron or eagle swooping down in dreadful judgment on her own child. It has been suggested that Eva in her fiery manifestation displays the protean character of the Indian goddess Shiva; her first relation to Plum is as a benevolent lifegiver. Burning him for heroin addiction, she becomes the fiery avenging face of the goddess.

Her act, whether god-like or more secularly murderous, places her on a plane with Bigger Thomas who rationalizes his murders in the name of an achievement of "personal" space. Eva tells Hannah: "He was a man, girl, a big old growed-up man. I didn't have that much room. . . . I done everything I could to make him leave me and go on and live and be a man but he wouldn't and I had to keep him out so I just thought of a way he could die like a man not all scrunched up inside my womb, but a man" (72). One imagines a more intelligent Bigger talking of Bessie Mears' "solace in death," of his having helpfully removed her from the "scrunched up" confines of a narrow existence. Eva, in her throne-like chair in a child's wagon, is an imperious and arrogant agent of vengeful death, just as she is the willful namer of man's fate, labelling and constricting the three Deweys to an unindividuated, libidinal existence and mocking the moutainboy of beautiful voice with the disagreeable name "Tar Baby."

She is, finally, a mythic character, not quite allegorical, and not fully developed as an avatar of some non-Christian pantheon. She is, nonetheless, a positer of a creed that literally defines her daughter and granddaughter. She is also, as we have seen, the absolute controller of more than one fate in the novel. Ironically, with all of her self-defining hatred of BoyBoy ("it was hating him that kept her alive and happy," 37), she is the chief advocate for monogamous marriage, telling her newly-married women boarders just what they should do for their husbands and counselling her granddaughter Sula to settle down into marriage and a family. The admixture of advocacy and hatred, inversive survival energy and arrogant murder, make Eva the type of morally ambiguous character that Morrison seems so adept at creating and so astute in evaluating. Of Eva, she says: "[She] plays god, names people and, you know, puts her hand on a child. . . . She decided that her son was living a life that was not worth his time. She meant it was too painful for her; you know the way you kill a dog when he breaks his leg because you can't stand the pain. He may very well be able to stand it, but you can't, so that's why you get rid of him" (Morrison 1979: 218).

Aware of Eva's god-like response to the incumbencies of survival in 1895, Morrison draws us to her as Milton leads us to his darkly-majestic Satan, only to show us, in time, the morally culpable will to power that has conditioned our own identification with evil. For Morrison, Eva is not, finally, an empowering model of Afro-American liberation but a self-absorbed and imperious survivor of disaster.

II

When we arrive at the year 1922, we are aware that Morrison, like her most readily identifiable male precursor Jean Toomer, has presented characters and details of a setting that is meant to suggest an ancestral village. Polarities have been established, rituals described, and village origins and occurrences subjected to subtle scrutiny. The emergent world of the Bottom is not unlike the Dixie Pike village in Toomer's Cane (1923). For, as in *Cane* there is from the outset of *Sula* a strong sense that an era and its kinship and expressive structures are in decline. Toomer's narrator speaks of a "plaintive soul, leaving, soon gone" (p. 12), and Morrison's narrator opens her story with word of deracination — nightshade and blackberry bushes being torn away along with the rambling, commercial structures of an erstwhile neighborhood. Further implicating the tone and texture of *Cane* in *Sula*, are the similar appearances in the two works of grotesques — symbolic characters who carry a burden of significance and who are, even when most lyrically described, bereft of wholeness. Toomer's Becky is an isolated whitewoman who violates traditional southern sexual taboos. His Fern is a sexually liberated hysteric who combines the landscape's beauty with the resonances of a Jewish cantor's singing. The men and women of *Cane's* three sections share the qualities of beauty, strangeness, imcompletion, hysteria. All tremble, at points, on the verge of the outrageous — whether in their passivity, their obsessive search for rootedness, or their distraught determination to make something — anything — happen.

What Toomer implies is that "village values" may produce an exceedingly resonant folk harmony when there are no radically competing sounds. At evening fall, after the sawmill has blown its final whistle, the supper getting ready songs of blackwomen are perfect correlatives for a sensual landscape. But in the glaring light and blaring dissonances of southern industrial day and northern urban noon, village values and their expression may stand, with all their haunting nostalgia, merely as a promise — "a promise of a soil-soaked beauty; uprooted, thinning out. Suspended a few feet above the soil whose touch would resurrect . . ." (96).

In truth, Toomer's Georgia hamlet and his Washington world of the black bourgeoisie are not chosen places controlled by blacks. Rather, they are, like *Sula's* Bottom, functions of slavery. Their apparently tranquil intimacy and autonomy remain romantic mystifications if they are not read as reaction formations of certain Western confinements. It is all too easy, for example, to blink the denial that is always co-implicated in definitions of "village values." The "joke" is as much a factor, finally, in *Cane* as in *Sula*.

What is compelling about comparison of the two works is that Morrison would, indeed, seem to emanate from a tradition different from that of Wright and Ellison. Henry Louis Gates, Jr. describes *Cane's* lineage as a lyrical or "speakerly" tradition in black letters, distinguishing writers such as Toomer and Zora Neale Hurston from realist writers such as Sterling Brown and Richard Wright (295-96).[9] And nowhere is *Sula's* situation as lyrical and symbolic narrative better observed than in the chapter entitled "1922," which begins with the statement: "It was too cool for ice cream."

III

It is "too cool for ice cream" because Nel and Sula, as twelve-year-old black girls "wishbone thin and easy-assed" (52), are not yet mature enough to participate physically in the sensual, sexual mysteries signified by ice cream. The location of Edna Finch's Mellow House (the ice cream parlor) in the community is at the end of a gauntlet of young and old black men who stare with "panther eyes" at the young girls. All of the men are thinking of images summoned by the phrase "pig meat," but one twenty-one year old black "pool haunt of sinister beauty" named Ajax, actually utters the phrase, stirring the budding sexuality of the two girls like confectionary ice on warm and eager tongues.

The opening scene of "1922" is, thus, rife with sexuality. And while the surname "Finch" carries connotations of a delicate flight and extends the bird imagery of *Sula* (we recall Eva's "heron" or "eagle"), "mellow" indicates "ripe," or "mature." The oxymoron marked by "sinister beauty" for Ajax is complemented by the innocent lust of adolescent girls and the almost blues innuendo of Morrison's handling of "ice cream." Surely, Edna's mellow confections appear more like the male equivalent of the blues' "jellyroll" than Baskin-Robbins' twenty-one flavors. Vanilla and lemon come together as follows:

> The cream-colored trousers marking with a mere seam the place where the mystery curled. Those smooth vanilla crotches invited them; those lemon-yellow gabardines beckoned to them. They moved toward the ice-cream parlor like tightrope walkers, as thrilled by the possibility of a slip as by the maintenance of tension and balance. The least sideways glance, the merest toe stub, could pitch them into those creamy haunches spread wide with welcome. Somewhere beneath all of that daintiness, chambered in all that neatness, lay the thing that clotted their dreams (51).

This mutual dream of Sula and Nel is scarcely one of real "ice cream." What brings the two girls together, in a word, is the Phallus, the Law of the Fathers whose "mystery" makes it a creamy veil for their adolescent dreams.[10] Now the PHALLUS in psychoanalytic terms is to be distinguished from the penis. For it is not a material object but a discursive signifier of the Father, or better, of the Father's LAW. In the writing of Freud, infantile drives institute a tripartite pattern of lack-absence-differentiation. Originally "at one" with the breast of the Mother, the child experiences hunger (lack) as an absence of the breast. Eventually, he or she discovers in the Mother's absence his or her *difference* or differentiation from the Mother. A dyadic, or two-fold relationship is the result.

The child makes demands; the Mother has desires. The child wishes to become the desired of the Mother. (A simple instance is alimentary — the child demands food; the mother desires toilet training.) In order for CULTURE to occur, this dyad of desire must be interrupted by a third term. That term is the Father as PHALLUS, as the LAW. Here we come to the Oedipal stage in which those children possessed of a penis come to want to be the absent PHALLUS *for* the Mother but find the Father always already there. Hence, they tremble before the thought of death (castration/lack) and subjugate themselves to the master, the LAW of the PHALLUS. They know that they will accede to Fatherhood in due course. Children without a penis substitute a baby — as a sign of presence and satisfaction, and a possible fulfillment of desire — for the absent PHALLUS. What Jacques Lacan makes of the traditional corpus of Freud is a signifying drama in which the PHALLUS represents the condition of possibility of socio-sexual differentiation and cultural production by *standing for* the third term, or Father. It is the marker, as it were, of male power and familiarly patriarchal discourse. It is both pre-cultural and culture-founding.

Based on a myth of pre-historic murder of the Father (e.g., Freud's *Totem and Taboo*) who had hoarded the women of the clan and denied the sons, the LAW of the PHALLUS is totemic. It represents the cultural necessities of incest-avoidance and submission to the dread of death (castration). The PHALLUS, in a word, is the signifier that institutes male-dominant cultural discourse and mandates a division of physiologically differentiated children into two, unequal sexes, instantiating in any of its appearances a problematic of desire. To create a habitable space beyond the LAW of the PHALLUS, symbolic manipulation — an unveiling — is *de rigeuer*.

In fact, what causes the discourse of "1922" to coalesce (or clot) is the triple repetition of Sula and Nel's ritual of the Phallus. It is important to say at the outset, however, that Sula and Nel, for all their apparent bonding, do not share a single perspective. While the Phallus may be an object common to their dreams, how very different their dreams are! Nel lapses easily into a "picture of herself lying on a flowered bed, tangled in her own hair, waiting for some fiery prince. He approached but never quite arrived" (51). Sula, by contrast, "spent hours in the attic behind a roll of linoleum galloping through her own mind on a gray-and-white horse tasting sugar and smelling roses" (52). Different fantasies, to be sure. Sula is a rider and a taster of confections; Nel awaits a fire that never quite kindles. The visions of both girls, however, include not only an implied relationship to the Phallus, but also the presence of some further person, a dream companion of the same gender.

This third party signals a traditional triangulation described by Nancy Chodorow in *The Reproduction of Mothering*: "Girls cannot and do not 'reject' their mother and women in favor of their father and men, but remain in a bisexual triangle throughout childhood and into puberty. They usually make a sexual resolution in favor of men and their father, but retain an internal emotional triangle" (140). Discussing the work of the psychologist Helene Deutsch, Chodorow explains that when women are involved in heterosexual, erotic relationships with men, relational triangles represent a reproduction of the type of mother-daughter bonding described in the foregoing quotation (200). There can be little doubt about both Nel's and Sula's erotic attraction to "the thing that clotted their dreams." Similarly, there can be little doubt about the "nontraditional" character of that signifier in their lives. For both girls are "daughters of distant mothers and incomprehensible fathers (Sula's because he was dead; Nel's because he wasn't)" (52). In a sense — and as a consequence, at least in part, of a "nigger joke" — Nel and Sula are *not* members of a traditional "family," and, hence, cannot play out the usual family romance.

For example, Sula cannot maintain any affectional preoedipal bonding with a mother who, pressed by the exigencies of her need for touching, admits to not liking her daughter, to seeing Sula (quite justifiably in the male-bereft economies of the Bottom) as a burden and a cross to bear. Hence, a rejected Sula watches her mother burn to death without so much as stirring a muscle. Similarly, Nel, as the diminished product of a mother bent on eradicating sexuality along with her daughter's distinguishing physical identity, is incapable of finding a maternal perch for her affections. The two girls, therefore, come to stand for each other as more MOTHER than their actual mothers. They enact their supportive displacement as a function of the incumbencies of a black "village" existence.

Similarly, Sula and Nel are required to construct the role of the FATHER from that assembly that marks the male gauntlet from the Time-and-a-Half Pool Hall to Edna Finch's Mellow House. This further displacement mystifies the Phallus even further in their mutual imaginings. And it is, ultimately, the displacements occasioned by the "nigger joke" that necessitate a three-fold enactment of Phallic rites in "1922."

First, there is a ludic enactment in which "the beautiful, beautiful boys

. . . [whose] footsteps left a smell of smoke behind" (56) are metaphorically appropriated as "thick" twigs peeled "to a smooth, creamy innocence," like ice cream (58). Sula's first act is an artist's response; she "traced intricate patterns . . . with her twig" (58). But soon, both Nel and Sula are hollowing out holes in earth. Their separate holes join, and Nel's twig snaps. Both girls, then, throw their twigs into the hole and collect all the debris from the clearing around them and bury it, with the twigs, in the earth. The first rite is completed. The Phallus has been metaphorically exposed and exorcised; its mystery has been appropriated by the absorptive (earth) womb, which seems capable of serving as the whole (as opposed to the broken or fragmented twig) ground of bonding between the girls. It is as though a "creamy" pleasure can be shared by a common hole. Demystification and burial (a purgative burial and "cleaning") are engaged as common ritual acts.

In the second instance of the Phallic rites, however, the girls' responses dramatically differentiate them. Chicken Little comes into the clearing, and while Nel badgers him about his polluting behavior (i.e., picking his nose), Sula accepts him as he is. In an adolescent figuration of her mother's relationship to male lovers, Sula suggests that Chicken "didn't need fixing." (p. 43) And it is Sula alone who climbs the tree with the little boy, showing him a world beyond the river. Nel remains on the ground and, hence, is not party to a Freudian reading of tree climbing.

In the section of the *Interpretation of Dreams* entitled "representation by symbols," Freud observes: "I added [in explanation of one of his patient's dreams] from my own knowledge derived elsewhere that climbing down, like climbing up in other cases, described sexual intercourse in the vagina" (401). Nel is further excluded from the scene when she takes no active part in burial. Sula alone responds in mocking revelry to Chicken's infantile boast of (sexual) achievement: "I'm a tell my brovver" (60). She "picked . . . [Chicken Little] up by his hands and swung him outward then around and around. His knickers ballooned and his shrieks of frightened joy startled the birds and the fat grasshoppers. When he slipped from her hands and sailed away out over the water they could still hear his bubbly laughter. The water darkened and closed quickly over the place where Chicken Little sank" (60-61). Morrison's own mocking designation of the Phallus, in all of its mystery, as a false harbinger of apocalypse — "Chicken Little" — begins the demystification that is completed in the little boy's burial by water. Immediately after he sinks below the surface, Sula rushes across the footbridge to Shadrack's shack. Overwhelmed by the neatness of its interior, she forgets to ask the mad ritualist if he has seen her throw Chicken Little in the river. He, thinking she seeks reassurance about the permanence of human life, speaks the single word "always."

Sula has just discovered the absence of benevolent design and the limits of conscious control in the universe. Hence, Shadrack's reassurance is absurdly comic. And in the absurdity of what is (given Shadrack's fiery history) a common knowledge of disorder, the two characters are bonded. Sula becomes one in the party of Shadrackian antinomianism.

The final enactment of Phallic rites in "1922" expands the categorization of "the mystery" from false herald of apocalypse to Christian sign of the Transcendental Signifier — the Law Itself. In its burial rites for Chicken Little, the community of the Bottom summons Jesus Christ as the metonym for the son — the son, who, as Eva tells Hannah in reference to Plum, is "hard to bear." "You wouldn't know that," she explains to her daughter, "but they is" (71).

The women of Greater Saint Matthews take Jesus "as both son and lover," and in his "downy face they could see the sugar-and-butter sandwiches and feel the oldest and most devastating pain there is: not the pain of childhood, but the remembrance of it" (65). Phallic mystery, even in its most transcendental form as the Law, has as its woman's redaction loss, pain, absence. The actual fathers are disappeared by a "nigger joke" in *Sula* that emasculates them and denies them any legitimate means of production. They desert children who, thus, become reminders of dismemberment, dispossession. The joke's consequences demand a compensating ritual, and in Sula, it is a funereal exertion of religious frenzy: "they [the women of Greater Saint Matthews] danced and screamed, not to protest God's will but to acknowledge it and confirm once more their conviction that the only way to avoid the Hand of God is to get in it"(66).

And so "in the colored part of the cemetery, they sank Chicken Little in between his grandfather and an aunt" (66). Butterflies mark the scene of this third burial — butterflies that signify graceful flight and sexual delight and unite, once more, at a higher level of abstraction and joke-compensation, the dreams of Sula and Nel: "two young girlfriends trotting up the road on a summer day wondering what happened to butterflies in the winter" (66).

The butterflies return as "lemon-yellow" delight when Ajax releases a jar of them in Sula's bedroom on one occasion when they make passionate love. And how, with his lemon yellow as sign, could we mistake Ajax as other than one of the party of New Orleans, Sundown House conjurations? Rochelle Sabat, in an early instance of Sula's bird imagery, appears as "the woman in the canary-yellow dress" wafting an ordor of gardenias (25).

IV

Morrison is such a careful artist and her prose is so richly nuanced that it begs attention to every detail. It would be a mistake, however, to obscure the importance of "1922" by pushing on immediately with further readings. For, it seems to me, the geneaological and thematic lines of the novel are practically all in place with the close of the third enactment of Phallic rites of that chapter. Nel, who passively and quite conventionally by the bourgeois gender standards of her heritage awaits the fiery prince, is a natural for the role into which Helene Wright has "scrunched" her. She will be wife and mother, not an artistic tracer of innovative designs.

Sula, by contrast, will be the daring heir of her grandmother and mother's easy sexuality, an ally of Shadrack in an absurdly boring world where a little "touching every day" may provide the only relief — and release. Nel will shout cautions while Sula climbs trees.

It is important, however, in marking out the dynamics of Afro-American PLACE, not to reinscribe uncritically the Law of the Father, to remystify the Phallus by insisting too strenuously on the significance of "1922." There is, in fact, a reading of *Sula* that claims heterosexuality in general is under erasure in the novel. In "Toward a Black Feminist Criticism,"[11] the Afro-American lesbian critic Barbara Smith writes:

> Despite the apparent heterosexuality of the female characters I discovered in re-reading *Sula* that it works as a lesbian novel not only because of the passionate friendship between Sula and Nel, but because of Morrison's consistently critical stance toward the heterosexual institutions of male/female relationships, marriage, and the family. Consciously or not, Morrison's work poses both lesbian and feminist questions about Black women's autonomy and their impact upon each other's lives (165).

Smith is surely correct about *Sula's* unflagging critique — in the strictest philosophical sense — of traditional heterosexual arrangements. If BoyBoy and Jude (Nel's whiny husband) are signs of the Father and Husband in *Sula*, then neither finds positive signification. Further, if Eva, Helene, Hannah, or Nel are taken as signs of the Mother and Wife, a similar absence results. Marriage does not work in *Sula* in the manner of, say, the implicit valorizations of that institution suggested by the Dick-and-Jane primer of white family life that appears in *The Bluest Eye*.[12] And it is surely true that Nel and Sula's relationship is the signal, foregrounded instance in the novel of productive and symbiotic human allegiance. The girls begin by loving each other with the uncritical acceptance and shared curiosity of adolescent adoration. They remain, as well, emotionally dependent upon one another — even when they are physically separated or distanced by seeming betrayal. As a representation of woman's bonding, then, *Sula* works toward Smith's specifications.

One question to be posed, however, is: How adequately does a lesbian reading, which foregrounds and privileges a loving and compatible relationship between Sula and Nel, explain the PLACE and dynamics of Morrison's village as a whole? I want to suggest that a lesbian reading, while persuasive in its description of the best aspects of the relationship between Nel and Sula, leaves too much of the novel's exquisitely detailed and richly imaged concern for the values of the Bottom out of account.

For example, though it is true that *Sula* does not contain a marriage that works like the Dick-and-Jane postulates of *The Bluest Eye*, it is also true that such postulates are subjected — in the very portrayal of black life in that novel and in the omniscient narrator's reduction of such postulates to gibberish-like epigraphs — to almost comic inversion. The mystifying ideality of such postulates becomes absurd in the face of lived black life. Moreover, if heterosexual arrangements that lead to a mindless and deserted reproduction of mothering are the only heterosexual arrangements considered by a critical reading of *Sula*, then it is fair to say that Morrison is unabashedly critical of them. However, there is a heterosexual relationship in *Sula* between the protagonist and Ajax that possesses — in Morrison's and her narrator's view — all of the skyward possibilities and potentially resonant camaraderie that would result if "Lindbergh . . . [were to sleep] with Bessie Smith" (145). The following quotation from *Sula* can scarcely be read as a condemnation of heterosexuality:

> He [Ajax] liked for her to mount him so he could see her towering above him and call soft obscenities up into her face . . . . She looked down, down from what seemed an awful height at the head of the man whose lemon-yellow gabardines had been the first sexual excitement she'd known . . . .
>
> If I take a chamois and rub real hard on the bone, right on the ledge of your cheek bone, some of the black will disappear. It will flake away

> into the chamois and underneath there will be gold leaf. I can see it shinning through the black. I know it is there.
>
> How high she was over his wand-lean body, how slippery was his sliding smile.
>
> And if I take a nail file or even Eva's old paring knife — that will do — and scrape away at the gold, it will fall away and there will be alabaster. The alabaster is what gives your face its planes, its curves. That is why your mouth smiling does not reach your eyes. Alabaster is giving it a gravity that resists a total smile.
>
> Then I can take a chisel and small tap hammer and tap away at the alabaster. It will crack then like ice under the pick, and through the breaks I will see the loam, fertile, free of pebbles and twigs. For it is the loam that is giving you that smell.
>
> She slipped her hands under his armpits, for it seemed as though she would not be able to dam the spread of weakness she felt under her skin without holding on to something (130).

"Weakness" translates in this scene as complimentarity, the protagonist's realization that she is the indispensable "water" for the man of sinister beauty's loam. The ritual of earth and twigs in "1922" rewrites itself as heterosexual pleasure and fulfillment, and woman is on top.

It is as though a woman blues singer like Bessie Smith flies, while a male pilot takes delight in sexual pleasure rather than achieving gratification from aggressively asserted power of the Phallus. Morrison's poetical and sensual writing of this heterosexuality suggests a bonding that might possibly bring a Bottom community down from its suspension," — that might re-root it in fertile loam. "He swallowed her mouth just as her thighs had swallowed his genitals, and the house was very, very quiet" (131).

The swallowing of the actual penis, rather than the burial of the Phallus, might produce a resounding quiet and a genuine Peace. In her engaging essay, "Sorceress and Hysteric," Catherine Clément writes as follows about accommodative strategies for the anomalous (for "dirt," or "residual categories") delineated by Lévi-Strauss: "The anthropoemic mode . . . consists in vomiting the abnormal one into protected spaces — hospitals, asylums, prisons. The other, the anthropophagic mode, examples of which are found especially in ahistorical societies, consists in finding a place for anomaly, delinquency, and deviancy — a place in the sun at the heart of cultural activity" (8). To "swallow" is to incorporate anomaly into the community as "place in the sun," not to confine it as burial. In Sula and Ajax's heterosexuality, we discover a model that rewrites the "joke" of a capitalism that emasculates the blackmale penis in the office of the Law of the Fathers.

Reclamation, thus, takes the form in *Sula* of an artistic, mystical, and inverted totemic feast that erases rather than reinscribes the Phallus. Sula, in the role of a male Pygmalion's deconstructor, rather than a female statue in passive transformation, goes through layers and layers of suppression in order to arrive at the soil of community. Her swallowing is beneficently anthropophagic. Is, then, Ellison correct in his claim that black male genitals offer salvation for technological society?[13] Scarcely. Genital display in *Invisible Man* is a homosexual occasion; only men are present. In *Sula* woman is on top as the domestic flyer, the ritual blues purifier and cleaner of congestive layers whose excavation leads, finally, to fertile and reclaimed "dirt."

An interested reading of the Sula/Ajax relationship — one that led, say, to the assertion that the resonant combination of flight and blues signalled by their merger is a heroic writing of Afro-American PLACE — might well be accused of overprivileging a male principle. But such an accusation would be justified only if Ajax's real majesty was ascribed, exclusively and quite mistakenly, to some self-generating source. A right reading of Sula's lover does not cast him in the role of the romantic and autonomous streetcorner male. Ajax is properly understood, in a very cogent sense, not as "his own man," but as the offspring of his mother's magic:

> . . . [Ajax's] kindness to . . . [black women] in general was not due to a ritual of seduction (he had no need for it) but rather to the habit he acquired in dealing with his mother, who inspired thoughtfulness and generosity in all her sons.
>
> She [Ajax's mother] was an evil conjure woman, blessed with seven adoring children whose joy it was to bring her the plants, hair, underclothing, fingernail parings, white hens, blood, camphor, pictures, kerosene, and footstep dust that she needed, as well as to order Van Van, High John the Conqueror, Little John to Chew, Devil's Shoe String, Chinese Wash, Mustard Seed and the Nine Herbs from Cincinnati. She knew about weather, omens, the living, the dead, dreams and all illnesses and made a modest living with her skills. Had she any teeth or ever straightened her back, she would have been the most gorgeous thing alive, worthy of her sons' worship for her beauty alone, if not for the absolute freedom she allowed them (known in some quarters as neglect) and the weight of her hoary knowledge.
>
> This woman Ajax loved, and after her — airplanes. There was nothing in between. And when he was not sitting enchanted listening to his mother's words, he thought of airplanes, and pilots, and the deep sky that held them both (126).

The magical, black Conjure Woman as source of knowledge, as teacher of respect for women, as hoary sage whose attraction is *not* physical beauty, progenitor of seven sons who may yet seed the earth with possibilities of camaraderie for black women and a conjure-inspired love of flight — this is the village value, or locational pause, the PLACE, as it were, that provides conditions of possibility for successful heterosexual bonding in *Sula*. Of Ajax's perception of Sula, we learn: "Her elusiveness and indifference to established habits of behavior reminded him of his mother, who was as stubborn in her pursuits of the occult as the women of Greater Saint Matthew's were in the search for redeeming grace. . . . [He suspected] that this was perhaps the only other woman he knew whose life was her own, who could deal with life efficiently, and who was not interested in nailing him" (127).

But as pleasantly sanguine for a vernacular reading of *Sula* as Ajax's conjure associations may sound, we know that the heterosexual bliss of the novel comes only after Nel has discovered Sula naked and alone with her husband Jude. This discovery blasts Nel and creates a permanent rift in the friendship between the two women. Further, we know that the same materially possessive drive that makes Nel unable to forgive Sula, forces Sula herself to transmute egalitarian flights of pleasure into a plan to "nail" Ajax. When the conjure woman's son senses her intention, he returns to a male dominant position in intercourse and heads for a Dayton, Ohio air show: "He dragged her under him and made love to her with the steadiness and the intensity of a man about to leave for Dayton" (134).

Finally, then, both Nel and Sula are victims of village values that define a "pure" woman as an adoring and possessive holder of her man, a glad bearer of sons, even though the labor required to produce a boychild is exceedingly difficult. Early in the Vietnam war, noting the number of children she has borne, a French woman says to Adrienne Rich: "*Vous travaillez pour l'armée, madame*?"(11)

And the sons — so difficult to bear — are always leaving for wars, leaving to encounter Shadrack's and Plum's fates. In their wake lies only the "remembrance" of innocence. It seems apt with this description of the sons to note Morrison's dedication to *Sula*: "It is sheer good fortune to miss somebody long before they leave you. This book is for Ford and Slade [the author's sons], whom I miss although they have not left me." From a psychobiographical perspective, the author plays a series of dramatic maternal roles — from arch-destroyer, through dismembered single parent, to magically artistic conjure woman bequeathing a love of flight. It is not, however, the biographical that forms the crux of the novel.

What Morrison's novel ultimately writes in the failure of a potentially redemptive heterosexuality — a relationship in which flight is a function of black woman's conjure and not black male industrial initiative. When this failure becomes apparent, Sula has already been branded pariah by the Bottom and has assumed her role as a "witch" or sorceress who, in effect, defines boundaries of the domestic. Women become stolidly traditional mothers and loving wives under the threat of Sula's pollution: "Once the source [defined as Sula] of their personal misfortune was identified, they had leave to protect and love one another. They began to cherish their husbands and wives, protect their children, repair their homes and in general band together against the devil in their midst" (117-18).

We return with this quotation to the concept of purity and danger advanced by Mary Douglas. Sula is a domestic; she is an ironic agent of sytemization and purity. Her force lies, finally, in a heritage and allegiance that enable her to serve as a defining anomaly, a marginal check on the system of community. As heir to the *manlove* of the Peaces and self-possessed arrester of conjure's sinisterly beautiful offspring, she is a natural cohort for the thunderingly obscene Shadrack. Her hermeneutical richness is signified by the mark above her eye which is variously read as a rose, a serpent, a tadpole, and funeral ash from the seared Hannah. When she dies in a closed room, not unlike a suffocating hole, she assumes the foetal position of one who, like the riddled subject of Sophocles' Sphinx, has come almost full circle. She slides back into the watery womb.

It is Shadrack, the mad ritualist, then, who carries the day. The most energetic defender against dismemberments and absurdities of a "nigger joke" he all but erases the joke by leading a rebellious group of Bottom inhabitants on a winter suicide parade. Like inversive Luddites, or kamikaze pilots of another war, they march against the very signs of their denial, attacking the construction from whose labor they have been barred, moving like banshees through the very center of Medallion. Many of them are killed when the ground shifts and the incomplete tunnel fills with water. Like Sula, they expire in the womb of their genesis — they are doomed victims of a joke-work that kept them "running."

Shadrack remains above the cacophony, ringing his bell, saddened by the death of Sula whom he believed would endure "always." And, perhaps, Sula does fully endure in Nel's vomiting forth of the bolus of mud and leaves, the terrible loneliness for a friend, that emerges as the circling cry and penultimate sound of the novel: "O Lord, Sula, . . . girl, girl, girlgirlgirl." (p. 174) The cry's repetitions, like other repetitions and eternal returns in the novel, is a bare human talisman against life's signal and absurd arrangements.

But this is not the end.

It is important to note that Nel's final appearance is appropriated to a narrative "present." *Sula's* final chapter is entitled "1965," and we become aware that the very chronicle of *Sula* is the difference within a larger history. The Bottom's story is the always already remainder constructed by an interested voice from selected and residual categories, significant details, actively foregrounded heroisms.

In short, there is an inexorable history ruled by the "joke" inscribed in *Sula*. It runs from *present* (the opening pages of the book as "prologue") destruction and reversal of value to *present* (the final chapter, "1965," as epilogue) destruction and reversal of value. Just as the master has duped the black slave into accepting barren hill land by manipulating language, so the narratively present-day white citizens of Medallion reverse the acceptable scale of material values and declare the hills a desirable locale. Nigger heaven, one might say — a segregated point of conjure, community, and conspicuous ritual — becomes the imminent domain of white leisure, "room for the Medallion City Golf Course."

In a sense, one might say that *Sula* effects a resonantly adept refiguration of discursive priorities in which the narrator foregrounds not the historical "joke," but the selectively chronicled Afro-American PLACE that is the eternal and residual redaction of the joke. The Bottom is the difference, the objectified differentiation in productive expressive display that raises Sula's name above the very medal and commemoration of whiteness marked by the place-name "Medallion." As in Toomer's fascinating short sketch entitled "Esther," "the town [of Medallion] has completely disappeared" during most of the text in Morrison's writing of the village values of its Bottom. The Bottom's existence and signifying difference are notable because they are marked and remarked at the moment of their demise by one who appreciates their ancestral resonances and domestic codifications of "purified" black experience.

Morrison's *Sula*, in its brilliantly adept employment of language, becomes the signifying difference within Afro-American discourse. Reversing a traditional iconography of airplanes and flying in black fiction, it suggests that folk interiors may contain domestic conjurations that unite Lindbergh and Bessie Smith in resounding glory. Rather than a cadaverous remainder, Afro-American folk history carried by black woman's rituals signifies a symbolic difference within Afro-American discourse. And, finally, in the domain of the signifier and the signified, PLACE becomes not a matter of matter, but a question of symbolic manipulation. Rather than adopt an extant historiography, Morrison plays over and beyond and behind and below history, symbolically chronicling the domestic, ordering rituals of black life. *Sula*, as a result, bears little resemblance to a traditional black male historicizing of a standard story.

Morrison describes Sula as an artist without a medium, and hence a dangerous figure (121). What she seems to imply in this characterization is the problematic of, say, Jacques Lacan.[14] Rather than the Conjure Woman as medium, I think she means to suggest the expressivity of language. Language is always coextensive and coterminous with the emergence, and, ironically, the alienation, of the subject.

Briefly, Lacan claims that when the child (between six and eighteen months of age) sees his image in the mirror, he responds with a "flutter of jubilant activity" at the discovery of what he believes to be "myself," or "me" (Certeau 56). Ironically, the "self" captured by saying "I am *that*" is already alienated, a secondary identification in which the SUBJECT is subjugated to language. There is, only, a secondary identification in which language remains the differentiating difference within. In *Heterologies*, Michel de Certeau captures this Lacanian problematic as follows: "the lie [represented by literature or myth or iconography] is the element in which the truth can emerge, the truth that the Other always institutes the subject by alienating it" (56).

In terms of the dynamics of Afro-American PLACE, these formulations translate as follows: language, myth, iconography constructed by Afro-American expressive traditions are locational mirrors to which we point in our intellectual and affective assertion — "I am *that*." Such "secondary identification" is only alienating when it fails to accord with, at least, an Afro-American REAL that is gender diversified, characterized by village values as well as urban technological spaces — energetic laborers as well as living domestics. It is a terrain where the great American joke of denial has always held sway, but where more than one black woman has inversively decided, like Bessie Smith, or Rosa Parks: "Mm: I can't move no moe/ There ain't no place: for a poor old girl to go."[15]

V

Refusing to give way to historiographical myths of an erasure of race by the mechanistic glories of technological flight, black women have settled down to business. Either they have appropriated flight to gainful ends like Willa B. Brown, whose Chicago flying school was one of the first of its kind in the United States.[16] Or, they have transformed the joke of Western capitalism in the manner of Sarah Breedlove, whose lineage includes the millionaire cosmetologist A'Lelia Walker.[17]

At the heart of *Sula's* Bottom stood, among other businesses, Irene's Palace of Cosmetology, a woman's place where they "used to lean their heads back on sink trays and doze while Irene lathered Nu Nile into their hair" (3). A'Lelia Walker's "business" was to remake herself, to stop her hair from falling out, and to get away from the scarred domestic knees and the reddened hands that had marked her mother as maid, as laundress. What she did was energetically to take care of business by taking the result of her dream life (an old man from Africa conveyed a formula for renewal to her in a dream) and doing something about her own, and all blackwomen's hair. The mirror produced a "flutter of jubilant activity" — "I am *that*!"

Similarly, Morrison takes care of business by constructing the very mirror that holds us together, that offers a communal PLACE where we can come to see ourselves. Her work metaphorizes the energies of the persona framed by the Washington, D. C. poet, Ethelbert Miller in the words with which I want to end these reflections on the dynamics of Afro-American PLACE. Miller's poem "Only Language Can Hold Us Together" reads as follows:

only language
can hold us together

i watch the women
bead their hair
each bead a word
braids becoming
sentences

she would
never comb her hair
it was always wild

like new poetry
it was difficult
to understand

she would enter
rooms where old women
would stare & mumble
& bold ones would say

"where's her mother"

she never understood why
no one ever understood the
beauty of her hair

like free verse
so natural as conversation
so flowing like the french
or spanish she heard or
overheard she thought she knew

"i want to go to
mozambique" she said one day

combing her hair
finding the proper beads
after so long

"i want to go to
mozambique" she said

twisting her hair
into shape the way her
grandmother made quilts
each part separated &
plaited

"i want to go to
mozambique or zimbabwe
or someplace like luanda

i need to do something
about my hair

if only i could
remember

the words
to the language
that keeps
breaking in my
hands"

Morrison "remembers" and enables us to know our PLACE and to be cool about our hair. For, in truth, it has often seemed in black male writings of a putatively asexual Western technological world as our proper PLACE, that the dominant expressive impulse has been more toward an escape from "bad hair" than from "bad air." Morrison's linguistic cosmetology allows this very basic "badness" to be refigured as village value, as a mirroring language — a springy "lying" down if you will — in which we can find ourselves, and where especially black men may yet make a jubilant response, saying, "We are *that*!" Or, in more vernacular terms:

> I will pack your water: from the boggy bayou
> Hey now tell me sweet baby, who may your manager be
> Before many more questions, won't you please make
> arrangements for me,
> Your hair so doggone curly and your eyes ain't blue.
> That's why baby, I'm making a fool about you.[18]

Morrison has enabled us to know precisely our Afro-American PLACE by showing us just what we need to do with words, values, language that we have too often allowed to break in our hands. She brings us to the founding Bottom of our lives by showing us precisely what to make of our hair. Her manipulations of the symbolic, thus, bring her into fine accord with her captivating protagonist of whom we are told: "Sula never competed; she simply helped others define themselves" (95).

NOTES

1. It seems important at this juncture to differentiate Morrison's "intimate" place from the spaces of confinement described in the magnificently suggestive study of women writers and the nineteenth-century literary imagination offered by Sandra M. Gilbert and Susan Gubar. Gilbert and Gubar write in *The Madwoman in the Attic* (New Haven: Yale University Press, 1979) as follows: "literally, women like Dickinson, Brontë, and Rossetti were imprisoned in their homes, their father's houses; indeed, almost all nineteenth-century women were in some sense imprisoned in men's houses. Figuratively, such women were, as we have seen, locked into male texts, texts from which they could escape only through ingenuity and indirection. It is not surprising, then, that spatial imagery of enclosure and escape, elaborate with what frequently becomes obsessive intensity, characterizes much of their writing" (83). The thesis of Gilbert and Gubar stresses "escape" by imprisoned women authors as a writing of the "madwoman," the mad double who is id energy or the wantoness of the unlawful. Bertha of *Jane Eyre* is the *ur*-madwoman double. She, in Gilbert and Gubar's view, expresses the anxiety of authorship of Brontë and other women writers and represents, as well, the woman's escape from patriarchal houses and male texts into a peculiarly woman's imaginary. The specifically Victorian and white Western psychosexual orientation of this thesis — for all its resonant clarity and persuasiveness — seem to remove it from the type of ancestral, folk codifications of space and place implied by Morrison's writing.

2. I am referring to the historian Deborah White's observation (*Ar'n't I a Woman? Female Slaves in the Plantation South*. New York: W.W. Norton, 1985: 63) that African women who were victims of the European slavetrade were not confined to the holes of ships but were allowed to go unshackled on the half and quarter decks. This, of course, rendered them not "free," but accessible to the European crew of traders.

3. The discussion of the joke that follows relies heavily upon the observations of Sigmund Freud in *Jokes and Their Relation to the Unconscious* (trans. James Strachey, New York: W. W. Norton, 1960).

4. In *Purity and Danger*, Douglas writes: ". . . our pollution behavior is the reaction which condemns any object or idea likely to confuse or contradict cherished classifications. We should now force ourselves to focus on dirt. Defined in this way it appears as a residual category, rejected from our normal scheme of classifications" (36).

5. "Then Nebuchadnezzar came near to the mouth of the burning fiery furnace, and spake, and said, Shadrach, Meshach, and Abednego, ye servants of the most high God, come forth, and come-*hither*. Then Shadrach, Meshach, and Abednego, came forth of the midst of the fire." *Daniel*, iii, 26, of the Bible. The ironic resemblance that Morrison's antihero bears to the biblical Shadrach lies in his seeming idolatry before the power of death, while the Shadrach of the book of Daniel is condemned by the king for his refusal to worship the golden image. Insofar as Morrison's character is a partisan of an *ordering* ritual, however, he does construct an alternative to the capitalist disorder of war.

6. The three women who work in the Dead house are Ruth (the wife) and the two daughters of Macon Dead — Magdalene called Lena and First Corinthians.

7. Otto Rank reports and interprets a dream as follows in the *Interpretation of Dreams*: "If we bear in mind that Freud's researches into sexual symbolism . . . have shown that stairs and going upstairs in dreams almost invariably stand for copulation, the dream becomes quite transparent" (405).

8. Shadrack's followers increase yearly; the first to join his inversive parade are Tar Baby and the Deweys.

9. Gates refers to the quality of Toomer and Hurston's prose as "lyrical" (295) and goes on to designate what he calls a "speakerly" text (296). (The Afro-American equivalent of Barthes' "writerly" text.) Hurston's work, then, like Toomer's would consist of the lyrical production of talking books.

10. For valuable accounts of the PHALLUS in the work of Freud and Lacan, see: Mitchell, Juliet and Jacqueline Rose, eds. 1982. *Feminine Sexuality: Jacques Lacan and the école freudienne* (New York: W. W. Norton); Juliet Mitchell. 1975. *Psychoanalysis and Feminism: Freud, Reich, Laing and Women* (New York: Vintage Books); Jane Gallop. 1982. *The Daughter's Seduction: Feminism and Psychoanalysis* (Ithaca, New York: Cornell University Press).

11. Adrienne Rich in her essay "Compulsory Heterosexuality and Lesbian Existence" also makes the mistake of speaking of *Sula* as a novel of "lesbian existence." Rich's essay appears in *The Signs Reader*. ed. by Elizabeth Abel and Emily K. Abel (University of Chicago Press, 1983).

12. *The Bluest Eye* begins as follows: "Here is the house. It is green and white. It has a red door. It is very pretty. Here is the family. Mother, Father, Dick, and Jane live in the green-and-white house. They are very happy." Quickly, however, the normal spacing and

typeface are run together, and, finally, reduced to mere strings of letters. The novel, thus, begins with a deconstruction of the representation of "traditional" (read: WHITE PATRIARCHAL) family structures that greeted so many of us as we were just learning to read. Morrison's artistry suggests another (a BLACK) reading of the family.

13. In *Invisible Man*, the final scene before the "Epilogue" is a nightmare vision of castration in which the protagonist's testes are launched into the air by his male adversaries and false guides and hang floating over a technological civilization as possible salvation (556-558).

14. Juliet Mitchell and Jacqueline Rose, eds., *Feminine Sexuality*, and Jane Gallop, *The Daughter's Seduction*, are excellent sources for discussion of the Lacanian problematic, as is Luce Irigaray. 1985. *This Sex Which Is Not One* 1977 (Ithaca, New York: Cornell University Press).

15. Bessie Smith, "Back Water Blues."

16. Nalty, Bernard C. 1986. *Strength for the Fight: A History of Black Americans in the Military* (New York: The Free Press, 143). I must thank my extraordinary Research Assistant, Claire Satloff, for this reference and for her very dedicated work in securing sources necessary for the completion of this entire essay.

17. Giddings, Paula. 1984. *When and Where I Enter: The Impact of Black Women on Race and Sex in America* (New York: Bantam Books). Giddings' history seems to me essential reading for anyone interested in feminist, or Afro-American, or general historical contours of the United States of America. Her account of Walker is my source for the discussion that follows.

18. Bo Chatman, "Arrangements for Me — Blues." For my blues citations, I have relied on the remarkable work of Michael Taft. 1983. *Blues Lyric Poetry*. New York: Garland.

REFERENCES

Certeau, Michel de. 1986. *Heterologies: Discourse on the Other*. Minneapolis: University of Minnesota Press.

Chodorow, Nancy. 1978. *The Reproduction of Mothering: Psychoanalysis and the Sociology of Gender*. Berkeley: University of California Press.

Clement, Catherine and Cixious, Helene. 1986. *The Newly Born Woman*. Trans. Betsy Wing. Minneapolis: University of Minnesota Press: 3-59.

Douglas, Mary. 1966. *Purity and Danger, An Analysis of the Concepts of Pollution and Taboo*. London: Routledge and Kegan Paul.

DuBois, W.E.D. 1965. "Three Souls of Black Folks". In *Three Negro Classics* ed. John Hope Franklin, 233-234. New York: Avon.

Ellison, Ralph. 1965. "Invisible Man". In *Three Negro Classics* ed. John Hope Franklin. New York: Avon.

Gates, Henry Louis, Jr. 1984. "The Blackness of Blackness: A Critique of the Sign and the Signifying Monkey." In *Black Literature and Literary*

Theory, ed. Henry Louis Gates Jr., 285-321. New York and London: Methuen.

Miller, Ethelbert. 1986. *Where Are the Love Poems for Dictators*.

Morrison, Toni. 1972. *The Bluest Eye*. New York: Pocket Books.

———. 1974. *Sula*. New York: Alfred A. Knopf.

———. 1977. *Song of Soloman*. New York: Alfred A. Knopf.

———. 1981. "City Limits, Village Values". In *Literature and the Urban Experiences* ed. by Jaye, Michael C. and Watts, Ann Chalmers, 35-43. New Brunswick: Rutgers University Press.

Rich, Adrienne. 1976. *Of Woman Born: Motherhood as Experience and Institution*. New York: W. W. Norton, and Co.

Smith, Barbara. 1982. "Toward a Black Feminist Criticism." Hull, Gloria T., Scott, Patricia Bell, and Smith, Barbara, eds. *But Some of Us Are Brave: Black Women's Studies*, 157-175. Old Westbury, New York.

Stepto, Robert. 1979. "'Intimate Things in Place': A Conversation with Toni Morrison". *Chant of Saints* ed. by Harper, Michael S. and Stepto, Robert B., 213-29. Urbana: University of Illinois Press.

Sterling, Dorothy, ed. 1984. *We Are Your Sisters, Black Women in the Nineteenth Century*. New York: W. W. Norton.

Toomer, Jean. 1977. *Cane*. New York: Liveright.

Sieving the matriheritage of the sociotext

Myriam Díaz-Diocaretz
University of Utrecht

1. Preliminary remarks

The topic for this occasion concerns further propositions within a more general framework around what I have previously called "social text" in writing by women.[1] This term was introduced not as a static structure but as a set of variable functions to account for some common factors in poetic texts of different periods, each one in its own historical context. *In the frame of the textualization of the woman's point of view, the constructs of woman's voice and strategic consciousness were described and shown to be part of the represented world in which patriarchal and cultural sociolects as well as the poet's idiolect are conjointly interacting.*

To sift a woman's world-vision in contradistinction with the world-vision of patriarchy, the notion of strategy in the poet's artistic program was essentially seen as a dynamic factor. Let us recall briefly the key elements. First, it was suggested that "to reinforce the strategy of the woman's voice, the poet also constructs a perspective of the represented world that may be expressed as being divided between the male and the female, or masculine and feminine, as a result of a perception (and inscription) that the voice speaks from one of these two segments of the world." Second, "woman's strategic consciousness consists of an attitudinal position in response to the social orientation of the dichotomy male/female (often taken for granted or ignored by male writers or a masculinist view); woman's strategy, then, is the textualization of the suggested correspondence between the represented world and empirical reality, inscribed within the text" (Díaz-Diocaretz 1986b). Given these major dominant features, the poetics of the social text invites analysis beyond or in addition to the thematic level to sift among the various tensions and relations of internal differences in texts written by women; it engages inclusion of systematic continuities and discontinuities in a given text in relation to other discursive practices. Viewed in this light, the "social text" allows us to apprehend instances of *representation and metatextual practices of writing*, linking in this way poetic discourse to the extra-textual world through the woman's voice. This link is valid in so far as the communicative status of a poem is taken in its intratextual and extratextual system of relations (cf. Lévine 1976:205-212). Aware of the need to elucidate further important points, and to complement those previous suggestions, in this present work I shall refer to the sociotext limiting myself to general correlations that are not the domain of representation but which have textual implications in artistic composition.

The first correlation will concern extraliterary dimensions of writing in the event of artistic creation; it situates the notions of *woman*, *self*, *social being* as constituent elements for the construction of the writing subject's sociality. Formal constraints and implicit norms in writing by women play a role that we still need to elucidate, particularly in the context of *social discourse* as a whole, since those frames are part of the horizon orienting and being oriented by the writing subject. In writing by women, this horizon acquires importance in the implications of assumed values that affect content (cf. Bakhtin [Volochinov] 1977:41-42). The general purpose is to find operational concepts that will allow us to recognize, situate and delineate the multiple variants and differences transversely inhabiting the notions of "woman" and "women" in poetic discourse. In the line of these arguments, some distinctions will be necessary, such as the question of the author and of the writing subject (*scripteuse*); likewise, woman as writing subject and *the other* in relation to "social being" and "social world" and to "the alien text" will be explored as another correlation. The next aspect will refer to specific uses of elements of poetic form that reveal the *function of the unuttered*. In the context of *cultural muteness*[2] and the boundedness of the writing subject in the principles of artistic standard and composition, writing by women contains a *verbally unmarked ideological evaluation by form* (cf. Volochinov [Bakhtin] 1983:22); therefore, I propose a development of this notion, from a consideration of the Bakhtinian feature of the enthymeme. Finally, as a part of the *enthymeme*, and related to evaluation by form and to an evaluation of a given collective within the utterance, focus on the writing subject's relationship with a given linguistic code as the national language(s) used in the work's composition — whenever relevant — will be proposed since a particular rapport resulting from this correlation is a dynamic condensor of social evaluations as well. This last point is meant to indicate that the variables of race, class and gender are not fully exhaustive, especially if the question of text production within the mechanisms of the semiotics of *culture* is ignored (cf.Lotman et al. 1975); those variables cannot be sufficient to describe production by a given group in the *context of discourse*. For instance, "American" culture has been a particularly appropriate sphere in which to analyze the internal movements of competing social forces because it sees itself and names itself by proclaiming its unity and homogeneity while the artistic and literary production emerging from a non-dominant perspective within that very culture constantly contradicts such an assumption. Texts by women from Afro-American culture may bring about significant divergences through a number of elements vis à vis texts by other "American" women poets; these texts may articulate not only a gendered voice, but especially a particular textualized experience and other strategic constituents foregrounding the poets' *de-territorialization* of hegemonic standards within a white dominant perspective.[3] This implies that the congenial and polemic relations within a text consolidate a given aesthetic and ideological world in the context of a heterogeneous society.

The general framework of the proposed dynamics of the sociotext includes an understanding of the probability within writing by women, of a specific signifying practice functioning as discourse in the social world. In an intersection between the extratextual and the textual, a meeting ground is crucial between *self*, *social being*, *writing subject* and *subject of the utterance* — all of them conditioned by and yet themselves modifying the mechanisms of discursive production. Social evaluation, implicit norms and formal constraints interact in the horizon of reception both in the event of artistic creation and of the historical matrix through the "changing phenomenon of language" (Mukařovský 1977). The sociotext refers to the multiple dimensions of a given discourse in which external hierarchies are dismounted or accepted, and a new dynamic order proposed from the internally contextualized critical attitudes towards those hierarchies.

Equally important for consideration of the sociotext is the aesthetic correlation between the notion of woman as language user and text-producer who transforms and participates in the development of the *sociostatics* and the *sociodynamics* in discourse. Although literary conventions and poetic standards are, by definition, in constant change, in the event of artistic creation these appear — especially for the woman writer — as already fixed, pre-formed, already established, therefore static since they are already part of the social forces seeking to preserve the preexisting dominant balance in a given society. As a response to this phenomenon, the poet in her function as a writing subject looks for contextual relations of opposition, strategies of resistance and other elements that will, through innovations, unsettle such stasis; in this way, the dynamics is activated, and it counteracts the already-existent discursive practices. The sociotextual correlations will engage disclosure of the subject's aesthetic project and its textual bounds within or outside a given community or society.

Alongside the synchronicity inherent in the sociotext, the ideological construction of the subject may be explored in a diachronic direction. Given all the variables that come into play in the sociotext, the *represented* and the *empirical* worlds meet as two correlatives without becoming fused. By now I hope it is evident that the sociotext does not refer to an instance derived from sociocritique (yet both meet at crucial points), or from sociology, or sociolinguistics, or social psychology.

A sociotextual analysis invites integration not only of aspects apprehended and interpreted in particular poetic texts and discourses, but it also makes way for critical discourse to provide a wider evaluation of the discourse in question. Poetic and critical discursive practices are set in interaction as ideological products; both the text being analyzed and the text that is analyzing bring about the interrelation of the writing subject and that of the critical subject. Both constitute two distinct signs; the first and most immediate implicit relationship as practiced in semiotics is that of the subject as social unity which is above all ideological. This aspect is also relevant in the criticism of poetic discourse, particularly in the poetics of the lyric.[4]

The sociotextual dimensions interweave a strategic discursive space where certain key concepts are to be contextualized according to the *critical subject position* and the supposed difference in discourse; these dimensions, moreover, bring together correlations generated by a given text's position in relation to other texts,[5] to discourse and to the texts of culture in the social world. This is particularly important if we remember that in the event of artistic creation the writing subject constructs a world-conception in the text; the latter in its turn conveys a proposed world-view; the domain of the interpreter's own conception of the world will activate another world-view in the reading practice. Therefore, writing, text, and reading practice as a part of a process relate to each other in dynamically different ways (see Iser 1978; Harari 1979; Suleiman 1980; Tompkins 1980). In artistic creation, the notion of writing by women is in itself a condensor of internal differentiations, marked not just and not necessarily by gender, but by other juxtaposing factors. It will be important to remember that "Discourse, taken more broadly, as a phenomenon of cultural intercourse, ceases to be a self-sufficient thing and cannot be understood independently of the social situation which engendered it" (Volochinov [Bakhtin] 1983a:8). This social situation is the extratextual which the sociotext incorporates as the unuttered, without denying importance to the contents of a given work; this content is situated in a wider framework of underlying evaluations providing an ideologically oriented function. The thematic aspect, implicitly, is one element among others, and it is determined by several other dominant interrelations working from within and outside the text.

2. Slovo and writing by women

There is a challenging problematic proposed by feminist criticism which uncovers numerous problems in the domain of textual theory. Consider the fact that in the 1970s the "death of the author" and of the subject is declared in the same period when the woman writer is being reclaimed in an act of revision from a feminist perspective.[6] Such a crucial phenomenon is not without theoretical consequences. Among other questions, it unsettles the total (Formalist) separation of the text from its producer, by reasserting it as a product of human construction and a medium of expression for consciousness of gender paradigms; it introduces the critical approach to gendered modes of socialization in the domain of the psyche (e.g. psychoanalysis) and the psychosocial forces, and their actualization in language use; it breaks open the assumptions about text production, interpretation and reception dividing discursive practices between those of *patriarchy* and those of *woman in patriarchy*, with the consequence, among others, of a new field of academic research being institutionalized as Women's Studies. In such a wide area of critical discussions I would like to invite you to veer our attention to the theoretical approach of the dialogic and its potential development from the practice of writing by women as a point of departure, in a critical interaction that may reveal further aspects to be explored. This means that when we confront a number of aspects from both the dialogic and the critical position that acknowledges theoretical questions raised by feminist critique and writing by women, new questions will be unbounded. The Bakhtinian School's critique of Saussure's notion of the arbitrariness of the sign makes way for a revision of all practices derived from that trace (see Eagleton 1983). A systematic feminist critique that would attend to this radical challenge would provide a re-formulation of the Bakhtinian School's principles — which are not free from a masculinist view; yet those foundations of the dialogic do not exclude a feminist position as a legitimate focus. The encounter between a feminist perspective and the dialogic is in itself inherently political; and both viewpoints convey the conditions for and engagement of the ideological at the core of their arguments.

An initial reasoning of significant implications that underlies the present inquiry involves two aspects referring to verbal interaction, from the Bakhtinian School. Let us now look at both aspects in turn. First, there is the notion that the word is the most neutral sign in that it does not have a specificity in any sphere of ideological creation (Bakhtin[Volochinov]1977: 32); therefore it is a phenomenon open to the fulfillment of all kinds of ideological functions (31). Given this assumption, to suppose a "difference" of writing by women is to suppose a specificity for *the word*, which, then, cannot lie in language per se or in an innate female authorial voice, but in specific uses of discourse. The semiotic nature of writing by women is to be explored in the dialectics between the writing subject and the word, the latter understood as the phenomenon of the dialogic.

The second important aspect from the Bakhtinian School is the idea that the word in written discourse is part of an ideological argument, in a constant process of transferral, since the word does not forget where it has been and can never wholly free itself from the context of which it has been part (Bakhtin 1973:167). This former place and space of the word constitutes the *alien* word, which in a transformative textualization becomes the alien text.[7]

The writer's verbal medium obtains a function that constitutes the work's literariness, and in this event a "world-semantic component" serves to establish coherence in the correspondence between *text-structure and world-structure* (cf. Beaugrande and Kessler 1981:25-6). In poetic discourse, the utterance is a textual resultant between the "self" existing in society and its new articulation in the represented world. Being an artistically organized unity, the text does not lose, or eliminate, or annul "the social quality of its medium but is, through new evaluations, given a new social orientation" (Volochinov[Bakhtin]1983b; see also Todorov 1981). In contemporary poetic discourse by women, for example, certain texts can contribute to an expansion of tradition and to ideas inherited from the patriarchal world, including an implicitly congenial dialogue with contemporary voices; or, as in feminist discourse, the new evaluation may be reflected in a polemic dialogue in which the very texts from patriarchy are used for a critique of those received ideas; or, as in woman-identified and woman-oriented discourse a congenial dialogue with texts by women may refract yet another ideological construct in the artistic text.[8]

Writing, a reality not independent of human activity, is historically saturated and organized, embedded with the domain of productivity, and the word is "the ideological phenomenon par excellence"(Bakhtin [Volochinov]1977:31). Every supposition made about the nature of writing — including writing by women — elicited from a single writer's work or from a group of texts by several authors, is simultaneously an assumption about social discourse at large. It is important to recall the relationship between writing (in the event of artistic creation), with a given text, and discourse in the social world in general, to consider the meaning of the notion of "writing by women." For purposes of the present discussion I shall proceed to delimit what we will understand by "social discourse" and its relevance to the sociotext. Acknowledging his debt to Benjamin, Gramsci, Bakhtin, Foucault and others, and to situate the intertextual analysis in a general context, Marc Angenot (1983:101-112) introduces an expanded notion of social discourse, understanding the latter as a problematic. Angenot's objective has a much wider range than that of the intertextual, since it applies to discourse and its modes of production at large, and it is in this potentiality for expansion of the term that I would like to emphasize its usefulness. From Angenot's problematization, I stress the following aspects: social discourse is everything that is written (printed) in a given society, arranged through narration and argumentation as the two fundamental modes of the *mise en écriture*; it encompasses "the discursive and topical rules" organizing what is written; it contains *the dicible*, that is, "what can be said about the instituted discourses, and the themes assigned acceptability and capacity for 'migration-mutation' at a historical moment in a given society" (105). This entails a synchronic *coupage* of discursive typologies (philosophical, political, scientific, literary, and so on) and "its recognizable borders, as well as the limits being challenged, contested" (Angenot p. 105, cf. Bakhtin[Volochinov]1977); it includes the interdiscursive factors working in "coexistence and interference" (105). In this synthesis, Angenot points to the roles of the individual and of the collective, not only with their respective doxa but their paradoxes as well (106). Moreover, discourse and actual practice are shown to be related to each other through the historical production of acceptability and the social status of those practices (106); from this, the canonical divisions of social discourse arise, and the social divisions of the subject of the utterance and the division of the different types of audience (e.g. the public) are organized. Therefore, in the hegemony of social discourse, the role of the addressee (*destinataire*) emerges as significant.

All these points are of relevance to the interaction between writing by women and the transformations of social discourse; we are aware that this relationship has not been one of reciprocal interaction, but rather dominated by patriarchy; social discourse functions and is practiced from a masculinist view; therefore, the internal dynamics of the problematic of social discourse from within the mechanisms of production *of patriarchy* works, setting Angenot's words in my context, as follows: "Le discours social ne produit pas seulement des objets, mais il institue les destinataires de ces objets en les identifiant; pas seulement des objets pour des sujets, mais des sujets pour ces objets" (Angenot 1983:106). At times this may originate a dual orientation towards the object and the subject. Prescriptive literature in nineteenth century Spain, for example, mainly produced by men or under their authority, and written *for women*, conveyed a double message, one directed at women (how they should be), and the other — which had a great importance in the role of social expectations — was aimed at the male readers themselves to instruct them on how they should prefer and expect women to be. The latter remains as one of the clearest instances of men's internalization of patriarchy's prescriptions, reinforced in the complementary production of other forms of discourse in the same period such as legal documents, commercial texts (advertisements in journals and popular magazines, catalogues), medical and didactic treatises and many other texts. Both social discourse and woman as subject and object are historically bound; woman as writing subject is marginalized and constrained by patriarchy's modes of legitimizing itself, and at the same time it is within and from those margins and constraints that her own resistance and freedom begins in her discursive practice.

The sociodynamics in which a given artistic text is placed at the moment of its production conveys several concomitant mechanisms that emerge from the "self" and the "social being" correlating to social world (as organized empirical reality) and the textual world. The writing subject originates from and is oriented towards verbal and extra-verbal horizons. The text produced is partly determined by the previously existing discourses and initiates new transformations in the situation it obtains in discursive practice (Kristeva 1974). The "sexual differential," that is, the *gendered socialization and its articulation in the textual world*, is a major factor in writing by women; but it cannot be the only element, since there are discourses in which the textualization of a gendered figuration is not present, or at least is not a constant because it may appear in the practice of discourse by male poets (see Díaz-Diocaretz 1985b, 1986b). An understanding of a line of matriherital continuity in writing by women requires an approach to each text as sign in relation to other texts already known; on the level of critical discourse, it is a line of understanding that links the response and interpretation of a given sign by means of other signs, that is, relating the production of one individual consciousness and linking it to the product of another individual consciousness (Bakhtin[Volochinov]1977: 28). Therefore, the matriheritage studied through the sociotext (as a working concept) implies not a tradition but a *gender-specific and sociohistorical problematic* in the continuity of cultural muteness exerted upon women. The functions of ideology and artistic program necessarily interrelate in the literary text and its internal structure. An exploration of language as the word, as *slovo*, in a dynamic sense, in the terms proposed by the Bakhtinian School, proves to be adequate to set writing in the act of communication rather than in the ahistorical system based on Logos (Godzich 1986). Wlad Godzich's significant critique of the meaning of community and communication in Western thought offers a fruitful argument in that direction. Godzich emphasizes the Bakhtinian notion of slovo in its ideological orientation as a "concept of motion, of that agency that overcomes inertia and standstills." The operation of "running a discourse through the word," in the true meaning of the dialogic, Godzich affirms, is "always political since it usurps the place of one discourse by another with the resulting reorientation of the entire set." Here in a line of agreement with Godzich we recall Terry Eagleton's description of the sign in Bahktin as a "form of struggle and contradictions," and of language as a "field of ideological contention, not a monolithic system" (Eagleton 1983:116-7). If we consider the notion of woman as social being whose writing practice conveys the actualization of her artistic and ideological program as a result of an underlying sociopolitical praxis, we can take the writing subject's discourse in the framework of the semiosis of writing by women in the above mentioned activity, "through the word."

In the historical continuity of social discourse, the matriheritage supposes a possible, hypothetical community joined by a common line in women's situation as sociopolitical beings in the multiple cultures of civilization(s). Here as elsewhere I shall insist that we favor not the issue of gender of the empirical individual signing as author determining certain assumed characteristics of writing; rather, that we pay close attention to textual features that activate semiotic operations; these correlations are generated in the practices of writing and the reading experience, and in the poetics of writing where we can trace implied structures of interpretation. The semiotic function of the work of art as sign cannot exist without either production or perception.

Indispensable for the delineation of the matriherital hypothesis is the consideration of writing as an activity among other psychophysic and material forces in the social relations of the productivity of communicative acts.[9] Writing by women, be it absent, emerging, suppressed, censored, recognized and accepted or acclaimed, needs to be reformulated from an understanding of the forces that are internal to the act of writing and of communication and those that are external but which have a bearing in the production of the text as well. As one way to approach this problematic we shall reflect on how the notional fields of "woman," "self" and "social being" are essential as correlators among the extra-literary dimensions of the sociotext in the event of artistic creation in the general context of social discourse and the word, and within the major paradigms of critical theory in feminist debates.

3. Woman, self, social being

> More and more I become acutely aware that in what I call *my text, my writing*, my voice is one and many, and at times it is no voice at all, yet I know I am there. But even in the moments when I gather phrase after phrase, word after word from the most personal, from the deepest images, thoughts, feelings, and ideas to engender a world I struggle to claim as *my own*, I sense, here and there, a stranger's words that I must also draw out and use if I am to speak at all.
>
> — "after", "from"? —

Writing: to know the stranger within, the familiarly unknown, the phantom of contradictions —

I speak through you but I cannot speak with you...

Writing to change the course of exile from silence into the word(his), from the named to naming with the only instrument we have, language, the divider —

— "we"? "have"?...

Writing: to create spaces for evidence that I received and perceived something from the outer and the inner worlds —

— for "whom"?

Writing: to execute one's own reciprocal relationship between self and social world, to occur and be present; to happen in discourse?...

Writing: to mark the boundaries between the self and the void which the self refuses to be.

— *between* —

A woman, writing: and the poem of my youth looks back at me, emerges, *super facies*, in the surge of a sleepless night, and I keep reading its tale: *if I was yours, why didn't you give me your voice, your body*? And now, with a blurring sight, slowly blooming in white hair and tiny wrinkles, and feeling tired in new ways, I remember — and as you read this the story will be the same — I remember the land between the dark ocean and the fearful beauty of the mountain ranges, the disconnected villages, the shut off microphones, the rumor that murders in uniform at 2 a.m., the squint-eyed muffler, details we no longer write about because, they say at the headquarters, it has become a cliché, because, I say, it still happens... *I was afraid of you*...and the text, speaking now by and from itself, ebbs, *you deprived me of you...does it hurt to have a body? I would not hurt you*
In silence, I write in the blank page:

others would

When far away from there, you did it over and over the text insists

On the page, my second thought:
A woman's passport in the continents of musts.

Writing. A woman, writing:caught between the "free subjectivity" and the "subjected being."
Woman: I, the scriptural paradox, *a relative construction*.[10]

In this new country, my promise never to silence you again — *dannoe*! *sozdannoe*![11]

The problematizations of "the self" and "woman" as concepts have been meeting points and places of separation in the critical construction of feminist discourse and discourse on women, whether from the French or Anglo-American scene, whether psychoanalytic, psychiatric, legislative, literary, linguistic approaches; I shall, to use E. Meese's phrase (1986:137) — "speak within paradigmatic constraints" by taking the key concepts as notions of sameness and the very place of difference.[12]

Between the closed system of woman's nullity in the cultural muteness caused by the powers of patriarchy and the infinitude of possible discourse, the "self" textualizes and constitutes the writing subject in a semiosis of transreferented events. The text comes to modify the prevailing discursive domain; it is an instance of separation from the self as it obtains its new relations in the larger domain of the texts of culture. The two principles, of nullity and infinitude, are virtual horizons in the event of artistic creation, in which the writing subject is formed as the self intends, towards separation and fusion of and in discourse, to cease being merely the discourse of the other, to mark off the writing subject by its very existence in relation to all other discursive practices.[13]

The virtual and actual separation of the self from the infinitude of discourse is not realizable but remains a paradoxical move essential for the writing subject to exist. The two poles that initiate the activity of signifying practice are the self (immaterial) and its immediate other, the body (material). Every being has these two poles; *the sexual differential* occurs subsequent to this first relation since every socialized being receives the masculine and the feminine to be embodied in the semiotic assignment as referent in relation to the (man's or woman's) body, and the construction as social being. A given set of ideologies comes to be integrated in the domain of the social being and its relationship with the social world where language (as expression of *the other*) pre-exists. Ideologies and their socio-cultural structures of implicit norms, internalized codes, modes of assimilation and indoctrination, modes of resistance and specific evaluation, are reoriented in the social being and articulated through the subject in the act of writing. The event of artistic creation is a dynamic constellation in which the self's inner expression and experience are transmuted into an externally manifest form as utterance. Thus, *dramatis personae*, characters, and lyric personae in the represented world are not independent from the above mentioned variable junctures from self to writing subject; they are representations of *the other* as well, but dialogized and subjected to the writing subject's textual dimensions, given and giving a discursive evaluation. In this process numerous variants appear inscribed in the writing subject and these concern another complex relationship between the self, social being, and *experience* as part of the *inner world and its articulation into a form of the external world* (in a given language). Here the social orientation is posited: "The transition from experience as inner expression to the externally manifest utterance is the *first* stage in ideological and [...] literary creation. At this stage the *social orientation*, which is already laid down, or whose possibility is hinted at in the experience, becomes fixed" (Volochinov 1983b:110). This transition, no doubt, is fully dynamic. Ideology, as well as form in the event of artistic creation, are not devices that are *given*, but rather come to be *positioned* in direct relation to the writing subject (cf. Medvedev 1983:58).

By exploring the conscious and the unconscious forces in the self through the word, the writing subject introduces connections and boundaries thereby situating it paradigmatically and syntagmatically, both as a product of history, and as the material for subsequent signifying practices. When the construction of "woman" enters into the aesthetic domain of poetic discourse, it becomes also a concretization of a specific social being, neither a normative entity, nor a transcendent notion; as representation it may appear as a given identity achieving coherence in its individuality, its unity of relationships.

The writing subject is product of the inscription of ideations of the self that bring into the represented world that which constitutes a portion of the sphere of material reality and material forces (including daily experience and ideas); the latter are assigned a new value as an outcome of selection from a given reservoir of abstract and virtual systems of signifying practices where the subject did not exist, or existed as *the other*. In order to place the writing subject in the context of social discourse, I shall revert the focus from the common feminist paradigm of WOMAN AS THE OTHER[14] to that of WOMAN AND THE OTHER. The two major correlations functioning in this paradigm are:

THE ONE WHO IS NOT I [ME] === THE SOCIAL BEING
(celui/celle qui n'est pas moi)
THE OTHER:
THAT WHICH IS NOT I [ME] === THE SOCIAL WORLD
(ce qui n'est moi)

The sociality of *the other* correlating with the writing subject occurs as a discursive positional inscription rather than a static presence, as instances of identifying rather than identity.[15] For example, Afro-American discourse engages from its inception the discursive practice of the subject position within the slave-holding system in the activity of the discourse of the excluded, and *the other* — as alien text — as the discourse excluding it; in the first part of the twentieth century, the move to a subsequent appropriation of the discourses that were formerly constituting the other is provoked when the writing subject is no longer a function of the discourse of the marginal, or of the marginalized; and especially from the 1960s the subject position in Afro-American discourse undergoes a radical transformation creating a metadiscourse that foregrounds new semiotic appropriations of *the other* in an interdiscursive polemic practice (Díaz-Diocaretz 1985a; 1985c; 1986c).

Perception and awareness of *the other* in the form of alien text and discourse[16], and the will to inscribe and communicate it, and its incorporation into the signifier are an ideological response to the cultural manifestations existing outside of the self and apprehended as already socially organized; that is, they are already given a logic of order by dominant practices. The event of writing in artistic creation is, from this perspective, an activity of sign production in which the I and THE OTHER are dialogized, the self and the alien text are confronted in a resulting regrouping of values. The transformations of inner expression into *the other* as *alien discourse* reestablish new correlations within the problematic of cultural muteness.

The two dimensions, "self" and "social being" infix within discourse the communicative structures in and through a variety of subjects according to each utterance, and can only represent themselves in what seem to be "projections" or ideations from their sources (cf. Benveniste 1966:133). The speaking subject is not just the active or passive agent but a *deictic sociality*, a sociodynamic force (not center) orienting the correlations between "self" and *the other*, between writing subject and speaking subject. *The other*, — as *alienus* — becomes articulated in discourse, transformed from a text of the social world to a feature of the writing subject. The alien voice may take its position as (another) speaking subject; as utterance, it may come to be integrated into the textual world as representation, or it may be textually implied as "the unuttered." Consequently, the historical specificity of the writing subject and its correlation with its intratextual speaking subjects are not and cannot be fixed structures, nor are the sociotextual functions that activate new texts in the readers, static. They are ever changing in a constant interplay and movement of intersections and adjustments being reshaped in the aesthetic organization and production of the text. In the context of the notion of woman as social being, a distinction unfolds between woman as *author* (a static condition), and as writing subject ("scripteuse") ever different and no longer the empirical being, yet not totally detached from the social world; likewise, the social being is not entirely independent from the structured represented world. The author functions in the social world, while the scripteuse belongs to the domain of signifying practice.

Reflections on the writing act and the ideological nature of the subject evidently includes consideration of the question of the author but in its true domain: in the activity of production that belongs to a specific category determined by socioeconomic structures. Whether it is as intellectuals, literary persons, or authors, women also function according to particular ideologies and social status, therefore according to class factors within social groups. However, even in the most radical social and political changes, the patriarchal structures remain an uninterrupted continuity of discursive practice. The matriherital factor calls for the critique of this historical dominance of interruption in social discourse. Of equal importance is the particular reservoir acquired through cultural, geographical, economic, historical, gendered, and racial markers and other conditions which constitute the social being and inform the world of experience. This double domain of socioeconomic structure and reservoir is the context external to the text that explains why a feminist perspective cannot avoid dealing with patriarchal notions. A feminist critical vision works precisely with the space of juxtaposition where the writing subject — in the articulation of self and of the other — and every social form and every instance of representation embedded with patriarchal notions, are grounded in discourse as competing forces. Both the innate and the acquired memories on the one hand (the latter inherited from and instilled by patriarchy) and the relation of the body and social being are two sets of opposing conceptions and major dynamic social forces working within text production. Woman, as a sociocultural being, can be understood from the frontiers and from the very ground of contradictions, where assimilation, indoctrination, and especially modes of internalization are the mechanisms by which relations, divisions, and splits occur between self, social being and social world.

The dynamics in the articulation of the subject provoke a voice that is *multiple* (never one, or univocal, but contradicting and contradictory) and *changing*, transforming the previous voices as well as those that are ulterior to it in the activity of reading. Writing is above all an acquired consciousness of the will to cease to be silent, mute, of the refusal to be merely *the other* in discourse; it is the act of changing the discursive practices of *l'autrui*. In the relation between the self, the writing subject with the social world in the historical intersection and the textual dynamics at the crossroads of multiplicity and change, *the alien text* (as discursive structures of the other) may be perceived and restructured with a foregrounding of its patriarchal propositions. The discursive strategy of displacing the patriarchal and other types of texts as *the other* and appropriating it in a variety of forms reveals the multiple nuances of the feminist, non-feminist, woman-oriented, masculinist factors in poetic discourse.

4. La femme qui parle: "Madame Texte"[17]

Formal constraints and implicit norms — as unuttered forms of the alien text — play a major role in the relationship between self, social being, writing subject and artistic text. The position of writing subject *vis à vis* those constraints is not simply a virtual one in the symbolic order, or a transcendental one in the constant replacing of signifiers, but rather it is a concrete operation that has effects in the dialectics of sociotextual production and reception.

Given that "all human activity is governed by constraints," writing is not exempt from them. In the communicative act initiated by the writing subject within the dialogic continuum of discourse, there exists a horizon in which the virtual completion of the text is oriented towards an implied reader, where the text proposes new strategies (Volochinov[Bakhtin]1983a; Iser 1978; Eco 1979). In the internal communicative situation of the artistic text, the addressee's presence is an implied subject; an absence made explicit in the text may constitute the very horizon of the "ideated" completion of the communicative act for the writing subject; yet this implied subject is perceived quite differently in the reading process as an ideated discursive feature, since it is transformed from the aesthetic to the artistic pole (cf. Iser 1974:274). To choose a female speaking subject implies both the incorporation of a gendered social being as representation (the writing subject may be male or female) that is to be distinguished from the social being and the self that conceives such construction. The empirical physical body of woman and the physical body as symbol, come to be closely attached by means of the referent linking and separating the world of natural reality from the one of social reality. It is in this sense that the notion of woman's writing, like the notion of the woman's body in its multiple representations, is a subject constituted as sign and ideological product; texts by women reflect a reality conceived from a specific strategic consciousness, refracting another social reality which is sifted through the word (cf. Bakhtin[Volochinov]1977:27). The ideological in the subject concerning woman as social being introduces an orientation worthy of consideration in another area where the textual and the extratextual juxtapose, but which refers to structures interacting within the artistic work for the constitution of the aesthetic: the relation of formal constraints and the unuttered as evaluation by form.

In contemporary writing by women (since the 1970s), we find the textual articulation of the writing subject's *consciousness* that the event of writing occurs in a predominantly patriarchal medium; we can observe how this non-artistic reality is refracted through the event of aesthetic creation into poetic texts. In counteraction with the dissemination of addressees and objects created by patriarchy and texts instituting their subjects (cf. Angenot 1983:103), the articulation of such consciousness not only designs a horizon of socially constituted readers, but also provokes a series of discursive practices that nowadays we can assemble under the type of "discourse of feminism" with a variety of text-types, forms, and genres (letters, speeches, autobiographies, literary works, criticism). Such a phenomenon — of consciousness — has become the very topic of the discourse being produced. We need to distinguish clearly, however, between the enterprise of producing texts with a feminist consciousness set in the context of author, and supply-demand market[18] and the activity that concerns the writing subject and the nature of a given artistic form. External social constraints may permeate the consciousness of an individual in the event of creation. Semiotics can be useful to focus on the unspoken awareness of external forces from the social world and their transmutation into the text; we can investigate from that approach whether this awareness is predominant or not in texts by women, and whether it cooperates or intervenes in the internal structural elements. It would be a methodological error to search for differences in gendered awareness of social constraints in the intrinsic characteristics of language or in women's practice per se. Instead we must look for distinctions in the systems of relations in which texts by women situate themselves in the general context of social discourse. We may explore, for example, the forms in which the ideologically constituted horizon of implied recipients would be refracted in the event of writing and would give shape to the subject's own structures. In contemporary feminist writing, the rise of a specific interpretive position leaves no doubt that there exist textual strategies that induce such readings (e.g. Heilbrun 1971; Edwards and Diamond 1977; Felman 1975; Fetterley 1978; Kolodny 1980; Showalter 1981; Culler 1982).

From recent studies in language, we have learned that women and other discriminated groups in a given society are able to have and develop a sociolinguistic sensitivity when confronted with social norms and formal rules (cf. Conklin 1974); this suggests the ability to put to work strategies in order to manipulate circumstances in a speech situation, and to accommodate their participation to either "correctness" or "appropriateness" (Thorne and Henley 1975). This phenomenon, obviously, does not occur only in situations in natural speech, but in the activity of writing as well. The question of "correctness"' may be translated into other restrictions, which function as aspects of constraints and conventions governing, for example, the fulfillment of standards of textuality. Here, I shall (mis)use Frake's notion of "the formal" (1983:299-304).

In the light of an "already existing tradition," writing by women encounters a strong field of constraints; "the nature of the texts, the tools, and their manipulations, are specified in advance. What is happening is predefined, over-determined, securely bounded" (301). Writing in patriarchy is in itself an activity that is rigidly framed. Feminist writing incorporates itself in this field of constraint as the very ground from which to proceed. A major force for a feminist orientation to exist is this very knowledge; once aware of constraints, the articulation of such phenomena becomes "the very field of advantage to the constrained."

As a response to the aforementioned constraints, the discursive strategies of the writing subject subordinate certain elements of a text's aesthetic organization, of its composition; it is a process in which options are utilized in particular structures towards the verbal and also towards the extra-verbal horizon such as those of semantic nature and of values (Todorov 1981; Bakhtin 1984:298). The "value-horizon" is of significance in the selection of elements of textuality, acceptability, and coherence (cf. Beaugrande and Kessler 1981). The search for matriherital factors calls for siftings of textual implications that concern the blocking and interruption of women's activities as *collective subjects* in the two interacting poles of sender and addressee (*destinateur-destinataire*; cf.Greimas 1976:10). In other words, patriarchy's maiming of women's emissive and receptive acts has played a role in both competence and performance in discourse. In studies on formal constraints and of the nature of discourse the patriarchal factor constantly perpetuates this phenomenon. Consider, for example, the following definition: "le discours n'est que la langue en tant qu'assumée par l'homme qui parle." These are A. Greimas's words (1976:10), quoting Benveniste, to place the subject in the system of discourse. The coherence of the patriarchal system is clearly seen in the comfortable correspondence between the restrictive hypothetical identity of the gendered speaking subject, and the general internal referent in scientific discourse at large. The simple substitution: "le discours n'est que la langue en tant qu'assumée par la femme qui parle," is more than a change in gender, it unfolds a sociocultural dimension. *La femme qui parle, the woman who speaks, the woman who writes*; in this actualization of the female speaking subject, a dual horizon appears: "the world" at large, and the world in patriarchy. The woman's word speaks from this duality.

5. The enthymeme in writing by women

Both the utterances in real-life and in the poetic text consist of two parts: that which is verbally realized, and its non-verbal situation, the implied (*podrazumevaemoe*, lit. under-mind-ed). To explain this reciprocal embeddedness in the utterance, Volochinov (1983a: 5-30) suggests an analogy with the old term from logic, *enthymeme*. The term consists of a syllogism in which one of the premises is not stated but implied. This aspect of the non-verbal is not an external cause; it constitutes the very structure of the utterance (12). The significance of the enthymeme consists of its determining "the very *selection* of words and *form* of the verbal entity" (13), and each instance of selectivity of the linguistic material conveys a specific evaluation and an intratextual orientation within the artistic event. I will borrow the term to re-examine and explore the role of the implied evaluation in poetic discourse by women, which can lead us to discover a multiplex system of valuational positions that the writing subject takes with regard to poetic form as it is closely intertwined with what is spoken about or actually expressed. To delineate a matriheritai *aesthetics*, the very arrangement of artistic material must be taken as central. An "*evaluation by form*" (22) whether radical or not, presupposes subordination of all elements in the structure of the text itself.

It is important to stress the fact that the presence of the "unuttered context of life" in the artistic work is bounded by the interaction of three essential participants in discourse: the speaker, the listener, and the topic (the latter, the "one of whom [of which] they speak," is called the "hero" by the Bakhtinian School). The interaction of these three co-participants constitutes and determines the form of the text from within.

To start with, one aspect of speaker/addressee relationship involves the particular feature of the speaker in the first person singular, as expression for the individual I-experience from which the lyric voice is to be perceived. Moreover, it provides an orientation of content and has a role in the interrelationships with the two other co-participants of the utterance. However, this paradigm operates on the explicitness of *the uttered*, not on the implicitness of the enthymeme, while being determined by it.

What I wish to emphasize is the function of the unuttered listener in relation to the topic of the utterance as an evaluating act which determines form; the importance of the speaker in poetic discourse by women should not be neglected, and I will ask you to keep it in mind. The changing hierarchies in the relationships between speaker(s) and person(s) addressed, as I have proposed elsewhere (1985b), can determine the type of feminist or non-feminist orientation of the poet's discourse, or may reveal the use of internalized patriarchal conventions.

The "listener" will be understood as an addressee imagined by the writing subject, as the element in relation to whom the work is angled (Volochinov 1983a:22); it is a poetic factor, a constituent component having a "regulatory role" as a "constant structural element of artistic creation" (27). Thus, the "listener" is part of the non-verbal field, one that can appear as an added implied identity, as an enthymeme. By focusing on this element we can trace the spectrum of evaluations of, for instance, the system of formal constraints on the implicit norms actualized in the use of poetic conventions as they are structured in the artistic text.

The enthymeme provides a way to look for accepted "common assumptions" and especially the role of a "commonly assumed evaluation" being accepted and which may be part of the inner voice of the writing subject (cf. 1983:12-15). It is socially objective, that is, it does not originate in the individual; therefore the evaluation is not a singular one, but corresponds rather to a given commonality. In a general sense, it can contain the implied "atmosphere of shared feeling," of support from a given period, or an artistic movement; or from a given collective according to a specific cultural sphere (e.g. "American," "Black," "Chicano," "Caribbean," "Native

American"), or to a specific race classeme (black, white, Indian), or to a specific nation or continent (Africa, Latin America, Israel, India) or according to a specific social class. The wider the range of the shared viewpoint and the wider the social group, the more general and constant the enthymeme appears in the implied elements of the utterance. When writing by women in a given period contains all structures of tradition as accepted, as something inherent, the form of the text in itself is a manifestation of the "unhesitating confidence in the sympathy of the listeners/readers" from that tradition.

Yet the enthymeme may take the form of a "shared discontent," through the assumption of an antagonistic rather than supporting chorus; here, another participant (besides the expressed listener) emerges as an *enigmatic feature*. If the commonality of evaluations is centered upon patriarchy, the speaker may challenge the implied through the unspoken tone of vexation (e.g. Sylvia Plath). In other instances, the enthymeme determines the production of a viewpoint containing the implied as evaluations in agreement with a collective of women. When the enthymeme is oriented towards patriarchy or towards women, for example, it must be considered as closely interrelated with the other variant co-participants in the text.

Along the lines of this proposed framework, we shall recall that the writing subject's relationship with *the other* had a dual unfolding, in "the one who is not I=social being" and "that which is not I=social world," both aspects external to the work. In the internal structure of the artistic text, these are concomitant to the Bakhtinian "listener" and the topic. *The other* in the artistic utterance takes the form of the "listener," to make way for the point of view of another implied participant. Volochinov defines this listener in the following terms: "This constant *co-participant* in all acts of our consciousness determines not only its content, but, this is the most important to us, the very *choice* of content, the choice of what we are conscious of, and what also determines those *evaluations*, which permeate consciousness (27)."

A case in point is the discourse of Phyllis Wheatley which has been amply studied in terms of internalized literary canons. Even though there are encoded instances of awareness of difference in the writing subject's being "an Ethiop" in a white world, which indicate an attempt to break certain constraints, that which dominates in her poems is precisely a particular role of the *other as enigmatic feature*. In the structures of her poems this "listener" is revealed fully in the use of poetic conventions. The constant assumption of a supporting chorus is given a clear angling through diction, and semantic metaphors, as well as tone, all of which are in agreement with the unuttered context which in extratextual historical retrospective we identify as the world that educated her and encouraged her to become a writing subject in spite of her being part of a collective of the excluded. Not all "listeners" are as explicit or unambiguous as in Wheatley's discursive strategies.

One of the important functions of this "listener" is that the writing subject may ideate it and textualize it in the form of an implied co-participant featured as an ally, or as an adversary, and this in its turn provokes changes in the intonational patterns and the tone itself (e.g. the presence of humor, irony, satire). This function can be set in another interacting sociotextual correlation with the following: "all phenomena of being which surrounds us are fused together with our evaluations of them. If an evaluation is in reality conditioned by *the very being of a given collective*, then it is accepted dogmatically as something understood and not subject to discussion. Conversely, where the basic evaluation is expressed and demonstrated, it has already in that case become equivocal, it has become separated from the subject; it has ceased to organize life and, has, in consequence, lost its connection with the conditions of that collective's being" (13; my emphasis). From this we can extrapolate some observations which were not developed or predicted by the Bakhtinian School, in relation to writing by women, if we understand the notion of a "given collective" in at least three ways: a) as a patriarchy-oriented and dominated collective; b) as a dominant collective (which may include patriarchy, but which is structured and controlled by hegemonic forces within a sociopolitical and economic order); and c) as a non-dominant collective. The three are quite distinct yet one does not exclude the presence of the other in a given text. Let us consider an example.

The inclusion of dialect, of colloquial forms and the vernacular in Afro-American poetry at the end of the nineteenth century is a sign of the movement of the enthymeme from the "white" collective and its socially accepted assumptions, towards those of the commonality of evaluations excluded, up to that moment, from the domain of poetic form. Quite interestingly, as Gloria T. Hull (1979: 169) points out, the dialect verse, in that period, is practiced exclusively by male poets. The fact that the tone of dialect poetry might have seemed "unladylike" to the women poets is one plausible explanation Hull offers, considering the social constraints towards the feminine. In agreement with Hull's idea, I am inclined to believe that given the articulation of woman's strategic consciousness, the enthymeme in writing by women may contain the *unuttered fundamental valuational contexts conditioned by the very being not of one collective* as the Bakhtinian School suggests for all utterances but *that it is conditioned by the very being of at least two collectives*. In the case of women poets who refuse to write in dialect in the nineteenth century, we might venture to say that it is an implied evaluation, by refusal to practice it, of the strongly male-dominated character of Afro-American discourse in that period. The two collectives, in this case, would be patriarchy (in its dual form determined by race) and the dominant world of white society.

Another interesting example appears in the discourse of Gwendolyn Brooks, with the opposing orientations between the choice of her topics — racial discrimination, enforced poverty of black people in urban life, alienation, and her attempt to understand a rigidly organized society indifferent to the conditions of the black community. The transformations in the interaction of actual speaker and addressee within the poems can be better appreciated through the role of the "enigmatic feature" which reverses the system of hierarchies internal to the texts. The trajectory of the enthymeme and the aesthetic effects which it determines in Brooks's discourse show the gradual veering of the unuttered evaluations. At first, from *A Street in Bronzeville* (1945) to *The Bean Eaters* (1960), the writing subject accepts standard literary practices but does not fully conform to them, translating this tension into a technical achievement of, for example, off-rhyme and the hybrid form (as an innovative poetic deviation) that results from her fusion of the ballad and the sonnet. On a macrostructural level, the choice of topic around the lives and experiences of black people begins to emphasize in her discourse the semantic context of her represented world. Especially since *Riots* (1968), the unuttered shared support from the dominant collective of the "white world" is set in the background to give room to the implied identity of the black community itself. This movement explains Brooks's new position as writing subject in relation to her choice of topic, and in her use of free verse and variations in the structure of the intonational patterns.

The decisive change in Brooks's discourse is not an isolated fact, since it directly corresponds to a radical innovation introduced as *evaluation by form* in Afro-American poetic discourse of the 1960s which in texts by women obtains its specificity in the discursive strategies of the woman's voice. In the texts of that period the speaker becomes more emphatically situated within the sphere of the black community. This social orientation and its corresponding set of strategies needs to be correlated with the transformation of the enthymeme in reference to intonation.

The choice of intonational and rhythmic units of Black English, oral discourse, and colloquial expressions, verbally present in the Afro-American poetic utterance is indeed a valuational act in which the enigmatic feature of the Black community, as ally, determines style from within. Equally important are the cases in which this particular linguistic material (Black English) is not chosen. It may be totally absent from the discourse of a given poet or it may appear alternated with the use of standard forms. Thus, it should be stressed that a specific intonation is an important element of the enthymeme in Afro-American discourse underlying the implied element of metaphor of performance, foregrounded as a significant part of the work's composition. The texts require not just the relation with the co-participants they may evoke; in fact, the supporting chorus that will share the social evaluation of the elements chosen and towards which the artistic event is also oriented emphasizes the poetic practice of Afro-American discourse.

If I stress the poetic practice of Afro-American discourse it is because the function of the enthymeme in poetry by Afro-American women needs to be distinguished in these aspects of form from the poetic discourse of women whose identity of assumed evaluations are oriented from and towards other collectives.

For a valid exploration of the discursive practices by women in the United States, the operational concepts and notional fields that will account for the individual constitution of the writing subject must consider the function of each text in the context of social discourse in "American" culture. In the case of Afro-American discourse, the transformations throughout two centuries of production have occurred from within the development of a culture emerging from the African diaspora, and outside of a dominant sphere, in spite of the slave-holding system that confined those practices to justify a supposed "extracultural" nature. The matriheritage in writing by black women and the transformations of the multiplicity of corresponding writing subjects are to be situated first in their difference within the patriheritage shared also by black men as writing subjects.

In contemporary discourse by women the division of the world into either a male-oriented or female-oriented set of implied evaluations may appear not only in the represented world but also in the design of the unuttered participant constituted as "patriarchy." If aware of this, the subject becomes separated from the patriarchal collective and acquires a consciousness that reorients the utterance. In texts of a feminist orientation, the enthymeme of patriarchy as adversary determines the tone of irony, or may take the direction of the collective evaluations of women, as in the poetry of Judy Grahn and Adrienne Rich (e.g. in *The Dream of a Common Language*).

In the poetic discourse of Adrienne Rich since 1951, the enthymeme serves as example of the transformations of the evaluative act by form which go intimately connected with the ideological reorientations of her writing subject. First, the enigmatic feature in the 1950s and the 1960s determines the stanza forms, choice of lexicon, and regular use of iambic pentameter lines, from the Anglo-American tradition. After the 1960s, the texts begin to reveal a speaking subject who no longer yields to the suggestions of "gentle tones," but begins to deliver variations from irony to reproach, to detachment, introducing intonation breaks sometimes without transition (e.g. in "The Phenomenology of Anger") that set in motion syntactic factors and changes of semantic relevance. When her enthymeme becomes inhabited by the women's world, the tones formerly addressed at patriarchy are deferred, no longer foregrounded.

When the enthymeme that dominates the choice of poetic form contains the firm assumption of a supporting chorus from the collective of women, contemporary poetic discourse offers another varied spectrum of differences. For example, the woman-oriented and woman-identified viewpoint that gives coherence to the choice of historico-mythical elements in the discourse of Audre Lorde is quite distinct from those in the discourse by Judy Grahn.

If my suggestion is accepted, the enthymeme is a necessary element which in writing by women breaks open the possibilities of tracing in detail textual features that may contribute to finding some paradigms of matriheritage within differences in poetic discourse, thus linking ideological evaluation with poetic structure.

I would like to add to this an important factor for the apprehension of the enthymeme. It refers specifically to the *cultural situation of the writing subject* correlated with that of the speaking subject, in the choice of a given national language as linguistic material; that is, I am proposing the rapport between the writing subject and the role of the unuttered evaluations conveyed by the chosen language as part of the ideological released from within the linguistic material and its uses in a particular text. A few examples will suffice. It includes the relationship of the writing subject in Afro-American discourse with standard English; or the unuttered evaluations in texts such as *Abeng* and *The Land of Look Behind* by Michelle Cliff, in correlations with the cultural spheres of Jamaica and Britain; in the United States, the rapport of the writing subject originating from any of the ethnic communities *vis à vis* standard language, such as the work by Native-American and Asian-American women; in the writing by Chicanas there is a specific rapport with the Mexican and the Spanish culture, in addition to "American" culture (see, for example, Ordóñez 1984); in the same way women from ethnic groups of European origin include a variety of distinct communal evaluations in their language.

Important in this context is the case of Puerto Rican women writers who decide to write in Spanish or in English, and the texts by Nuyorican poets in a language embedded with their own evaluation of standard practices; in another cultural sphere in the context of "American culture," this concerns the textual rapport of Olga Broumas with the English language and with Greek culture. It includes also consideration of the occasional use of foreign expressions (in relation to English) of, for example, French and Latin in the poetry by Marilyn Hacker and by Adrienne Rich, or of Spanish in June Jordan, Ntozake Shange, and Lorna Dee Cervantes (on the latter see Monda 1984). By the same token, the aesthetic function of texts in Latin, English, Italian, French, and Greek in the novels in Spanish by Iris M. Zavala (Puerto Rico) and in a larger domain the textual function of English in writing from India and South Africa. Each particular language has its position within the hegemony of a given society, because woman as writing subject obtains a position within this context and the forces of patriarchy. All these aspects of the social being may suggest a variety of angles of structural aspects in the aesthetic organization of a text. A correlation with one or more languages implies relationships with one or more cultures, and in the context of the dialogic in discourse and its transformations, the writing subject is actively taking position through unuttered evaluations. The linguistic and aesthetic forms that preexist a text are given new orientations, are de-territorialized, de-privileged, forced to a maximum degree of expression (cf. Deleuze and Guattari 1975) to release new signifying practices. Artistic form, determined by the enthymeme, will shape internal polemics. Thus, the supposed "tradition" of a given dominant order is challenged, its tendency to preserve its balance is shaken, and newly transformed, this time, by the woman who writes the uttered, and through it, the unuttered.

I would like to close with the general conclusion I suggested at the beginning, that in order to analyze specificity in poetic discourse by women, the gender factor, a useful constant, must be taken in correlation with all other elements in the internal structure of the artistic text. To allow for the place of differences among women in poetics, the notions of class, gender, and race are not sufficient unless they are placed in a more operational framework where texts by women become contextualized in the production of social discourse as a whole. In the framework of the dialogic and of semiotic practice, the element of *culture* needs to be reformulated from a feminist perspective — not simply in the sense of "women's culture" — in the context of the mechanisms of the cultural and the extra-cultural spaces in the social world at large. In this semiotic dialectics we can understand the variety of mechanisms and forces of social discourse that each one of us is evaluating and which are evaluating us. The dynamics of the sociotext, as a critical tool for correlations, makes it possible to *integrate* rather than exclude elements that may not seem compatible. In this sense, the sociotext is a crossdisciplinary factor, leading us to a recognition, in the differences within writing by women, of the strangers within.

NOTES

1. See my articles (1985a), and especially (1986b).

2. "Cultural muteness" will be used in this essay whenever a critical position is assumed in reference to "silence" in writing by women in order to distinguish the practice of the critic from that of the writer. See Díaz-Diocaretz (1986a, b).

3. The concept of "de-territorialization," introduced by Deleuze and Guattari (1975) has proven useful to analyze Afro-American discourse in the context of the semiotics of culture (cf. Díaz-Diocaretz 1984b, 1986c).

4. Among the few studies exploring ideology in lyric discourse, Easthope (1983) is particularly valuable.

5. Here the relevance of J. Kristeva's *intertextualité* is evident. However, in one of the many departures from the Bakhtinian School, Kristeva's notion of signifying process is articulated as the functioning of the *semiotic* ("a linguistic signifier signifying an *object* for an *ego*," 1974:67) and the *symbolic* in the direction of the psychoanalytic discursive system; in my perspective, I take these notions in their relation to the social world; therefore, the bond between one text to another comes to be placed in the interdiscursive context of the ideological function within *the* word itself.

6. Compare, for example, Rich (1972) and Barthes (1972); Foucault (1979) and the publications of the *Tel Quel* group, with the essays in Gilbert and Gubar (1979).

7. See Díaz-Diocaretz (1984a, 1985a, 1985b).

8. For a more detailed discussion of those notions as three types of discourse, see my references (1984a, 1985b).

9. "Material forces" constitute a *correlation of forces* which transform concrete historical praxis in a multi-leveled dialectics, including the transformations of those conditions producing in turn their own subsequent existence. Cf. Gramsci (1953), Texier (1966:48-49).

10. Both "free subjectivity" and "subjective being" explain the ambiguous meaning of the term "subject." See Althusser (1971:182).

11. In Russian, "what is given" (*dannoe*), "what is created" (*sozdannoe*).

12. The constructions of "women," "writing" and "the body," have, of course, existed in all forms of feminist analysis. For example, Chodorow (1980); Gallop and Burke (1980); Gallop (1982a, 1982b); Jones (1981); Wenzel (1981); and, most recently, Brooke-Rose (1985); Jardine (1985); Kristeva (1985); Miller (1985); Suleiman (1985); Stimpson (1985), and Meese (1986).

13. In Kristeva (1969), poetic language presents itself, for the writer, as a potential infinitude, the set of realizable possibilities. For the problematic of a model of the poetic language Kristeva follows the notions of "space" and "the infinite" from mathematical theories. What I propose is not in opposition to such a model; however, it needs to be stressed that the correlations suggested in my essay are closer to "the infinitude" as a dimension of existence originating from the recently emerging science of psychophysics.

14. E.g. Woman as man's other in Simone de Beauvoir's existentialist *Other*, Lacan's psychoanalytic other and Other, Irigaray's logic of the same. See Feral (1980); Makward (1980); Gilligan (1980) has explored the conflict between "self" and "other" as a central moral problem for women in concrete experience, proposing, for example, that abortion decisions center on the self; Moi (1985) provides an interesting discussion.

15. Both configurations of *the other*, as presented in the diagram, appear as signs of the non-person situated outside of the writing subject. Cf. *Ce/celui*, "that which," "the one who," as third person signify a non-person, a sign of absence, "situated outside of discourse"; cf. Barthes (1972:139), Benveniste (1966:252).

16. The alien text as an intertextual factor within the framework of the dialogic has an important function in contemporary feminist discourse (Díaz-Diocaretz 1984a, 1985b, 1986a). In a different approach Baron (1986) presents the notion of "alien tongue" as equivalent for the language of women within the development of grammar-gender related forms in the English language.

17. Here I am in implicit intertextual polemic with Hartman's title "Monsieur Texte" (1981:1).

18. As we know, books and literary productivity are assigned very different functions and values, and the practice of oral or written discourse obtains a position within a given culture, distinctions we must keep in mind when we study the work by women from either the Third World, or the First World.

REFERENCES

Althusser, Louis. 1971. *Lenin and Philosophy*. New York: Monthly Review Press.

Angenot, Marc. 1983. "Intertextualité, Interdiscursivité, Discours Social." *Texte: Revue de Critique et de Théorie Littéraire* 2: 101-112.

Bakhtin, Mikhail. 1973. *Problems of Dostoevsky's Poetics*. Trans. R.W. Rotsel. Ann Arbor: Ardis.

——— [V. N. Volochinov]. 1977. *Le Marxisme et la philosophie du langage* (1929). Trans. Marina Yaguello. Paris: Les Editions de Minuit.

———. 1984. *Esthétique de la création verbale* (1979). Trans. Alfreda Aucouturier. Paris: Editions Gallimard.

Bakhtin School Papers, Ann Shukman (ed.). Russian Poetics in Translation 1983 No. 10.

Baron, Dennis. 1986. *Grammar and Gender*. New Haven: Yale University Press.

Barthes, Roland. 1972. "To Write: An Intransitive Verb?". In *The Structuralist Controversy*, ed. by Richard Macksey and Eugenio Donato, 134-156. Baltimore: The John Hopkins University Press.

Beaugrande, Michel de and Kessler, Wolfgang. 1981. *Introduction to Text-Linguistics*. London: Longman.

Benveniste, Emile. 1966. *Problèmes de linguistique générale*. Paris: Gallimard.

Brooke-Rose, Christine. 1985. "Woman as Semiotic Object." *Poetics Today* 6(1-2): 9-20.

Chodorow, Nancy F. 1980. "Psychoanalytic Perspective." In *The Future of Difference*, ed. by Eisenstein and Jardine, 3-19.

Conklin, Nancy F. 1974. "Toward a Feminist Analysis of Linguistic Behaviour." *University of Michigan Papers in Women's Studies* 1(1): 51-73.

Culler, Jonathan. 1982. *On Deconstruction: Theory and Criticism after Structuralism*. Ithaca, NY: Cornell University Press.

Deleuze, Gilles and Guattari, Félix. 1975. *Kafka: Pour une littérature mineure*. Paris: Les Editions de Minuit.

Díaz-Diocaretz, Myriam. 1984a. *The Transforming Power of Language: The Poetry of Adrienne Rich*. Utrecht: Hes.

———. 1984b. "'Mijn naam is van mij van mij van mij': Zwarte noord-amerikaanse dichteressen in hun context" (in Dutch). *LOVER* 84(4): 188-197.

———. 1985a. "Black North American Women Poets in the Semiotics of Culture." In *Women, Feminist Identity and Society in the 1980's*, ed. by M. Díaz-Diocaretz and I. M. Zavala, 37-60. Amsterdam: John Benjamins.

———. 1985b. *Translating Poetic Discourse: Questions on Feminist Strategies in Adrienne Rich*. Amsterdam: John Benjamins.

———. 1985c. "On the Poetics of the Lyric: Strategy of the Black Woman's Voice." Paper for the conference The Black Woman Writer and the Diaspora. Michigan State University, East Lansing, October.

———. 1986a. "Estrategias Textuales: Del discurso femenino al discurso feminista." *Molinos*: *La mujer en cambio* (marzo): 38-48.

———. 1986b. "Poeticizing the Difference: The Social Text and Writing by Women." Trans. by Anita Kontrec, *Knjizevnost* (Belgrado) 8/9: 1471-79.

———. 1986c. "Proposals for a Crossdisciplinary Approach to Afro-American Literature." *Third Utrecht Summer School of Critical Theory*, University of Utrecht, June 16-21.

Eagleton, Terry. 1983. *An Introduction to Literary Theory*. Oxford: Basil Blackwell.

Easthope, Anthony. 1983. *Poetry as Discourse*. London & New York: Methuen.

Eco, Umberto. 1979. *The Role of the Reader: Explorations in the Semiotics of Texts*. Bloomington: Indiana University Press.

Edwards, Lee and Diamond, Arlyn. 1977. *The Authority of Experience: Essays in Feminist Criticism*. Amherst: University of Massachusetts Press.

Eisenstein, Hester and Jardine, Alice (eds). 1980. *The Future of Difference*. Boston: G.K.Hall.

Felman, Shoshana. 1975. "Women and Madness: The Critical Fallacy." *Diacritics* 5(4): 2-10.

Feral, Josette. 1980. "The Powers of Difference." In *The Future of Difference*, ed. by Eisenstein and Jardine, 88-94.

Fetterley, Judith. 1978. *The Resisting Reader: A Feminist Approach to American Fiction*. Bloomington: Indiana University Press.

Foucault, Michel. 1979. "What is an Author?". In *Textual Strategies*, ed. by Harari, 141-160.

Frake, Charles O. 1983. "Notes Toward a Cultural Analysis of Formal." *Text* 3/3: 299-304.

Gallop, Jane and Burke, Carolyn G. 1980. "Psychoanalysis and Feminism in France." In *The Future of Difference*, ed. by Eisenstein and Jardine, 106-121.

Gallop, Jane. 1982a. *The Daughter's Seduction: Feminism and Psychoanalysis*. Ithaca, N.Y.: Cornell University Press.

———. 1982b. "Writing and Sexual Difference: The Difference Within." In *Writing and the Sexual Difference*, ed. by Elizabeth Abel, 283-90. Chicago: University of Chicago Press.

Gilligan, Carol. 1980. "In a Different Voice: Women's Conceptions of Self and Morality." In *The Future of Difference*, ed. by Eisenstein and Jardine, 274-317.

Godzich, Wład. 1986. "From Community to Communication: Semiosis and Semiotics." *Third Utrecht Summer School of Critical Theory*, University of Utrecht, June 16-21.

Gramsci, Antonio. 1953. *Il materialismo storico e la filosofia di Benedetto Croce*. Roma: Einaudi. 5a ed.

———. 1972. *Cultura y literatura*. Barcelona: Ed. Península.

Greimas, Algirdas Julien. 1976. *Sémiotique et sciences sociales*. Paris: Editions du Seuil.

Harari, Josué V. (ed.). 1979. *Textual Strategies: Perspectives in Post-Structuralist Criticism*. Ithaca, N.Y.: Cornell University Press.

Hartman, Geoffrey. 1981. *Saving the Text: Literature/Derrida/Philosophy*. Baltimore: Johns Hopkins University Press.

Heilbrun, Carolyn. 1971. "Milletts' *Sexual Politics*: A Year Later." *Aphra* 2: 38-47.

Hull, Gloria T. 1979. "Afro-American Women Poets: A Bio-Critical Survey." In *Shakespeare's Sisters*, ed. by Sandra M. Gilbert and Susan Gubar, 165-182. Bloomington: Indiana University Press.

Iser, Wolfgang. 1974. *The Implied Reader: Patterns of Communication from Bunyan to Beckett* (1972). Baltimore: Johns Hopkins University Press.

———. 1978. *The Act of Reading: A Theory of Aesthetic Response*. (1976). Baltimore: Johns Hopkins University Press.

Jardine, Alice. 1984. "Gynesis." *Cahiers de Recherches* 13: 65-71.

———. 1985. *Gynesis: Configurations of Woman and Modernity*. Ithaca, N.Y.: Cornell University Press.

Jones, Rosalind. 1981. "Writing the Body: Toward an Understanding of *l'Ecriture Féminine*." *Feminist Studies* 7: 247-63.

Kessler, Suzanne J. and McKenna, Wendy. 1985. *Gender: An Ethnomethodological Approach*. Chicago: University of Chicago Press.

Kolodny, Annette. 1980. "Reply to Commentaries: Women Writers, Literary Historians, and Martian Readers." *New Literary History* 11: 587-92.

Kristeva, Julia. 1969. *Semiótica* 1. *Semiótica* 2. (Recherches pour une sémanalyse, 1978). Trans. J. M. Arancibia. Madrid: Editorial Fundamentos.

———. 1974. *Revolution in Poetic Language* (1984). Trans. Margaret Waller. N.Y.: Columbia University Press.

———. 1985. "Stabat Mater." *Poetics Today* 6(1-2): 133-152.

Lévine, Y. I. 1976. "Le statut communicatif du poème lyrique," In *Travaux sur les systèmes de signes*, ed. by Y. M. Lotman and B. A. Ouspensky, trans. Anne Zouboff, 205-212. Bruxelles: Editions Complexe.

Lotman, Jury et al. 1975. "Theses on the Semiotic Study of Cultures (As Applied to Slavic Texts)." In *The Tell-Tale Sign: A Survey of Semiotics*, ed. by Thomas A. Sebeok, 57-84. Lisse: Peter de Ridder Press.

Makward, Christiane. 1980. "To Be or Not To Be...A Feminist Speaker." In *The Future of Difference*, ed. by Eisenstein and Jardine, 95-105.

Medvedev, Pavel N. 1983. "The Formal (Morphological) Method or Scholarly Salieri-ism" (1925), trans. Ann Shukman. In *Bakhtin School Papers*, 51-65.

Medvedev, Pavel N. [M.M.Bakhtin] 1983. "The Immediate Tasks Facing Literary — Historical Science" (1978), trans. C. R. Pike. In *Bakhtin School Papers*, 75-91.

Meese, Elizabeth A. 1986. *Crossing the Double-Cross: The Practice of Feminist Criticism*. Chapel Hill and London: University of North Carolina Press.

Miller, Nancy K. 1985. "Rereading As a Woman: The Body in Practice." *Poetics Today* 6(1-2): 291-299.

Moi, Toril. 1985. *Sexual/Textual Politics*. London and N.Y.: Methuen.

Monda, Bernadette. 1984. "Interview with Lorna Dee Cervantes." *Third Woman* 2(1): 103-107.

Mukařovský, Jan. 1977. *The Word and the Verbal Art: Selected Essays*, trans. (ed.) John Burbank and Peter Steiner. New Haven and London: Yale University Press.

Ordóñez, Elizabeth J. 1984. "The Concept of Cultural Identity in Chicana Poetry." *Third Woman* 2(1): 75-82.

Rich, Adrienne. 1972. "When We Dead Awaken: Writing as Revision." In A. Rich, *On Lies, Secrets, and Silences: Selected Prose 1966-1978*, 33-49. New York: Norton.

Showalter, Elaine. 1981. "Feminist Criticism in the Wilderness." *Critical Inquiry* 8, 179-206.

Suleiman, Susan and Crosman, Inge. (eds.). 1980. *The Reader in the Text: Essays on Audience and Interpretation*. Princeton, N.J.: Princeton University Press.

Suleiman, Susan. 1985. "(Re)Writing the Body: The Politics and Poetics of Female Eroticism." *Poetics Today* 6(1-2): 43-65.

Stimpson, Catharine R. 1985. "The Somagrams of Gertrude Stein." *Poetics Today* 6(1-2): 67-80.

Texier, Jacques. 1966. *Gramsci*. Paris: Editions Seghers.

Thorne, Barrie and Henley, Nancy. (eds.). 1975. *Language and Sex: Difference and Dominance*. Rowley, Mas.: Newbury House.

Todorov, Tzvetan. 1981. *Mikhail Bakhtine: le principe dialogique*. Paris: Editions du Seuil.

Tompkins, Jane (ed.). 1980. *Reader-Response Criticism: From Formalism to Post-Structuralism*. Baltimore: Johns Hopkins University Press.

Volochinov, V. N. [M.M.Bakhtin]. 1983a. "Discourse in Life and Discourse in Poetry: Questions of Sociological Poetics" (1926), trans. John Richmond. In *Bakhtin School Papers*, 5-30.

———. 1983b. "Literary Stylistics," trans. by Noel Owen. In *Bakhtin School Papers*, 93-152.

Wenzel, Hélène Vivienne. 1981. "The Text as Body/Politics: An Appreciation of Monique Wittig's Writing in Context." *Feminist Studies* 7: 264-87.

The power of division

Jonathan Culler
Cornell University

One of the most common complaints in the world of criticism and scholarship is that publication is getting out of hand and that the critic cannot keep up with his or her field but risks drowning in the flood of publications. A genuine field, it seems, is one in which one can drown, or at least get lost. By this measure, feminist criticism has indeed established itself as a field. Bookstores are full of new books on feminism and feminist theory — American, French and other — not to speak of studies of women writers or of women's writing. Even those committing themselves full-time to this area would find it very hard to keep up — to survey potentially interesting publications and engage the best with the attention they require to pursue dialogue in or with a developing field.[1]

Under these circumstances it is tempting for a critic — especially a male critic — to treat the proliferation of publications in feminist criticism as a symptom of confusion and turmoil and to stand back from a mass he cannot master, asking, "What does woman want?" Historically that question has been a way of deflecting attention from the multifarious requests and projects women might be pursuing by positing a deeper hidden and unifying desire that would make all clear, if only a sustained and detached theoretical enquiry could reveal it to us. Thus male theorists may suggest that they cannot really take feminist projects and arguments seriously until the theoretical position of feminist criticism is clearly articulated. A feminist may justifiably reply, as Elizabeth Meese writes in *Crossing the Double-Cross*, that she "refuses to compress the problematics of feminist criticism into a single theory, not because these kinds of arguments cannot be or are not being made, but out of the belief that such constructions prematurely delimit the possibilities of our intellectual and social products" (ix).

More frequently, however, we find a less rarefied form of resistance to the proliferation of feminist debate, an impatience or apparent confusion before the diverse claims of feminist criticism: What on earth do these women want? Do they want more women writers in traditionally conceived literature courses or do they want separate courses on women's writing? Is feminist criticism the study of women writers, a separate activity, or is it a perspective on literature of all sorts, and other discourses as well? Are men being enjoined to adopt feminist perspectives or to keep away lest they appropriate and contaminate a discourse that must arise from woman's own experience? Let women get their act together, runs this version of "what does woman want?"; let them decide on a program for feminist criticism or feminist literary studies, and then we will take it seriously and consider how to respond. Male critics frequently — though perhaps more often in discussion than in print — cast resistance to feminist programs and proposals in this form, asking women to make up their minds.

The implication such requests carry is that male colleagues and readers would be more receptive, and that feminist criticism would therefore make more progress, in those areas where progress depends on the acquiescence of males, if it produced a unified program. I suspect, however, that this is not the case. If feminist criticism did present a united front, those who have resisted by asking it to make up its mind would seek arguments to oppose or at least slow down the implementation of the agreed-on projects. A single position or demand might be easier to resist than several different demands at once. Feminist critics may do better, as Elizabeth Meese suggests, to resist the request that they make up their minds, that they reduce feminist criticism to a unified program. What some male critics might call a refusal to make up one's mind, perhaps better thought of as a group's insistence on being of two minds, carries certain dangers but also what I propose to call a "power of division," substituting this term for the *difference* in the title of this volume. The conception of the "difference within" feminism or feminist criticism frequently leads to a celebration of heterogeneity that seems ultimately to appeal to individual difference and ground itself in an ideology of individualism: there are differences within because we are all different, and no one's difference should be compromised or suppressed by discourse or institutions. The role of these differences in feminist criticism is a question not easily resolved, but I am interested above all in divisions in feminist criticism — competing programs, positions, and claims — and the effects of such divisions on criticism and on literary study in general. The power of division is a power of ongoing argument, in which incompatible positions work to focus attention on a set of issues, set the terms of an entire field, articulating a space of exploration and debate. The power of division works to arrange an entire area of concern around sets of competing programs or purposes, whose divergent strengths and costs cannot be easily accommodated in a synthesis.

Much of the success of feminist criticism in recent years, I would argue, has been due to this power of division, though authoritative essays have often worked to reduce or recast division, transforming a series of disputes and divergent projects into an intelligible history, translating debates about feminist criticism into a series of historical stages, in effect assuring male readers especially, but also doubtless women readers as well, that they need attend only to the latest stage in the evolution of feminist criticism.[2] The drive to establish a sequential narrative of feminist criticism no doubt comes in part from a commitment to the idea of progress towards a goal: feminist criticism must be conceived as an historical progression rather than as dispute or debate. Such histories can also perform the useful function of creating a past for feminist criticism — a "trajectory of our own," as it were. But an effect of narrativization is the reduction or elimination of debate within feminist criticism as a vital force. Disagreement becomes the persistence of stages that should have been transcended — with feminist criticism preserving some valuable lessons but incorporating them into a further stage of feminist criticism. Sometimes this takes the form of an account of different generations of feminist criticism, with a naive first generation devoted to the rehabilitation of women's writing succeeded by a sophisticated second generation founding a theoretically-based "gender studies." But such accounts often work as appeals to history or the production of historical representations in literary studies generally do: to reduce what this volume calls "the difference within" by representing a space of debate and disagreement as a historical narrative, in which readers need not concern themselves with arguments about critical priorities because history has done that for them. Not only men's misogynistic questions but also women's feminist narratives may thus work to put at risk an important aspect of feminist criticism's power, which is precisely the power of division.

Feminist criticism, in its different varieties, has had considerable success both within universities, where it has substantially affected arrangements for the teaching of literature and the character of a good deal of that teaching, and in the larger context of American society, where it has brought new sorts of literature to cultural prominence — more successfully than any other critical movement of the past twenty years. I suggest that its success is due in part to a power of division, a series of differences within that divide a domain into competing positions, each of which has plausible arguments and an energy of commitment in its favor, but whose disadvantages are not easily discounted, and which together do not give rise to a synthesis. I propose to identify swiftly a series of important divisions within feminist criticism, where reconciliation or resolution would in my view be purchased with a loss of power. If feminist criticism did present a united front, that unified position would itself be caught up in a debate of which it would be only one pole — which would be a weaker position than that of dividing a field so as to set the agenda and pull others into its space of debate.

First, the political success of feminist criticism is due in part to its ability to remain divided about its relation to women's experience. Much of the leverage of its criticism, much of the appeal of courses on women's writing comes from the assertion of a continuity between women's experience of social and familial structures and their experience as readers. Literary works are conceived above all as representations of women's experience, to which women respond because they answer to their experience. This aspect of feminist criticism, summed up in the title of Arlyn Diamond and Lee Edwards's anthology, *The Authority of Experience*, gives literary study and literary criticism an immediacy that often seemed to have been lost (Heilbrun). The insistence on a direct connection between women's writing and women's experience is also responsible for a good deal of the success of feminist criticism outside the academy: in bringing a series of new writings and of older, neglected works by women to the attention of the reading public.

Yet for other styles of feminist criticism, ranging from Judith Fetterley's *The Resisting Reader: A Feminist Approach to American Fiction* to Shoshana Felman's "Rereading Femininity," experience is precisely the problem rather than the answer: culture has offered women only a male definition of their condition, so that they have not been able to read "as women," and the task of a feminist criticism is above all to make that possible, debating the possible characteristics and enabling conditions of reading as a woman, writing as a woman, living as a woman.[3] Works of feminist criticism which address these problems and interact with the most sophisticated Marxist, psychoanalytic, and post-structuralist theory, have made feminist questions central to contemporary theoretical debate about the production of subjects and of meaning and compelled even those critics of both sexes who might have little interest in women's writing as such to engage with feminist claims. This aspect of the feminist critical enterprise, complex and highly theoretical in its moments, speculative and experimental, even bathetic, may lack the broad and immediate attractiveness of criticism which appeals to women's experience, with which it cannot be easily reconciled, but without it feminist criticism would not have entered the realm of theoretical discourse in an expansive or decisive way or established a debate about woman's experience and its relation to the discourses of literature and culture. In short, feminist criticism is divided about the status of women's experience and of appeals to it, but this division has led to its success in different critical realms, and agreement on this issue would have made the impact of feminist criticism considerably less broad.

Next, there is the division between two claims of feminist criticism and literary pedagogy: first, that the process of canonization has excluded women writers from the domain of great literature, so that the canon and literature courses must be expanded to include more women writers; second, that women's writing belongs to a separate tradition that must be studied on its own terms, which are not those of "great literature" as men have defined it, and thus in separate courses, separate anthologies. This is the point on which male teachers of literature may be most inclined to ask women to make up their minds: How do they want women writers to be taught? There are certainly arguments to be given for each position, and the costs of adopting one or another seem relatively clear, but clear also, from the perspective of feminist criticism, is the advantage of pressing both arguments simultaneously instead of pursuing only one: by pressing two irreconcilable claims, feminist critics compel both male critics and other women critics to situate themselves in relation to the terms of this debate about how to teach women's writing. If feminists took one position or the other, attention could focus instead on whether the particular authors or courses they champion should be included at all, not on which mode of inclusion is preferable.

Third, there is the question of what role feminist criticism proposes for men: are they enjoined to address feminist issues, to do feminist readings, to teach writing by women, or should they, on the contrary, be discouraged from doing so lest they appropriate and dilute or compromise a feminist discourse which should be linked to women's distinctive experiences or perspectives? Elaine Showalter's account of gynocritics turned gender studies offers men an unproblematical position; they can pursue studies of the construction and representation of gender within literary and other discourses as they can pursue any other academic subspecialty. But the special power of feminist criticism, it seems to me, is linked to the fact that while on the one hand indubitably becoming an academic field or professional focus, it has simultaneously, on the other hand, questioned the possibility and productivity of a feminist critical inquiry divorced from the experiences of marginalization which women have undergone. It seems important that feminist criticism appear both as an academic activity to which anyone versed in the appropriate texts can in principle contribute and as a discourse whose authority is linked to the special positions and experiences of women. These two conceptions are difficult to reconcile, but feminist criticism would be considerably less capacious and efficacious if it were to opt for one or the other.[4]

Fourth, within gynocriticism itself there is a division of a more recondite sort. Gynocritics, as Elaine Showalter defines it, is based on the idea of the distinctiveness of women's writing. It is certainly possible to question this presumption of distinctiveness, and the result is both confusion and defensiveness about the status of the assumption of the distinctiveness of women's writing, women's creativity. In fact, there seem to be two positions here, which are in conflict: on the one hand, the question of the distinctiveness of women's writing can be treated as an empirical question to be examined through comparative studies of various sorts. This is especially important for preventing the institutionalization of accounts of the distinctive features of women's sentences, or women's imagination, which can easily become the bearers of dubious ideological positions. There are also important questions about the relations, in different periods and literary modes, of supposedly distinctive features of women's writing to other textual and non-textual factors. But on the other hand, feminist criticism can also be based on the a priori assumption of the distinctiveness of women's writing, treated no longer as an empirical question but as a methodological necessity, the delimitation of a tradition whose marks may not always be detectable — it may have been repressed or rendered invisible in certain times and circumstances — since it is a tradition based in part on marginalization, a tradition whose very nature is to be occasionally invisible. The two options or approaches are necessarily in conflict, but both seem crucial to pursue, and each is likely to gain in alertness and circumspection from the existence of the other.

If the power of feminist criticism has in fact been in part a power of division — a function of divisions within feminist criticism — then one might wish to resist the assumption that feminist criticism should be working towards the development of a new disciplinary paradigm, in which it would become a "normal criticism" working within well-defined parameters with agreement about the evidence, rationality, and goals. That is the vision that Elaine Showalter's accounts frequently suggest: a feminist criticism devoted to elucidating the distinctive character of women's writing, for instance. But feminist criticism's special power in the past decade or so — and to my mind for the foreseeable future — has been linked to internal divisions that resist its reduction to an academic discipline and establish instead a series of ongoing arguments which engage readers and thinkers in a different way, preventing practitioners, observers, and opponents from settling into assumed positions.

As an illustration of the productive divisions within feminist perspectives, of a power of division, I would like to take up briefly the relation of Alice Walker's *The Color Purple* to Zora Neale Hurston's *Their Eyes Were Watching God*, which offers, I think, an allegory for, if not of, feminist criticism. These two magnificent novels by black women are books which male critics and teachers of literature ought to read and which they should not, in my opinion, hesitate to speak about. I am not qualified to place these works in the powerful recent tradition of black women's fiction or in the broader context of black writing in America: focusing only on features that emerge from comparing them in a discussion of feminist issues, I wish to use them to illustrate divisions about goals and priorities within feminist writing. In speaking about black women's writing, I do not, of course, speak for black women, whose perspectives on these novels would necessarily be different.

I want to consider *The Color Purple* as a rewriting or transformation of *Their Eyes*, though this is only one way of approaching that book. Henry Louis Gates has emphasized the way in which Shug Avery in *The Color Purple* is a transformation of Zora Neale Hurston herself: compare the description of the picture of Shug Avery that Celie gets from her father's new wife — "Her face rouge. Her hair like something tail. She grinning with her foot up on somebody motocar" — with the photograph of Zora that Alice Walker describes: "I have a photograph of her in pants, boots, and broadbrim that was given to me by her brother Everette. She has her foot up on the running board of a car — presumably hers, and bright red — and looks racy"(88).

One might begin with the figure of the tree which, as Gates notes, connects the two books — a figure with which the nature of woman has been entangled since the garden of Eden. In *Their Eyes* Janie's awakening sexual feelings are evoked through a virtuoso description of a blossoming pear tree, and then in this passage: "Oh to be a pear tree — any tree in bloom! With kissing bees singing of the beginning of the world! She was sixteen. She had glossy leaves and bursting buds and she wanted to struggle with life but it seemed to elude her. Where were the singing bees for her?" (25).

Her later adventures are told through repeated variations on this figure: "She had no more blossoming openings dusting pollen over her man, neither any glistening young fruit where the petals used to be" (112); "He could be a bee to a blossom — a pear tree blossom in the spring" (161). *The Color Purple* takes up the dynamic motif of woman as tree — woman as a blossoming tree in her relation to the man in her life — but draws out a more sinister implication. Celie reports that when Mr. ——— beats her, "It all I can do not to cry. I make myself wood. I say to myself, Celie you a tree. That's how come I know trees fear man" (30). It is as though Walker's novel shows that the terms in which Hurston conceives of woman's fulfillment (the blossoming pear tree) presuppose a relationship that is asymmetrical and, since man can be a woodsman as easily as a bee, oppressive.

The point is complicated by a later passage that carries the debate further. Shug reports, "When I found out I thought God was white and a man, I lost interest" (177). "My first step from the old white man was trees. Then air, then birds. Then other people. But one day when I was sitting quiet and feeling like a motherless child, which I was, it come to me: that feeling of being part of everything, not separate at all. I knew that if I cut a tree my arm would bleed" (178). Here the identification with trees is presented not as a way of relating to men (as in "she was not petal-open any more with him" [Hurston 111]) but as an escape from a man-centered — androcentric — universe. Indeed, in the next chapter when Celie leaves Mr. ——— and goes off with Shug, she curses him with words that come from trees: "Until you do right by me, I say, everything you dream about will fail. I give it to him straight, just like it come to me. And it seem to come to me from the trees" (187). Celie, like Janie, has visionary moments, as as the medium for a voice of nature, but that voice from the trees may also be the voice of the object to which Mr. ——— had reduced her: "Celie you a tree." The tree of knowledge and the trees that fear man help with the first step away from a middle-aged black man as well as from the old white man. "You have to git man off your eyeball, before you can see anything a'tall," says Shug. "He on your box of grits, in your head, and all over the radio. He try to make you think he everywhere" (179). The identification with trees is presented as a way of helping to do this: "You ever notice that trees do everything to git attention we do, except walk?" (179).

By this move *The Color Purple* connects Hurston's image of fulfillment in a relation with men to the issue raised by the title of her book. The phrase "their eyes were watching God" comes from the scene in which a devastating storm strikes when Janie and her lover Tea Cake are working in the Everglades. In the house "Six eyes were questioning God" (Hurston 235). "The wind came back with triple fury, and put out the light for the last time. They sat in company with the others in other shanties, their eyes straining against crude walls and their souls asking if He meant to measure their puny might against His. They seemed to be staring at the dark, but their eyes were watching God" (236).

The questioning of God is accompanied by the persistent anthropomorphism which posits God as a person-like being, a "He" one can watch and question even if there is apparently nothing but darkness to see. Although the novel occasionally personifies other natural forces — "Night was striding across nothingness with the whole round world in his hands" (234) — this anthropomorphism, which takes on special prominence and significance, is also andromorphic, positing a male god whose human attributes figure crucially in the novel's reflections on order and meaning. This andromorphism is reasserted in the passage which does most to develop the significance of the novel's title, when Tea Cake's attack of rabies (he was bitten by a mad-dog in the flood following the storm) makes Janie question God.

> She looked hard at the sky for a long time. Somewhere up there beyond blue ether's bosom sat He. Was He noticing what was going on around here? He must be because He knew everything. Did he *mean* to do this thing to Tea Cake and her? It wasn't anything she could fight. She could only ache and wait. Maybe it was some big tease and when He saw it had gone far enough He'd give her a sign. She looked hard for something up there to move for a sign. A star in the daytime, maybe, or the sun to shout, or even a mutter of thunder. Her arms went up in a desperate supplication

> for a minute. It wasn't exactly pleading, it was asking questions. The sky stayed hard looking and quiet so she went inside to the house. God would do less than He had in His heart (264).

That concluding sentence presupposes a male deity with a heart and maintains that presupposition by placing relations on the plane of visibility: watching darkness or the sky for exterior signs, whose absence may be read as evidence of a disjunction between inside and outside — exterior manifestation and inner intention or meaning. The consolation of "God would do less than he had in his heart," which converts the absence of external signs to evidence of an inner intention exceeding this absence, depends upon the hierarchy of inner meaning and outward signs — the superior authenticity of the former — and this depends, Alice Walker's astute rewritings show us, on an anthropomorphism: God as a man with an inside and outside. That is to say, the only way this consolation can work is on the assumption that what is in one's heart is more important and authentic than any outward show, and thus on the postulation of a He formed on a human model. Walker's book displaces the question of God from the plane of visibility (and the hierarchical relation between invisible inside and outward manifestation) to that of language, specifically writing: in *The Color Purple* "He" is the destination of Celie's letters, and in the place of questions about external signs and inner feelings there arises the question of whether he gets the message: "When I found out I thought God was white, and a man," says Shug, "I lost interest. You mad cause he don't seem to listen to your prayers. Humph! Do the mayor listen to anything colored say? . . . . I know white people never listen to colored, period" (177).

When God is the reader or listener rather than a potentially visible figure with an inside and outside, the situation changes. "It ain't a picture show," says Shug. "It ain't something you can look at apart from anything else" (178). While Janie takes the absence of external signs as evidence of a reticent interior, Celie draws no such conclusion from the evidence that God doesn't listen ("If he ever listened to poor colored women the world would be a different place, let me tell you" [175]). Once the question of God is posed in this fashion, the anthropomorphism is easier to expose. Celie herself stops writing to God and writes instead to her sister Nettie, an important development. And Celie and Shug, exposing the anthropomorphism of the old white man, can be read as suggesting that Janie has not succeeded in getting man off her eyeball, if those eyes are watching God. Her world is still man-centered. "He try to make you think he everywhere.

Soon as you think he everywhere, you think he God. But he ain't. Whenever you trying to pray, and man plop himself on the other end of it, tell him to git lost, say Shug. Conjure up flowers, wind, water, a big rock" (Walker 1983a:179).

Both books put their heroines in touch with natural objects, but if the tree helps Shug take her first step away from the old white man, Janie's images of the woman as pear tree show that there is still the potential for a man-centered universe here, and the passage in *The Color Purple* from the tree, through other natural objects, to "a big rock" shows the work that must be done to achieve liberation. "But this hard work, let me tell you," Celie continues. "He been there so long, he don't want to budge. He threaten lightning, floods and earthquakes [as happens in the crucially relevant passages of *Their Eyes*]. Us fight. I hardly pray at all. Every time I conjure up a rock, I throw it" (179).

In this perspective, then, *The Color Purple* sets up a debate with *Their Eyes were Watching God* that disputes its conception of women's liberation, challenging its androcentrism on several levels. The shift carried out by the plot itself is especially significant. The beautiful, articulate heroine of *Their Eyes*, who longs to join "the big-picture talkers" who laugh and brag with her husband Joe Starks on their front porch, while she is sent back inside to tend the store, and who finally does attain a full role in the world of stories and talk with Tea Cake and his friends, is moved out of the center in *The Color Purple*, appearing as Shug: the dynamic woman for whom men fall. Janie's affair with a younger man, Tea Cake, which *Their Eyes* presents as a liberation that violates the taboos of respectable society, is transformed in *The Color Purple* into a brief fling, Shug's affair with Germaine, which the novel makes tangential to the project of liberation: this is not where freedom and fulfillment for women lie. By focusing on Celie — plain, silent, poor, in these and other respects much worse off than Janie — rather than on a Janie or a Shug, *The Color Purple* suggests that there is a good deal more to be done in the wake of *Their Eyes*. Freedom and fulfillment for the beautiful, articulate, talented woman is all very well, but there persists the predicament of the Celies, raped by their fathers or stepfathers, beaten and oppressed by other men. And the task is to "get man off your eyeball," in a way that *Their Eyes* does not even conceive, much less accomplish. At the end of *Their Eyes* Janie is back in her house with her friend Phoebe, but Phoebe is a listener only, not a lover, as Shug is for Celie, and she is excluded when Janie pulls "in her horizon like a great fish-net. . . So much of life in its meshes! She called in her soul to come and see" (288). *The Color Purple* centers on the sustaining relations between Celie and Shug, and Celie and Nettie. Alice Walker calls *Their Eyes* "one of the sexiest, most 'healthily' rendered heterosexual love-stories in our literature," but *The Color Purple* she calls a historical novel, the germ of whose "history," she says, is "one woman asking another for her underwear" (Walker 1983b:88, 356).

In describing one novel as a rewriting of another I want to emphasize first the displacements and disagreements within a tradition of women's writing — differences within that are by no means irrelevant to the debates of feminist criticism. Both novels make the freedom of their heroines dependent on money — Janie's inheritance from her husband Joe Starks, Celie's success as a maker of pants — but beyond that they stage a debate which has a power of division — a division between powerful, competing models of liberation — which, unlike a heterogeneity whose appeal relies on an ideology of individualism, draws others into the discussion in a domain it articulates, channeling thought along the lines it delineates. That the dispute between *Their Eyes Were Watching God and The Color Purple* is not just a correction imposed by the latter's emphasis on the need to get man, including an andromorphic God, off your eyeball emerges when one considers how *Their Eyes*, in its turn, offers a critical assessment of key moves on which the argument of *The Color Purple* depends. The break with the white male God in *The Color Purple* is based on the claim that "God ain't a he or a she, but a It" (178). "I believe God is everything, say Shug. Everything that is or ever was or ever will be" (178). But this view is one that *Their Eyes* has already characterized as empty rhetoric: "So when speakers stood up when the occasion demanded and said 'Our beloved Mayor,' it was one of those statements that everybody says but nobody believes, like 'God is everywhere.'" A formula like this, the passage continues, is "just a handle to wind up the tongue with" (Hurston 77). *Their Eyes* can be read as suggesting, accurately in my view, that the formula on which the struggle against an anthropomorphic God relies is of dubious truth, a handle to wind up the tongue and permit further speech — further speech in which an anthropomorphic God returns, as in the subsequent sentence that supplies the book's title: "I think it pisses God off if you walk by the color purple in a field somewhere and don't notice it" (178). The presumption of a God modeled on a person — someone who gets pissed off — slides back in here in a passage whose role in supplying the title compels us to treat it as exemplary rather than trivial. If *The Color Purple* seeks to get man off your eyeball by representing love between women, *Their Eyes* may do so at another level, in its exploration of language and memory.

Their Eyes can also be read as predicting with an uncanny accuracy one of the side effects of getting man off your eyeball. After Janie's trial, when she has been acquitted by a jury of white men of murdering her rabid lover Tea Cake — used her narrative skills to secure her freedom by explaining that she would never willingly have hurt Tea Cake and acted only in self-defense — and befriended by white women who protect her from the blacks who had been barred from testifying against her, we hear this exchange:

--- "She didn't kill no white man, did she? Well, so long as she don't shoot no white man she kin kill jus' as many niggers as she please."

--- "Yeah, de nigger woman kin kill up all de mens dey want tuh, but you bet'not kill one uh dem. De white folks will sho hang yuh if yuh do." (280).

The success of *The Color Purple* among white audiences may possibly be linked, as has been suggested, to a deadly depiction of black men (the stepfather and Mr ———), which might seem to legitimate the worst racist stereotypes by presenting them as the experience of black women, whom it seeks to liberate from their oppression. That a compelling emancipatory analysis of the condition of black women might involve a ferocious critique of black male figures is an unfortunate irony that Hurston's novel astutely anticipates because it flirts with this mode itself in its portrayal of Logan Killicks and Joe Starks. *Their Eyes* initiates an exposure of the black man as oppressor, wanting to be served by his woman, but then takes another road in its daring and successful presentation of Tea Cake. Initially the type that white males are most likely to abhor — the black drifter in pursuit of women's money and sexual favors — Tea Cake in fact becomes for Janie a source of fulfillment. That move, which distinguishes the vision of *Their Eyes* from that of *The Color Purple*, is inseparable from the other differences I have emphasized and that *The Color Purple* seeks directly to transform: the man-centered universe within which Janie's freedom and satisfaction are achieved.

There is, then, between *Their Eyes* and *The Color Purple*, a genuine division, of programs and interests, but which by its force enlists us in their debate, articulating a space of discussion, as feminist criticism seeks to do: setting the terms of the argument and pulling us in, as Janie pulls in the "horizon like a great fish net. Pulled it from around the waist of the world and draped it over her shoulder. So much of life in its meshes" (286). The meshes of the difference within.

NOTES

1. I am grateful to Houston Baker for many helpful comments on an earlier version of this paper; he should not, however, be thought to endorse the views expressed herein.
2. In Elaine Showalter's "Towards Feminist Poetics," (1979) and "Feminist Criticism in the Wilderness," (1981) [in *The New Feminist Criticism*, ed. Showalter (New York: Pantheon, 1985)], the historicizing impulse is judiciously tempered. It emerges clearly however, in a lecture delivered at Dartmouth College, "A Criticism of One's Own," which describes the trajectory of feminist criticism as follows:

   > Before the Women's Liberation Movement, criticism of women's writing took the form of an *androgynist poetics*, denying female literary specificity. The women's movement initiated both a *feminist critique* of male culture and a *Female Aesthetic* celebrating women's culture. By the mid-1970's, academic feminist criticism entered a new phase of *gynocritics*, or the study of women's writing. With the impact of European literary and feminist theory by 1980, *gynesic* or post-structuralist feminist criticism, dealing with "the feminine" in philosophy, language, and psychoanalysis, dominated the field. And in the late 1980's, we are seeing the rise of *gender theory*, the comparative study of sexual difference.

3. I have discussed these problems in Culler, Jonathan. 1982. "Reading as a Woman". *On Deconstruction* (Ithaca: Cornell University Press) 43-63.
4. Here too the continuing debate prevents men from taking issue with a single feminist position and imposes on them a more complex and problematical position in relation to feminist discourse.

REFERENCES

Culler, Jonathan. 1982. *On Deconstruction*. Ithaca: Cornell University Press.

Felman, Shoshana. 1975. "Women and Madness: the Critical Phallacy." *Diacritics* 5:2-10.

———. 1981. "Rereading Femininity." *Yale French Studies* 62.

Fetterley, Judith. 1978. *The Resisting Reader*. Bloomington: Indiana University Press.

Gates, Henry Louis, Jr. Forthcoming. *The Signifying Monkey*. Oxford University Press.

Heilbrun, Carolyn. 1985. "Bringing the Spirit Back to English Studies". *The New Feminist Criticism*, ed. by Elaine Showalter. New York: Pantheon.

Hurston, Zora Neale. 1978. *Their Eyes Were Watching God* (1937). Urbana: University of Illinois Press.

Meese, Elizabeth. 1986. *Crossing the Double-Cross: The Practice of Feminist Criticism*. Chapel Hill: University of North Carolina Press.

Showalter, Elaine. 1985. "Towards Feminist Poetics" (1979) and "Feminist Criticism in the Wilderness" (1981). In *The New Feminist Criticism*, ed. by Elaine Showalter. New York: Pantheon.

Walker, Alice. 1983a. *The Color Purple*. New York: Washington Square Press.

———. 1983b. *In Search of Our Mother's Gardens*. New York: Harcourt Brace.

Notes on an alternative model — neither/nor

Hortense J. Spillers
Cornell University

Language has always been the companion of empire.
Antonio de Nebrija
1492 — "The Year of the Other"

In an inventory of American ideas, the thematic of the "tragic mulatto/a" seems to disappear at the end of the nineteenth century.[1] Even though certain writers in the United States have pursued this configuration of character well into the twentieth, with varying and divergent purposes in mind,[2] it is as though both the dominant and dominated national interests eventually abandoned the vocation of naming, perceiving, and explaining to themselves the identity of this peculiar new-world invention. A retrieval of this topic will, therefore, appear anachronistic and irrelevant to African-American critical projects at the moment. Furthermore, the term itself and the issues that it raises are so thoroughly circumscribed by historical closure and apparently bankrupt in the situation of their origin that my attempt to re-vivify them is burdened, already, in the beginning, with doubt, with the necessity to prove their revised critical point. But it seems to me that the mulatto figure, stranded in cultural ambiguity, conceals the very strategies of terministic violence and displacement that have enabled a problematics of alterity regarding the African-American community in the United States. Created to provide a middle ground of latitude between "black" and "white," the customary and permissible binary agencies of the national adventure, mulatto being, as a neither/nor proposition, inscribed no historic locus, or materiality, that was other than evasive and shadowy on the national landscape. To that extent, the mulatto/a embodied an alibi, an excuse for "other/otherness" that the dominant culture could not (cannot now either) appropriate, or wish away. An accretion of signs that embody the "unspeakable," of the Everything that the dominant culture would forget, the mulatto/a, as term, designates a disguise, covers up, in the century of Emancipation and beyond, the social and political reality of the dreaded African presence. Behind the African-become-American stands the shadow, the unsubstantial "double" that the culture dreamed *in the place of* that humanity transformed into its profoundest challenge and by the impositions of policy, its deepest "un-American" activity.

To understand, then, the American invention of the mulatto, a term imported from the European lexis,[3] is to understand more completely, I feel, the false opposition of cultural traits that converge on the binary distribution of "black" and "white." My further aim in exploring this topic, however, is to try to discover how "mulatto-ness," the covering term, explains the workings of gender as a category of social production that has not yet assimilated to women of color. Rather than proof of the point, I see these notes as a trial of it.

Before pursuing these observations further, I should point out certain difficulties of this analysis. Those historical subjects subsumed under "mulatto/a" cannot be so easily banished to the realm of the mythical, nor is it my wish to do so. I should make it clear that I am drawing a distinction throughout between historical figures like Frederick Douglass, or Lemuel Haynes, Vermont preacher of the early nineteenth century, and the *appropriation* of the interracial child by genocidal forces of dominance. The latter concerns a violence, or fatal ignorance, of naming and placing that is itself paradigmatic of the model of alterity, and to discover its ways and means is our persistent and urgent aim.

To compare, then, historical subjects with idea-forms, or iconographic content, or characters from novels might suggest an incommensurability, or even inaptitude of critical method, but the comparison could be instructive, since it alerts us to the subtleties that threaten to transform the living subject into an inert mass and suggests the reincarnations of human violence in their intellectual and symbolic array. The "mulatto/a," just as the "nigger," tells us little or nothing about the subject buried beneath them, but quite a great deal more concerning the psychic and cultural reflexes that invent and invoke them. I am suggesting that in the *stillness* of time and space eventuated by the "mulatto/a" — its apparent sameness of fictional, historical, and auto/biographical content — we gain insight into the *theft* of the dynamic principle of the living that distinguishes the subject from his/her objectification. Such difference remains evident in the institution of new world enslavement and the captivity and production of, for example, William Faulkner's narrator's "wise supine" female of *Absalom, Absalom*!

The questionable paternity of the mulatto character in fiction , just as its parallel in the historical sequence, demarcates the beginning and end of cultural and symbolic illegitimacy. We shall try to see more fully how and why that is the case. In a very real sense, America's historic mulatto subject plays out his/her character on the ground of a fiction made public and decisive by dimensions of the spectacular and the specular. In his/her face, the deceits of a culture are mirrored; the deeds of a secret and unnamed fatherhood made known: "My father was a white man. He was admitted to be such by all I ever heard speak of my parentage. The opinion was also whispered that my master was my father. but of the correctness of this opinion, I know nothing. . .(Douglass 21-22).

Frederick Douglass by any other name would tell the same tale over and over again with frightening consistency. But mulatto-ness is not, fortunately, a figure of self-referentiality. Neither the enslaved man/woman, nor the fugitive-in-freedom would call *himself/herself* "mulatto/a," a special category of thingness that isolates and overdetermines the human character to which it points. A semantic marker, already fully occupied by a content and an expectation, America's "tragic mulatto" exists for others — and a particular male other — in an attribution of the illicit that designates the violent mingling and commingling of bloodlines that a simplified cultural patrimony wishes to deny. But in that very denial, the most dramatic and visible of admissions is evident.

The site of a contamination, this marked figure has no name that is not parodic. Joe Christmas, for example, connected with the realm of immanence, of pure nature, makes no claim to rational force in the eyes of his maker (Faulkner 1959[1929]). Standing outside the ruined house of Joanna Burden, at the broken gate, in thightall weeds, Christmas, in an erection scene, engages gestures of alienation that overlap the erotic: "watching his body, seeming to watch it turning slow and lascivious in a whispering of gutter filth like a drowned corpse in a thick still black pool of more than water" (Faulkner 1959:100). Shortly following this bizarre moment, a car emerges in Christmas's hearing, as he observes his body "grow white out of the darkness like a kodak print emerging from the liquid." Just as the photograph discovers an inherent biochemical response, Christmas materializes the unarticulated, unaccommodated American identity — raw and fundamental in a portrayal of basic, unmitigated urge. We cannot even call Christmas's compulsion "desire" yet, since it is untouched by the mediations and remediations of culture. Transformed into naked, grotesque, hungry man at the world's margin, Christmas speaks the radical disjuncture of human experience as his own private chaos. Christmas's narrative takes hold of a conscious infinity of pain as we see him refracted through an endless regression of events in the re-encounter of former selves. We observe a figure drowning in a sea of phenomena, enacting and re-enacting a purposeful purposelessness of movement that is bizarre, madly pointed. Animated by forces beyond his knowing, Christmas provides an analogy to the deracinated person, fixed in cultural vestibularity. Time passes for him, over and around him, but it has no subjective properties that he might call his own.

A "unanimity-minus-one,"[4] who assumes the terror and crucifixion of his natal community's "expendable figure," Christmas is Faulkner's powerful effort to give a grammar to American race magic. But "race" itself is already a mystification by 1929, which year also witnesses the publication of Nella Larsen's *Passing*, another sortie into the intrigues of genetic determinism. "Race" becomes for Faulkner, as for Larsen and Jessie Fauset, a metaphor through which the chaotic and primitive urges of human community find systematic expression. In that sense, "community" comes weighted with the heft of irony, since, in Faulkner's case, its ultimate embodiment is one Percy Grimm, one's "perfect kamikazi." It is, therefore, both stunning and to be expected that, for Grimm and his kind, Christmas's jugular relocates in his genitals: the flight of Joe Christmas, arrested in the kitchen of the outraged Reverend Gail Hightower, ends in a blood bath. Grimm pursues him through the mob that wants his flesh for the death of Joanna Burden, but more precisely, his killing is a castration, as Grimm hacks away at the forbidden "cargo" in the name of white women's honor.

It would seem, then, that the mulatto in the text of fiction provides a strategy for naming and celebrating the phallus. In other words, the play and interplay of an open, undisguised sexuality are mapped on the body of the mulatto character, who allows the dominant culture to say without parting its lips that "we have willed to sin," the puritan recoil at the sight and the site of the genitals. In that regard, Percy Grimm is his culture's good little factotum, who understands on some dark level of unknowing that the culture, more pointedly, the culture of the Fathers, can never admit, as Joe Christmas's wildness reminds them, that the law is based on phallic violence in an array of other names and symbols. The term "mulatto/a, then, becomes a displacement for a proper name, an instance of the "paradox of the negative" that signifies what it does not mean. In Faulkner's work, at least, sexuality is literally monumental, with none of the antiseptic saving grace that psychoanalysis lends it. The unavoidable bedrock of human and fictional complication, sexuality is here restored to nearness to the terrible.

If, as old mad Doc Hines, in enraged and consistent babble contends, Joe Christmas — his probable grandson — describes "the mark and the knowledge," then Christmas is the first and last victim on his way out, given the peculiar occasion to understand history and culture, or those economies of violence that carefully differentiate "inner" and "outer," "order" and "degree."

In his *Conquest of America*,[5] Tzvetan Todorov distinguishes three dimensions of the problematics of alterity: 1) the *axiological* level — "the other is good or bad, I love him, or. . .he is my equal or my inferior (for there is usually no question that I am good and that I esteem myself.); 2) the *praxeological* level — the placing of distance or proximity between oneself and an imagined other — "I embrace the other's values, I identify myself with him; or else I identify the other with myself, I impose my own image upon him; between submission to the other and the other's submission, there is also a third term, which is neutrality, or indifference." 3) The *epistemic* level — "I know or am ignorant of the other's identity. Of course, there is no absolute here, but an endless gradation between the lower or higher states of knowledge."

As an instance of the exterior other in *negative* identity, Christmas, on Todorov's levels of analysis, is made the absolute equivalent of anomie. At no time in his fictional development do we not see him in clear association with wild, untamed plenitude, from Faulkner's version of terrifying female sexuality in the figures of Joanna Burden and Burden's good double in the pregnant Lena Grove, to the unspeaking, unspeakable neologism of filth — the "womanshenegro" of a particular Christmas nightmare — to the moonscape of urns, associated with the menses and Christmas's initiation into the rites of the sexual and sacrificial, to the cosmic infinity of days and space that swallow him up in a hideous repetition crisis that precedes his end. But if it is possible to say so, we observe in Faulkner instances of the exterior other in *positive* identity whose laws of behavior are much harder and more challenging to detect.

The exterior other in positive identity is, for Faulkner, a female, and in the Faulknerian situation of the female, we gain good insight into the processes of gender-making as a special outcome of modes of dominance. But even more importantly, we observe gender as a special feature of a racialistic ideology. In other words, the African-American female, in her historic identity, robbed of the benefits of the "reproduction of mothering," is, consequently, the very negation of femaleness that accrues as the peculiar cultural property of Anglo-American women, in the national instance, and more generally, of the female of not-color: Faulkner's *Absalom, Absalom* might be considered a case in point.

This novel renders a fiction of misplaced incestuous longings and the play of homoerotic motives by way of a Freudian family drama.[6] It is key that the children of unreconstructed Thomas Sutpen, the great obsession of Rosa Coldfield's furious speaking, are actually and symbolically "white" and "colored." In effect, this character out of the Virginia wilds, with a crucial *stop* in Haiti, lends an analogy on a Fatherhood that founds a "civilization" and a continuity that terminate in a version of Return of the Repressed — French *Bon*-become-black *Bond*, that Faulkner's Luster says the law puts on you when it catches up with you. The route from Haiti, to New Orleans, to Sutpen's Hundred, Yoknapatawpha County, is purposefully and gravidly suggestive, as it involves the worlds of subsaharan Africa, the Caribbean, and the United States in the replay of an economic triangulation whose wealth is built solidly on the backs and with the blood of captive human cargo. It is, then, not at all accidental, or academic, to the scheme of history implied by Faulkner's fiction that the savage and dangerous denial of Charles Bon's paternity has precedent in the cultural institution of new world enslavement, as attested by Frederick Douglass, and that this enslavement has a special place, meaning, and economics for the female, as witnessed in the narrative of Linda Brent.[7]

Vagaries of Faulkner's trammeled semantics aside for the moment, this novel quite simply concerns a man who had two sons, one of them the would be morganatic byblow of an obscure white male on the run, except that Sutpen did marry the mother of Charles Bon to discover, after the fact, that he had been "betrayed" by the makers of this contrived connubial arrangement. The overseer of a sugar plantation on the island of Santo Domingo — scored into historical memory by the successful revolt of Touissant L'Ouverture — Sutpen tells his version of his fiction to his contemporary, the grandfather of Quentin, and that, heroically, singlehandedly, he quelled a siege of insurgent African captives on the Haitian land.

The reward for his "bravery," the dowry of the marriage bed, so to speak, is the hand of the master's daughter, whose mother, in turn, is Spanish, the dark suggestion, not French. When Sutpen discovers that the woman to whom he is married has "Negro blood" in her veins, that single most powerful drop of dexyribose nucleic acid, he decides simultaneously that she cannot, for that reason, contribute to the increment of his "design." He then abandons her and her son, or repudiates them in the name of a higher social and moral purity, but compensates, he imagines, by relinquishing his legal right to various Haitian properties accruing to him as marital lagniappe. Said properties revert back to the plantation owner's daughter, who remains unnamed, as all the mulattas do, with the exception of Clytie, Sutpen's *other* daughter.

Leaving the "West Indies" for other new world territory, Sutpen arrives in Mississippi to take up land and build his "empire." With white Ellen Coldfield, of the indubitable blood, Sutpen has a daughter and son, Henry and Judith. But in Haiti a full decade before, Charles, the Good — forced into the estate of the prodigal — has been denied the name, if not the connubial inheritance, of the father. At "Ole Miss" on the eve of civil war, brother and brother meet — the marked and the untainted — their consanguinity not known to either. This disastrous encounter that possibly ends in fratricide bears the earmarks of sexual attraction, incestuously linked. But parallel to it is the complementing sybaritic tale, staked out in massive erotic display, of Charles Bon, installed with his mother in New Orleans under conditions of a severe and privileged privacy. In the narrative of Quentin Compson's father, not definitively informed by the apposite "facts" of the case, a probable fiction is hatched — or a fiction "true enough" — concerning Bon's unnamed octoroon mistress and the intricately manufactured arts of pleasure that distinguish the fictive New Orleans whorehouse (Faulkner 1951).

Compson's social and political sense makes a few things evident at once: he imagines himself the embodiment of that "heritage peculiarly Anglo-Saxon — of fierce proud mysticism." (Faulkner 1951:108). The world that he narrates through his son Quentin is permeated by notions of caste and hierarchy. This order of things, eminently linear, is fundamentally identified by its interdictive character, whose primary object of desire and placement is the female. But in this instance, "femaleness" is abstracted by legal practice and social custom into an idea that may be sealed off at any concrete point as forbidden territory. In other words, female, in the brain of the creating male narrator, allows access only insofar as she approximates physical/sexual function. A curious split of motives takes place here so that on the one hand the last woman in this hierarchical scale of values — the "slave girls," for instance — are both more and less female, while, on the other, the same may be said for the first "lady," albeit for radically different reasons. Compson's "ladies, women, females" specify an increasingly visual and dramatic enactment of male heterosexuality along three dimensions of female being — "the virgins whom gentlemen someday married, the courtesans to whom they went while on sabbaticals to the cities, the slave girls and women upon whom the first caste rested and to whom in certain cases it doubtless owed the very fact of its virginity" (Faulkner 1951:109).

In this economy of delegated sexual efficacies, the castes of women enter into a drama of exchange value, predicated on the dominant male's self-deceit. The third caste robs the first of a putative clitoral and vaginal pleasure, as the first purloins from the third a uterine functionality.[8] Only the latter gains here the right to the rites and claims of motherhood, blind to its potential female pleasure and reduced, paradoxically, in the scale of things to a transcendent and opaque Womanhood. In fact, we could say that whatever "essence," or "stuff" of the female genitalia that is lost in Compson's first estate of females is more than compensated by the third estate, inexorably fixed in the condition of a mindless fertility, just as bereft as the first of the possibilities of its own potential female pleasure.[9] But quite obviously the ways and means of domination are not adopted with cultural/historical subjects-become-objects in mind, nor is "gender" here any more than, or other than, an apt articulation of a divided male heteroticism.

Inside the split ego of the dominant male falls the "mulatta," or the "octoroon," or the "quadroon" — those disturbing vectors of social and political identity — who heal the rupture at points of wounding. Allowing the male to have his cake and eat it too, or to rejoin the "female" with the "woman," the mulatta has no name because there is not a locus, or a strategy, for this unitarian principle of the erotic in the nineteenth century mentality of Faulkner's male character. Bon's unnamed female forebear and his unnamed octoroon mistress, the unvoiced shadowy creatures that inhabit the content of the narratives of three male figures in the novel, suggest both the vaginal and the prohibitive pleasure.

The patriarchal prerogatives outlined by Compson are centered in notions that concern the domestication of female sexuality — how it is thwarted, contained, circumscribed, and above all, *narrated* — and not a single female character here escapes the outcome, from the infantilized, doll-like women of the master class, to the brutalized women who serve them. Under these conditions, sexuality is permissible, but silenced, only within the precincts of the father's house. We should say in the place of the *permissible* that sexuality is *clean* only in the father's house. Beyond the sphere of domesticity, the sexual — tenaciously named — effects synonymity with the illicit, the wild, the mysterious; without permutation.[10] And one of its signs is the "mulatta," who has no personhood, but locates in the flesh a site of cultural and political maneuver. Unlike African female personality, implied in her presence, the "mulatta" demarcates those notions of femaleness that would re-enforce the latter as an object of gazing — the dimension of the spectacular that we addressed before as the virtually unique social property of the "mulatto/a."

Noted for his/her "beauty," the "mulatta/o" in fiction bears a secret, the taint of evil in the blood, but paradoxically, the secret is vividly worn, made clear. Unlike Joe Christmas, whom we designated as an instance of the exterior other in negative identity, the mulatta, in positive identity, has value for the dominant other only insofar as she becomes the inaccessible female property that can be rendered, at his behest, instantly accessible. Teasing himself with her presence, the dominant other re-intersects the lines of sexuality and "civilization" forced to diverge by the requirements of the family, the private property, and the state. "Virility" reveals itself in the whorehouse as the scandal that is not only *sufferable*, but also primarily *applauded* as the singular fact and privilege of the phallus.

It doesn't matter if the principle of virility is, among living historic male subjects, an engagement fraught with *chance*, or the erection that occasionally fails, or the sporadic impotence about which living historic female subjects remain loyally silent. We are talking about *myth* here, or those boundaries of discourse that bound and determine belief, practice, and desire. To that extent, all "gendering" activity — "male," "female," and its manifold ramifications — constitutes the Grand Lie about which novels are written and for which cause history hurts.[11]

Even though Compson the narrator does not entirely grasp the political and ironic trenchancies of his own conjecture (as *reported* to Shreve by Quentin at Harvard), nor know in those recalled narrative moments that Charles Bon is not Anglo-Saxon male, he adequately identifies the complementary strands of relationship between chattel slavery and a eugenics of pleasure. Imagining what young Henry Sutpen, the Mississippi provincial, might have observed in his exposure to certain peculiarities of New Orleans life, Compson draws out the hidden exchange value of female use here as a commodification of the flesh that takes place according to intricate rules of gallantry. The caste/cast of octoroon females (in which Bon's mistress with child is installed) literally belongs to a class of "masters," who protect their "property" by way of various devices that cluster in notions of "honor." It would not do, for instance, for Henry Sutpen to call Bon's mistress a "whore," since he, or any other male committing the *faux pas*, would be "'forced to purchase that privilege with some of [his] blood from probably a thousand men'" (Faulkner 1951:115) The protection of chattel property in this instance occasions the ethics of the duel as the vertical version of the tumescent male. In other words, maleness is centered here almost entirely in sexual activity covered over by acts of courtesy and carefully choreographed through an entire "field of manners" from a certain architectural structure and accoutrements of the interior, to modes of dress and address.

This relocated mimesis of European courtly love traditions places "gender" squarely within the perspective of cultural invention whose primary aim is the gratifying appetites of the flesh. This materialist philosophy, modulated through various points of human valuation, would suggest that culture itself elaborates a structure of production and reproduction that posits, quite arbitrarily, "higher" and "lower" reaches of human society, immersed in the principle of desire in the Dominant Other. But it seems that powers of domination succeed only to the extent that their permeation remains silent and concealed to those very historical subjects — "higher" and "lower" — upon whom the entire structure rests, upon whom it depends. In other words, the fictions and realities of domination are not only opaque (not everywhere and at once visible) to the subjected (and *narrated*) community, but also remain evasive, in their authentic character as raw and violent assertion, to the dominant (and *narrating*) community. Compson, for example, as a materialized fictive presence, assumes a piacular, or religious, function of female use. His hyperbolic sense of "Anglo-Saxon" male mission is grammatically similar to Perry Miller's classic analysis of the puritan colonial's "errand in the wilderness" (Miller). That Compson's grammar crosses its wires with the "religious impulse" suggests not only the vanities of self-deceit, but also the implicit obscenities of an unironized view of any human and social arrangement. Further, his shortsightedness would problematize the "religious" itself as a special means of domination; as a dominant discourse hiding its hand, veiling its baser motivations.

But Compson initiates the first half of his analysis in correct assessment: the invention of the octoroon mistress rests on the "supreme apotheosis of chattelry. . .human flesh bred of the two races for that sale" (Faulkner 1951:112). That the sentence does not finish itself, overwhelmed by intervening and obstructing periods, ambiguates meaning: "that sale" *of*? "*that* sale," period? And no presumption of ignorance on the hearer's part — "we all" know *which* sale *that* is. "Apotheosis" proximate to "chattelry," however, gives rise to an untenable — one might even say godless — oxymoron. It is also a filthy joke. But none need call it "sacrilege," though, since, in Compson's view at least, this very discourse of contiguity has been ordained by God Himself.

A divine prosthesis, the narrator's "thousand, the white men — made [the octoroon mistress], created and produced them; we even made the laws which declare that one eighth of a specified kind of blood shall outweigh seven eighths of another kind" (Faulkner 1951:115). This refined prattle of a pseudo human science is not entirely misleading since it designates the *bestial* character of human breeding. If "mulatto" originates etymologically in notions of "sterile mule," then mulatto-ness is not a genetically transferable trait. It must be calculated and preserved as a particularistic project in "race." The southern personality's historic fear that the binary "races" might come together in the spawn of the "miscegenous" is absolutely assured and pursued in the presence of the "mulatto." In fact, it would seem that this presence describes that point of intersection between the *fulfillment* of the prohibitive wish and the *prohibition* itself[12] so that the narrative energies of the narrator's recalled text are part and parcel of an enormous struggle to ward off a successfully *willed* and *willful* compulsion:

> the white blood to give the shape and pigment of what the white man calls female beauty, to a female principle which existed, queenly and complete, in the hot equatorial groin of the world long before that white one of ours came down from trees and lost its hair and bleached out — a principle apt docile and instinct with strange and curious pleasures of the flesh (which is all: there is nothing else) which her white sisters of a mushroom yesterday fled from in moral and outraged horror — a principle which, where her white sister must needs try to make an economic matter of it like someone

> who insists upon installing a counter or a scales or a safe in a store or business for a certain percentage of the profits, reigns, wise supine and all-powerful, from the sunless and silken bed which is her throne (Faulkner 1951:116-17).

What Compson imagines concerning "the hot equatorial groin of the world" can be guessed only too well and has, embarrassingly, no historic basis and needn't, for the narrator, since the subject, one narrator remove, is addressing its own overdetermined sexuality. In the process, "black" remains unnamed except by implication in an imagined metonymic substitute. To return a moment to Todorov's dynamics of alterity, we observe that the narrator has (1) *epistemically* no valuable, or enviable knowledge of the female subjects in question; (2) distances himself *praxeologically* from the subjects so that they reveal to him no dynamic historical movement, remaining for the reader the fictional counters that they are; (3) accommodates *axiologically* to those subjects in a stunning act of obverted condescension that objectifies an other at the same time that the latter is isolated as potentially sacred feature.

What has been "created" here is not so much a fiction of the octoroon heroine as a text of an evoked "Anglo-Saxon" male presence *having*, essentially, a creation myth, not unlike one's giving birth or begetting. But this behaving as though the fictive text were "real," that it *ought* to give the reader valuable information about the historical sequence, contravenes the assumptions of our present critical practice, but the misstep is useful, nevertheless, in what might be abstracted from it. "White" women and those historical subjects trapped in the figuration of "hot equatorial groin of the world" modulate into the very same economic, if not cultural, principle by sheer semantic proximity. The distinction that I wish to make here between "economic" and "cultural" is meant to identify in the latter instance those social and political uses to which the subject is put, while the former is intended to define the translation of such uses in actual cash value, but more ordinarily, in the symbolic and figurative currencies released by such translation. The processes that I would keep discrete here so overlap in actual social practice that a distinction seems wrong. But the narrator's insistence on the "economic matter" of, by implication, a hired vaginal substance makes clear that dollars and ledgers are what *he* means as the materialized figurative value of the "white sister." It is less clear, from his point-of-view, though doubtlessly true, that the reign of the "wise *supine*" is just as costly and dear for the very same commodity, even if a "sunless and silken bed" carries a richer poetic and visual reverberation than counters and scales and stores and business.

Thrown down into the narrator's sentences as extended parentheses, these abrupt elaborations yoke "white" and "not-white" female in figurative alliance and likely, historic alignment that only the ahistoricity of "color," or the "proud fierce mysticism" of "Anglo-Saxon" race ideology, has excised. If the Compsons of the world enforce "order" and "degree" in their "casting" of women, then at least they suspect that fundamentally, the female substance — everywhere the same — acquires *different* value according to the very same standard of measure — its *imagined* and *posited* worth to a superior buyer, made supreme by his competence to command desire.

The missing *persona* from Compson's scheme is already there in what the metonymic figure keeps concealed. But "equator," in its cotermity with portions of the subsaharan African continent, proclaims the narrator's suggested meaning. But indirection in this case, which is itself a mode of figurative elaboration, brings us to a crucial point. In attempting to articulate a theory of difference regarding African-American women's community, we have begun the effort by looking at the terministic, or semantic "processes of appeal" that occur in certain textual evidence, including fiction. The Faulknerian excerpt, though isolatable in its persistent stylistic mannerisms, provides, in that regard, points of concentration in what we might call the historical narratives that refer to this community of women. I have in mind here not primarily, if at all, those written texts of history, or those texts based in self-conscious historiographical pursuit. I mean, rather, those configurations of discursive experience *about*. . . that appear dispersed across a range of public address and that may or may not find their way to topics of the historical discipline. These configurations, embedded in public consciousness, enact a "symbolic behavior" that is actually metatextual in its political efficacy, in its impact on the individual life-narratives of the historical subject.

Though "African-American women's community" and "mulatto/a" may appear to be widely divergent structures of human attention, the one claimed by the historical dimension, the other stalled on the terrain of the reified object, they discover common ground in two crucial ways: (1) the proximity effected between *real* and *imagined* properties. The "mulatto/a" *appears*, historically, when African female and male personality become hyphenated American political entities, at that moment when they enter public and political discourse in the Codes of slavery, the rise of the fugitive, the advertisement of the run-away man/woman.[13] (2) Both effecting a radical alterity with the Dominant One, they demonstrate the extent to which modes of substitution can be adopted as strategies of containment. In other words, if African-American women's community can be silenced in its historic movement, then it will happen because the narratives concerning them have managed successfully to captivate the historic subject in time's vacuum. By denying the presence of the African-American female, or assimilating her historic identity, more precisely, to a false body, ventriloquized through a factitious public discourse concerning the "blood" and "breeding," the dominant mode succeeds in transposing the real into the mythical/magical.

The situation of the "mulatta" in the same field of signification with the African-American female juxtaposes contrastive social and political uses, but their simultaneous appearance at the time of the national consolidation of slave-holding power is, on the one hand, no longer a secret — if it ever were — and a problem of meaning on the other. That class of historical subjects fathered by captive owners and following the condition of the mother were, color of skin aside, never surrogate Anglo-American, though they did stand in for black, for African. I am less interested in the class implications of this cultural phenomenon than its symbolic processes and their outcome. Subsequent to the intrusion of a middle term, or middle ground — figuratively — between the subjugated and dominant interests, public discourse gains, essentially, the advantages of a lie by orchestrating otherness through degrees of difference. The philosopher's "great chain of being" ramifies now to disclose within American Africanity itself literal shades of human value so that the subjugated community refracts the oppressive mechanism just as certainly as the authoring forms put them into place. This fatalistic motion that turns the potentially insurgent community furiously back on itself proceeds by way of processes we might call "archaizing." Faulkner's narrative voices provide examples of this trait when Quentin as Compson posits in the "hot equatorial groin of the world" and "those white ones of ours [come] down from trees and. . . bleached out" aspects of the magical, or the ahistorical, not at all responsive to context, or altering agency. The "mulatta," in prominent isolation from the living subject, just as, by hint, "black" and "white" women are, shows this process in concision. "Power" in this instance consists in the prerogative to name human value, to distribute and arrogate it.

The world according to captives and their captors strikes the imagination as a grid of identities running at perpendicular angles to each other: *things* in serial and lateral array; beings in hierarchical and vertical array. On the serial grid, the captive person — the chattel property — is contiguous with inanimate and other living things:

Anamboe 1736

. . . Nov. 24th Sold Capt. Hammond 4 women for Recd. the following goods

			Oz.	A.
Viz.	16	perpets	5	
	7	half Says	3	8
	3	half Ells		
	1	ps. Niconee	1	8
	4	qr bb powder	2	
	14	sheets	2	14
	2	paper Sleties		5
	112	galls rum	7	

(Donnan 130)

This itemized excerpt from an agenda of commodities in exchange vividly illustrates the dehumanization of African personality. Frederick Douglass, however, provides a narrative a full century later for such a scenario, remembering the division of property upon the death of one of his former masters. Having to return from Baltimore to the site of Captain Anthony's estate, he writes of the occasion: "We were all ranked together at the valuation. Men and women, old and young, married and single, were ranked with horses, sheep, and swine. There were horses and men, cattle and women, pigs and children, all holding the same rank in the scale of being, and were all subjected to the same narrow examination" (Douglass 59-60). 59-60).

From Donnan's accounts of the slave galley's logs and bills of lading and of sales, to Douglass' *Narrative* of the "peculiar institution," we discover time and again the collapse of human identity adopted to the needs of commerce and economic profit. But even more startling than this nominal "crisis of degree" (which renders an equality of substances not unlike the figurative collapse of disparities in metaphorical display) is the *recovery* of difference in a hierarchical and vertical distribution of being, as though this cultural "disarray" stood corrected, or compensated. In the intersection of these axes, at the point of "mules and men" — the human ownership and possession of other human beings — the notion of property so penetrates the order of things that the entire structure is undermined by a simple overwhelming paradox: those subjects located at this incredible juncture of saturation are both more and less human, the former because they enter into a wider ecumenicalism with named and claimed things, or vocabularies of experience; the latter because it is their destiny by virtue of Christ's church, by whom the country swears, and the spirit of national insurgence and constitutionality to be human first and only. That we find no comparable "list" of being, as we do the carefully accounted for commercial item, simply suggests to me that "laterality" had done its job, and no more needed to be said, if it were possible to rank human with animal. In effect, the humanity of African personality is placed in quotation marks under these signs and problematized as a leading public and philosophical issue.

Alterity, therefore, describes not only an inauthentic human status, but also the locus of an outright relationship between non-historical elements that come to rest beyond the veil of human and its discourses; this lack of movement in the field of signification seems to me the origin of "mulatto-ness" — the *inherent* name and naming — the *wedge* between the world of light and the step beyond — into the undifferentiated, unarticulated mass of moving and movable *things*.

Between these dualities, the "shadow" of the "mulatto/a" is interposed. It is a matter of surprise to me that there is in William Faulkner, writing in the twentieth century, and Frances E.W. Harper, writing in the nineteenth, a certain lexical recurrence that initiated my observations in the opening pages of this essay: Quentin/Compson the narrator describes Charles Bon in terms of appropriation that are just as apposite to his octoroon invention. In fact, Charles Bon is also thrice made — once by the attenuated concepts of history that haunt the characterization; once by the structure of mimesis that the character purports to display; and yet again by the appropriating speaker as a "shadowy" presence: "A myth, a phantom: something which [Ellen and Judith Sutpen] engendered and created whole themselves; some effluvium of Sutpen blood and character, as though as a man he did not exist at all" (Faulkner 1951:104). Frances Harper entitled her 1893 novel *Iola Leroy, or Shadows Uplifted*. Though it is appropriately not altogether clear what dramatic and rhetorical function the topos of "shadow" serves in the novel, it is at least probable that its ambiguity complements that of its topic — the fate of lola Leroy, mulatta girl remanded back into slavery and overcoming, at last, the pain and confusion of her biography. But the novel just as certainly concerns the reunion of mothers and children — the blood line of slavery — divided across the cleavage of "race."

In each instance of re-encounter, the pilgrimage that precedes it seems compelled by the mulatto status of the character, as though, as in comic resolution, the peace and order of the world were returned in *their* happiness. For Harper's narrator, at least, only the mulatto characters enter an ascension, as Iola Leroy, in the closure of the novel, is not only a character, but also Character Extraordinaire. These agents "too white to be black, too black to be white" share with Bon and Christmas the magical status of liminality, but in the case of Harper's eponymous heroine, the piously sacred overtakes her. And she assumes the equally ambiguous estate of the blessed: "The shadows have been lifted from all their lives; and peace, like bright dew, has descended upon their paths. Blessed themselves, their lives are a blessing to others" (Harper 281).

In effect, the law and the order of this world have not simply been fully regained. This world has ended as the character slips away from earth into the non-historical eternity of unchanged things, even if transcendent ones. This false movement takes us back to the notion of the intruded wedge between opposed dualities. In this instance, the mulatta mediates between dualities, which would suggest that at least mimetic movement, imitating *successful* historical movement, is *upward*, along the vertical scale of being. The only "black" in this case who can move is not quite "black" enough, or certainly not enough that the people who need to know can tell. We observe for the female a similar structure of assumptions at work in the Faulknerian instance.

The "shadow" as a center of ambiguity in Faulkner's and Harper's work might disclose the dramatic surprise that lends these divergent writings a stunning instance of mutuality. As a way of concluding those notes, I would observe three moments of crux: the lifting of the shadows from the one-dimensionality of Harper's characters' lives; the phantom-like, shadowy aspects that cluster in Compson's version of Charles Bon; the terrible, ascensive epiphany of Joe Christmas' slaughter: "Then his face, body, all seemed to collapse, to fall in upon itself, and from out the slashed garments about his hips and loins the pent black blood seemed to rush like a released breath. It seemed to rush out of his pale body like a rush of sparks from a rising rocket; upon the black blast the man seemed to rise soaring into their memories forever and ever" (Faulkner 1959:440).

In all three instances, the character achieves, at last, the superior talismanic force, a preponderance, or a preponderant lack, of humanity. This attribution of extraordinary humanity obviously works in contrastive ways: as we have seen in the case of *Iola Leroy*, the closural device points toward a divine and beneficent ground of potentialities; in the case of *Light in August*, toward a sacrificial torture. In *Absalom, Absalom*! Charles Bon, immersed in the secrecies of origin, is invested by effects of adoration, as he becomes the veritable love object of brother and sister Sutpen. But these opposing indices — pointing upward and downward — mobilize character to the very same region of finality. "Hell" is "heaven" turned upside down, as "heaven" comprehends "hell" in the classic scheme of cosmogony.

That the semantic field here clings tenaciously to notions of the transcendent without openly declaring them as such provides what seems an apt demonstration of Foucault's "enunciative field" by way of concomitance (1972:56-64). In this instance of discursive relations between what I would call a founding concept and "forms of succession," "quite different domains of objects" are involved that "belong to quite different types of discourse." Concomitance is generated "either because they serve as analogical confirmation [of the founding concept] or because they serve as a general principle and as premises accepted by a reasoning, or because they serve as models that can be transferred to other contents." The founding concept here may be generally regarded as a religiously discursive pointer, as we have observed in Compson's blank parody of the creation process. But the analogues on a religious discursivity in these works fracture in contradiction: the "sacred" mulatto figure simultaneously repels and attracts because of his/her blood-crossed career. Faulkner's narrators attribute to Joe Christmas the "pent black blood" and to the octoroon female "seven-eighths" of the *right* blood type. It is not until Bon's blood connection is revealed that Henry Sutpen most probably commits fratricide of the "blood" brother whom he has loved.

Throughout Harper's work the narrator refers to blood along various lines of stress: the "tainted blood" of "white Negroes"; the "trick of the blood"; "outcast blood in the veins": "traditions of blood" and the human estate; "the imperceptible infusion of Negro blood," etc. As the life essence, the human blood, for all that scientific knowledge teaches concerning it, persists in notions of the mysterious. At least one tends to regard it mysteriously, as if the scientific topicality of it were insufficient to exhaust its range of figurative possibilities.

The blood to which these fictive narrators speak has little to do with the scientific, even when they hint, and perhaps all the more so, mensurative dimensions of the substance, as in one-half, one-fourth, one-eighth "black." It appears that medical and scientific knowledge, after all, are not the arbiters of the blood *where we live*, nor yet the origin of recourse when geneaologies, or the "transfer" of time through children and properties are concerned. The blood remains impervious, at the level of folk/myth, to incursions of the "reasonable" and inscribes the unique barrier beyond which human community has not yet passed into the "brotherhood of man" and the "Fatherhood of God." But this very difficulty of the blood is the hinge upon which the concept of community, as we now understand it, appears to turn; extends itself.

Like the pharmikon, the blood is both the antidote and the poison,[14] as the intrusion of mystery in its place segregated the menstruating female, banished the outraged maternity of the unhusbanded woman,[15] and rendered "femaleness" itself the site of absence. On its basis, American Africanity was assigned to the axis of "thingness" in a vision of human community that replicates time and again notions of hierarchical and linear display. If there is mystery or spirit drooping down in the midst of things, then someone must safeguard its secrets; traditionally, the offices of the priestly function (and here I mean any structure of the esoteric), of the recondite in general, of the Dominant One, of a hyperbolean phallic status have fallen to the lot of the male. It is this inner and licit circle of a coveted and mystified knower and knowledge that determines the configurations of the law and the order — the name, the law of the Father.

But the mystery apparently yields its secret, despite the covering names, as the glorification of a male heteroticism, which designates the only "maleness" that can lay claim to the phallic principle. Under these conditions of culture and acculturation, we regard the "mulatta" as the recovery of female gender beyond the Father's house, beyond the lights of the female who falls *legitimately* within its precincts. The borders of the exogamous arrangement are extended without guilt. But the "master," not always sufficiently protected against the burden of incest, might well have discovered his daughter (by African female personality) in the bed of his wife. The invention of the American "mulatta" virtually assured his success.

NOTES

1. Winthrop Jordan. 1969. *White Over Black: American Attitudes Toward the Negro 1550-1812* (Baltimore: Penguin Books), remains one of the most thoroughgoing analyses of this subject from the point-of-view of the United States and its colonial antecedents. Part IV, "Fruits of Passion: The Dynamics of Interracial Sex" concerns specifically the historical context against which sexual mores, or an American behavior of sexuality, were played out. In this "cultural matrix of purpose, accomplishment, self-conception, and social circumstances of settlement in the New World," the mulatto child violated the strictest intentions of a binary racial function" (167). For Jordan, the situation of the mulatto reflects a persistent historicity: the configurations assumed by a cultural phenomenon, or structure of attention, against the perspective of time.

   Barbara Christian. 1980. *Black Women Novelists: The Development of a Tradition, 1892-1976* (Westport, Connecticut: Greenwood Press), looks closely at the theme of the mulatta in certain nineteenth and twentieth century fiction, including that of Frances E.W. Harper, William Wells Brown, Jessie Fauset, and Nella Larsen. See especially, "From Stereotype to Character," pp. 3-61.

   Mary V. Dearborn. 1986. *Pocahontas's Daughters: Gender and Ethnicity in American Culture* (New York: Oxford University Press):158, explores the specific connection between the thematics of the mulatta heroine in fiction and the act of incest: the denial of paternity and of blood rite to the interracial child creates an ignorance of identity that can redound to the distinct disadvantage of certain lateral kin relations. Even though Dearborn does not employ Judith and Henry Sutpen as an instance of the fatal unknowing, I think that a case can be made for it. Because they are ignorant of the existence of Charles Bon — their "black" brother — incest becomes a distinct possibility for all of Sutpen's children. Drawing out the symbolic and rhetorical resonances of the mulatto theme, Dearborn defines both the fictive character and the historical subject, we infer, as "a living embodiment of the paradox of the individual within society." She suggestively describes the "fictional mulatto" as the "imaginative conjunction of a cultural disjunction."

   Henry Louis Gates's guest-edited volume of *Critical Inquiry* [12(Autumn,1985)] does not propose to look specifically at the mulatto/a as an aspect of the problematics of alterity. But the various other issues of the latter explored in the volume are suggestive in a number of ways, specifically, Israel Burshatin's "The Moor in the Text: Metaphor, Emblem, and Silence," pp. 98-119. Burshatin's "moor," like the "mulatto/a" might be viewed as an already inspissated identity before the *particulars* of context have had an opportunity to do their vocation.

2. The following listing of fictional texts on the mulatto/a is not offered as an exhaustive survey. We regard them as "impression points" that the reader achieves in tracing the career of the subject from Harper's era through the 1930's:

   Johnson, James Weldon. 1960. *The Autobiography of an Ex-Colored Man*. New York: Hill and Wang, with an intro. Arna Bontemps.

   Toomer, Jean. *Cane*. 1975. New York: Liveright, with an intro. Darwin Turner. The reader should see specifically the closing section of this powerful work for the tale of Kabnis. Here, the exteriority of the mulatto figure has been revised and corrected into a structure of internal, or psychic complication.

   Larsen, Nella. 1928. *Quicksand*. New York: Alfred Knopf. Rpt. Negro Universities Press, 1969.

Larsen, Nella. 1929. *Passing*. New York: Alfred A. Knopf. Rpt.

Afro-American Cultural Series: The American Negro, His History and Literature, eds. Arthur P. Davis and Darwin Turner. Arno Press, 1969.

Fauset, Jessie. 1969. *The Chinaberry Tree: A Novel of American Life*. College Park, Maryland: McGrath Publishing Company. Rpt.1969.

Fauset, Jessie. 1969. *Comedy: American Style*. College Park, Maryland: McGrath Publishing Company. Rpt. from the 1933 copy at Fisk University.

The reader might consult the opening section of Barbara Christian's work for a more comprehensive account of the fiction of the mulatto/a. A fine study of Pauline Hopkins, contemporaneous with Frances Harper and in pursuance of the mulatto thematic, is provided by Claudia Tate. 1985. "Pauline Hopkins: Our Literary Foremother". *Conjuring: Black Women, Fiction, and Literary Tradition* eds. Marjorie Pryse and Hortense Spillers. Bloomington: Indiana University Press.

3. The Oxford English Dictionary on "mulatta" situates the term in Spanish. Born of a "Negra and a fayre man," "mulatta" in the English *lexis* appears c. 1622. Among its permutations in Portuguese is *mullato*, young mule, or one of a mixed race.

4. Girard's explosive work offers a background against which we might view the fundamental structuration of human community as the deployment of the dynamics of violence and the fear of violent reprisal. By isolating an "expendable figure," the "unanimity-minus-one," community purges itself of various impurities, including guilt. Community also discovers the One Man or Woman (or the substitute) whose elimination would not generate the operations of revenge. Faulkner's Joe Christmas is perfectly placed to carry out all the requirements of Girard's sacrificial program. Essentially unfathered, Christmas is Everyman/woman *before* the name of the Father "cleanses" him/her, or releases from the terrors of "unculture."

5. Todorov's interesting conceptual narrative concentrates in the career of the Native American at the hands of the European explorer, but its application locates a broader frame of reference.

6. John Irwin's brilliant structuralist reading of incest in Faulkner traces its manifestations in the agency of Quentin Compson. Overlapping *The Sound and the Fury* and *Absalom, Absalom*, Quentin reflects his own incestuous urges toward his sister Caddy (*Sound and Fury*) in the narrative that he "repeats" concerning Charles Bon.

   A critical reevaluation of Marxist theory in perspective with the contemporary scene of criticism occasions Fredric Jameson. 1981. *Political Unconscious: Narrative as a Socially Symbolic Act*. Ithaca: Cornell University Press. The opening chapter of the work questions the adequacy of a Freudian "Family Drama" as a comprehensive paradigm and theory of processes of social production.

7. The economic uses of African female personality under the onus of captivity are alluded to in Brent's chapter, "Sketches of Neighboring Slaveholders" (45-53). Not commenting specifically on the mulatta's value, the writer sounds, nonetheless, the profit connections between the female body/sexuality and the oppressive conditions of enslavement.

8. The informing conceptualization of the relevant paragraph here is suggested by the brilliantly speculative work of Gayatri Spivak in "French Feminism in an International Frame," *Yale French Studies*, No. 62: "Feminist Readings — French Texts, American Contexts," pp. 154-184.

9. Various aspects of female sexuality in conjunction with history and politics are examined in *Pleasure and Danger: Exploring Female Sexuality* ed. Carole Vance (Boston: Routledge, Kegan, Paul, 1984). My own essay here, "Interstices: A Small Drama of Words," looks specifically at the grammar of sexuality in relationship to African-American women's community. The essays here are based on papers delivered by the participants at the controversial "Feminist and Scholar Conference,IX," at Barnard College, Spring, 1982.

10. Foucault, re-opening the problem of Victorian sexuality, considers the discursivity of his subject. Victorian Europe was not, in his view, a sexually muted culture, but seized instead every occasion to induce and excite discourse about it. Illegitimate sexuality in the historic context he examines becomes one of the "forms of reality" subjected to a discourse that is "clandestine, circumscribed, and coded" in reference to the brothel, the mental institution, and other spaces of marginality (1978:4ff.). We would regard the site of the mulatta mistress as a marginalized class of objects erotically configured.

11. "History is what hurts" profoundly informs Jameson's sense that "History" is the "ground and untranscendable horizon [that] needs no theoretical justification." He offers its inexorability as the fundamental scene against which the critical praxis unfolds; against which we gauge the efficacy and completeness of any critical system (102).

12. The classic reading of the tensions engendered between the wish-fulfillment and its prohibitive mechanism is given in Freud's *Totem and Taboo*, Vol. 13. (*The Standard Edition of the Complete Psychological Works of Sigmund Freud*, trans. James Strachey. London: Hogarth Press, 1955).

13. The codification of law that underscores the institution of slavery in the United States is sporadically examined in numerous texts of history. But a work contemporaneous with the final days of the "peculiar institution" provides not only a detailed reading of the code, but also an instance of a parallel and *counter* sensitivity that takes on historic appeal in its own right: William Goodell. 1853. *The American Slave Code in Theory and Practice: Its Distinctive Features Shown by its Statutes, Judicial Decisions, and Illustrative Texts* (New York: American and Foreign Anti-Slavery Society). Apparently the "runaway slave" was neither rare nor forgotten. The plentifulness of advertisements describing the *person* of the fugitive — the model, we might suppose, for the contemporary "All Points Bulletin" of the Federal Bureau of Investigation and those mug shots that grace the otherwise uniform local post office — argue the absolute solidification of captivity — the major American social landscape, in my view, for two and a half centuries of human hurt on the scene of "man's last best hope": *Runaway Slave Advertisements: A Documentary History from the 1730's to 1790*, comp. Lathan A. Windley; 2 vols. Vol. I: Virginia and North Carolina; Vol. II: Maryland (Westport, Connecticut: Greenwood Press, 1983).

14. A description of the paradoxical nature of the *pharmikon* is provided by Girard in *Violence and the Sacred*.

15. The banishment, in Roman society, of the mother of the illegitimate child becomes a shocking item of anthropological use. See: Giambattista Vico, *The New Science*, trans. from 3rd. ed. Thomas Goddard Bergin and Max Harold Fisch, 1975. Ithaca: Cornell University Press Paperbacks.

REFERENCES

Brent, Linda. 1973. *Incidents in the Life of a Slave Girl* ed. L. Maria Child, with intro. Walter Teller. New York: Harcourt Brace Jovanovich Harvest Books.

Christian, Barbara. 1980. *Black Women Novelists: The Development of a Tradition, 1892-1976*. Westport, Connecticut: Greenwood Press.

Donnan, Elizabeth, ed. and comp. 1932. "Accounts from an African Trade Book, 1733-1736," from the Archives of the Newport Historical Society. *Documents Illustrative of the History of the Slave Trade to America*. 4 vols. Vol.III: "New England and the Middle Colonies." Washington, D.C.: The Carnegie Institute.

Douglass, Frederick. 1968. *Narrative of the Life of Frederick Douglass, An American Slave, Written by Himself*. New York: Signet Books.

Faulkner, William. 1951. *Absalom, Absalom*! New York: Random House Modern Library.

———. 1959. *Light in August*. New York: Random House Modern Library. First published in 1929.

Foucault, Michel. 1972. *The Archaeology of Knowledge and the Discourse on Language*, trans. A.M. Sheridan Smith. 1972. New York: Harper Colophon Books.

———. 1978. *The History of Sexuality: Volume I: An Introduction*, trans. Robert Hurley. New York: Pantheon Books.

Girard, René. 1977. *Violence and the Sacred*. Trans. Patrick Gregory. Baltimore: Johns Hopkins University Press.

Harper, Frances. 1893. *Iola Leroy, or Shadows Uplifted*. New York: AMS Press, repr. 1971.

Irwin, John. 1975. *Doubling and Incest/Repetition and Revenge*. Baltimore: Johns Hopkins University Press.

Jameson, Fredric. 1981. *Political Unconscious: Narrative as a Socially Symbolic Act*. Ithaca: Cornell University Press.

Miller, Perry. 1961. *The New England Mind*; 2 vols. Vol. I: *The Seventeenth Century*; Vol. II: *From Colony to Province*. Boston: Beacon Press.

Todorov, Tzvetan. 1984. *The Conquest of America*. Trans. Richard Howard. New York: Colophon Books.

Feminist historiography and post-structuralist thought
Intersections and departures

R. Radhakrishnan
University of Massachusetts

My purpose in this paper is to articulate the intersection of contemporary feminist historiography with post-structuralist theory and, furthermore, to develop this intersection as a point of departure for the affirmative programmatic of feminist historiography. In other words, my objective is to locate the "differential" politics of feminist historiography within post-structuralist "difference" and to develop this very location as the difference of post-structuralism from itself. My claim then is that feminist historiography, by assuming for itself both an identity under erasure and a determinate politics, succeeds in galvanizing post-structuralist thought beyond a fetishized indeterminacy towards what I call an affirmative or projective indeterminacy.

Why should feminist historiography even negotiate with post-structuralist theory? To answer this question synoptically: without the benefit of post-structuralist theory, feminist historiography (or for that matter, any adversarial, revolutionary, counter-hegemonic, or counter-mnemonic discourse/practice) is in danger of turning into a superficial reversal of forces of power that would leave untouched certain general and underlying economies of meaning and history (for example, identity, binarity, and representation), that constitute the ideological infrastructure for what I term "palpable historicity." I am suggesting then that feminist historiography and its "revisionist will" cannot but benefit by its interactions with, say, Lacanian psychoanalysis, Foucauldian counter-memory, and Derridean deconstruction. Each of these "male" modes operates oppositionally, critically, and deconstructively (and here I have neither the time nor the opportunity to go into the many differences among these modes), but experience a certain impoverishment of "will" (a kind of ascesis) and intention when it comes to envisioning and affirming or "identifying" an alternative to the regimes that are being critiqued so powerfully and relentlessly. These critical practices assume (a) that the negative or the "counter"-force in itself, in all its duplicitous and parasitic supplementarity, can and does operate as a new and creative emergence, and (b) that certain "protocols of vigilance," to use Derrida's phrase[1], guarantee successfully against the recrudescence of a whole range of basic structures and axiologies of oppression. There is then a demonstrable obsession with "that which is being critiqued." Obversely, the assumption seems to be that counter-mnemonic practices are best secured and empowered by way of their capacity to enact perennially their own doubleness, i.e., even as an agent of the counter-memory (Foucault; Nietzsche), the "present" ineluctably invokes memory, places it under erasure, and so on, *ad infinitum*. This results quite paradoxically and anomalously in the following predicament: post-structuralist thought perpetuates itself on the guarantee that no "break" (Althusser) is possible with the past even though its initial intentional trajectory was precisely to make visible this very "break," valorize it *qua* "break," and then proceed towards a different and differential creation.[2] Post-structuralist intentionality thus desiccates itself, allegorizes this desiccation, and offers this allegorically perennial revolution as the most appropriate defense against the reproduction of such categories and structures as, Self, Subject, Identity, etc.

But this program of action, quite laudable and even exemplary in its farsightedness, fails to ground historically this very capacity for far-sighted intervention. Rather than instantiate and exemplify the indeterminate by-way of the "determinate," in all its contingent circumstantiality, post-structuralist theory "over-looks"[3] the "determinate" altogether and in doing so forfeits the opportunity to ground its own perspectivity, i.e., to realize its perspectivity "perspectivally." Both indeterminacy and perspectivity get fetishized/reified/essentialized for lack of a clear sense of constituency. To sum it up, post-structuralist thought loses its capacity for intervention; instead, it begins to celebrate indeterminacy-as-such as though nothing were at stake. And here begins my own polemical intervention.

Feminist historiography has something at stake, i.e., feminist theory and historiography are a form of praxis. It is up to feminist historiography (and here I am intentionally equating revisionist historiography with critical theory in light of the post-structuralist disclosure that even the most disjuncted form of contemporaneity carries within it counter-mnemonic traces of discredited histories and temporalities)[4] to achieve critical practice as affirmation and coterminously, to radicalize this practice as its own potential auto-critique. Stated more generally, feminist historiography sets for itself the twin task of (a) of establishing, albeit contingently, its own "identity" even as it (b) offers battle to the algorithm of Identity-as-such. If such is the mission of feminist historiography/theory, it is of the utmost importance to conceptualize the relationship of feminist historiography to post-structuralist theory in axial or coalitional terms, and not in terms of domain, structure, and hierarchy. It is crucial that feminist critical practice not be identified within or hierarchically subsumed by post-structuralist thought. Such an identification or subsumption can only result in the depoliticizing of feminist intentionality.

And yet, this identification needs to be made provisionally and as a matter of strategy. If this strategic identification is not made, feminist critical practice stands in danger of lapsing into the naiveté of historicism and empiricism. On the other hand, an exemplary or synecdochal identification of feminist historiography with post-structuralist orthodoxy will have committed the feminist intervention preemptively as a juncture within the syntax of phallogocentrism.[5] In my reading, the post-structuralist feminist intervention has to walk the tightrope through and beyond post-structuralism and only as a function of such a competence valorize its critique as finally and definitively heterogeneous with what it critiques.

To begin then with a very fundamental question, "What do feminist critics want?"[6] This question makes two substantive claims: (a) that there is a demonstrable lack, and (b) that there is an objective whose fulfillment is desired and intended. Controversies can and will arise about how this objective is to be realized but not about the very reality of this objective. Thus there is a polemical and intentional specificity to the question that cannot be easily appropriated, generalized, dehistoricized, or allegorized. This specific potential for meaning cannot be deracinated from its historical context. This is another way of saying that there is a determinate exemplarity that characterizes a particular constituency at a particular time, but this exemplarity is not a privilege; on the contrary it is the kind of exemplarity that pertains to an entire axis, the axis of the oppressed. This displacement or deprivileging of identity into axis is in many ways a post-structuralist accomplishment, but unfortunately one that has not been allowed by institutional, textual and hermeticized versions of post structuralism to take on historical flesh and blood. But I claim that a question like what do feminist critics want, articulated both as an expression and as a differentiation of the post-structuralist quarrel with the basic structures of western thought, can achieve the determinacy of the indeterminate and the indeterminacy of the determinate.

To identify now a few themes and issues that are of great valence both to post-structuralist thought and the feminist endeavor, and then to demonstrate some of the consequential differences between the two at the level of strategy and practice.

Post-structuralist thought opens up an entire field where the feminist intervention may enable and empower its projects to the fullest. Post-structuralist thought is the newly opened up horizon within which certain practices may be conducted and actualized in their "own most" way, safeguarded as it were from epistemic violence from certain inimical and oppressive prehistories. This relationship of the horizon to what is in it or what constitutes it as horizon may also be seen as the relationship of a general theory to specific instances of it. Thus, "alterity," a post-structuralist theme, may be historicized, differentiated, and instantiated as "woman," "the ethnic," "the colonized," "the insane," etc., just as "binarity" itself may be unpacked and analyzed circumstantially as male/female, nature/culture, speech/*ecriture*, logic/rhetoric, etc. In rarefied epistemological terms, what we are talking about here is the semantico-syntactic tension between the "macro"logical and the "micro"logical. And here, clearly, there is a problem of rank, hierarchy, and precedence. Even post-structuralist thought with its indefatigable capacity for problematization and protocols of vigilance, finds itself heir to an entire tradition that has privileged *a priorism* of one sort or another, i.e., *a* priorism-as-such: the *a priorism* of mastery, transcendence, pure reason and of essences and categories and nomologies. So, confronted with its own "difference" and "difference-from" the tradition, post-structuralist thought in general and Derridean deconstruction in particular, does well to renounce ontology and logocentric authority of whatever provenance. In this particular context, and in this limited sense, it succeeds in activating all manner of discursive, rhetorical, and epistemological defense systems against the possible recrudescence of metaphysical and logocentric modalities, but unfortunately, it never gets beyond the discursive and the epistemological. It is arrested just short of history and worldliness; it remains a defense in theory, in principle, in gesture. Moreover, deconstruction's espousal of "pure difference" denies difference to the very ingredients that constitute "Difference." The metaphysical and onto-theological traces in deconstruction are influential enough to cause the plenary semanticization of "Difference" as a pure non-concept with the result that specific differences such as, the feminist difference, the ethnic difference, the Third-World difference, and so on, remain subtended, dematerialized and frozen under the mastery of Difference as ur-concept.[7]

Thus within its own economy (that it is an "economy," no thought can deny since this very denial contributes to the "economy"), deconstructive thinking perpetrates the violence of *a priorism*. If the differential indeterminacy of the post-structuralist horizon is trans-historicized, we then have a "pure" situation where the "general" has hegemonic precedence over the "particular," where theory dominates and pre-construes the significance of praxis and the temporality of the episteme preempts the pulsation of the critical and historical event.[8] The horizon instead of being an historically sensitive "construct" that is constantly formed, deformed and reformed by the happenings "within" it, hardens into an allegorical *ethos*, the incontrovertible *ethos* of the "always-ready." This overdetermination of the horizon into epistemic domain is structurally homologous with the essentialization of "Difference" and the allegorization of "counter" movements into the monolithic category of "alterity."

The difficult task that faces the revisionist perspectivity of feminist historiography is that of tapping on the one hand into the Utopian radicality of post-structuralist difference and alterity, and on the other, historicizing or semanticizing this very radicality by way of a here-and-now and a short-term program of affirmative transformation. Without this practical and historical dimension, the feminist intervention will find itself marginalized within the "contentless" romanticism of the perennial revolution, whereas without the theoretical component, it will remain trapped within the logic of identity and its corollaries. If feminist historiography intends to inaugurate what I call "axial temporality," and the "politics of heterogeneity,"[9] it has to deal with the benefactions and the perils of post-structuralist thought.

The critique of identity. This critique has been launched now for quite awhile. What is singular about the post-structuralist interrogation of identity is that it attacks identity-as-such and not just particular and isolated forms or versions of identity. This de-naturalization of identity (and the concomitant Benjaminian realization that every document of culture and civilization is coextensively a document of barbarism) is of undeniable critical value, but it is the beginning of a problem rather than the resolution of it. The real question is: on what basis or in the name of what should we produce "truths" and "identities" now that we know that all identities and truths are exclusionary and that all points of view including one's own are deeply ideological?[10] What does it take to achieve the kind of "meta-" or "second order" revolution that will enable the production of non-identical and non-authoritarian modes? How will this second-order transformation be its own content and furthermore, how does one inaugurate such a second-order change through and by changes in the first order?[11] What I am suggesting is that these concerns are extremely political and as such they need be aligned with the more immediate objectives of feminist historiography.

To situate this in the context of the feminist project, what is the purpose of revisionist historiography? If historiography is the unmasking of the ideological underpinnings of any seemingly transparent and natural history, how should such a critical or second order capacity be utilized to write a different history that will include differentially its own historiography?[12] Is not feminism in search of "identity," an identity, its identity, though not identity as ontological and essentialist, but identity as effectivity and as empowered and enfranchised constituency? If feminist theory intends to endorse identity provisionally, how should it negotiate with the blanket condemnation of identity prescribed by post-structuralist theory? There is a certain duplicity in the post-structuralist prescription that needs to be diagnosed elaborately. Radical enough as this prescription may be, the historical reality of the matter is that this very critique of identity and binarity is generated from a perspective that has been overdetermined by identity. There is even cruel irony in the fact that the total deconstruction of identity should be suggested as a remedy by post-identical interests for the betterment of constituencies that are as yet trapped in the temporality of the not-yet-self. It is indeed a self-arrogated privilege of overdetermined interests and systems of thought to underwrite radical nihilism or the perennial revolution as prototypical solutions for problems with different historical aetiologies.[13]

The pathetic anomaly of the situation is that the repressed constituencies have to play a game of catch-up and at the same time commit themselves to the overthrow of that very terrain that legitimates notions such as power, authority and ideological normativity. To put it reductively, the impact and consequences of deconstruction cannot be the same for different practitioners, agencies, and constituencies.[14] The alienation of the "other" and its namelessness has to be "named" before the very nomology of the "name" can be called into question and displaced. In the name of what then should feminist historiography be authorized? — both in the name of its self and namelessly whereby the emergence of its "identity" is made, by virtue of its capacity for auto-critique and a second-order transformation, to step beyond the closure of identity-as-such. In other words, the de-authorization of binarity has to take place in historically related but discrete phases. If this historical determination is not made, all adversarial discourses will be easily appropriated by the hegemonic discourse whose "always-already" displacement from itself (and the capacity of the hegemonic discourse to "nominate" and thus suborn its opposition) will only militate against the formation of historically actual oppositional forces. It is just not enough to say that post-structuralist theory has fractured the univocity of the self and that even the empowered self has been disclosed as "always already" eccentric and exotopic to itself. Such a totalization overlooks the reality of historical differences. For example, patriarchal discourse alienated from itself does not occupy the same space as the self-manqué of feminist discourse now threatened by further alienation.

With the word alienation, we enter complex territory. Depending on what historical period we are referring to or for that matter what system of thought, alienation comes out as good or bad, desirable or not. I would now like to focus briefly on the theme of alienation-by-language, a theme that occupies center stage in the post-structuralist theater. The Lacanian notion of the "lack," Derrida's notion of decentered play and the proto-Nietzschean impulse in Foucault to celebrate the perennial superannuation of the "subject of knowledge" by the will-to-knowledge (i.e., an epistemic momentum or temporality freed from nominalized securities and homes), all make great investments in the idea of disaccommodation by knowledge. Paraphrased simply, post-structuralist thought advocates strongly a model of knowledge not as home or domain, but as orphaned and exilic. In language and in thought we are rendered alterior to ourselves, alienated from all certitudes and modalities that conduce to the homely adaptation of knowledge. This is indeed a bold and radical thesis, but again this radicality has to be insured against rarefaction into a pure and unsituated radicality.

How can feminist theory both endorse alienation and at the same time lay claims to "its own" language? Again, I believe the strategy is a carefully calculated ambivalence. Feminist historiography finds itself confronted by two imperatives: to endorse in theory the thesis of language as ontological alienation and symbolic lack and to posit within the structure of this "lack" its own positivity. There is a socio-political urgency to the feminist cause that makes it unconscionable for it not to claim its own language and through this language make its own home, thus redressing centuries of silence, non-history, difference, forced otherness and representational violence. For women have always been the "other" and the "different," hierarchized and marked into inferiority and powerlessness by those very categories hailed as putatively radical by post-structuralist theory. To expect feminist discourse to alienate itself from its own potential language or to demand that feminist historiography not intend a safe and anchored home or constituency for itself is politically as vicious as it is vapid intellectually.[15] The same caution needs to be exercised in the context of the overthrow of the subject. Post-structuralist theory is quite correct in demystifying structures of subjectivity, but here again, feminist historiography has to go "beyond" by patiently accounting for different patterns of subject-formation and not just content itself with an algebraic repudiation of subjectivity.

The question of "woman" has taken on almost maniacal significance within male post-Structuralist discourse: Lacan, Derrida, and the many appropriations of the phenomenon of "woman" in Nietzsche. The upshot of it all, however, is the enigmatic and profound conclusion that "woman is unspeakable," which is to say that the reality of woman is unspeakable. We thus have the ironic and contradictory situation where the term "woman" is signified out of meaning. "Woman" who had been ostracized from historical, political, and philosophic presence by the dominant male tradition is now picked up by that very tradition, in the moment of its loss of self-certitude, and thematized into a state of allegorical infinitude. To put it in more physical terms, "woman" who had been raped and/or impregnated by the male pen into unhistorical oblivion, is now being picked up by the same "chivalrous" male will-to-knowledge and glorified and "disseminated" into the transcendent and ahistorical plenitude of allegorical unspeakability. The male will-to-knowledge, even when it operates oppositionally and deconstructively, is incapable of stepping out of the dialectics of ontology. I am not questioning or belittling for a moment the radicality of male critiques and deconstructions of the patriarchal tradition, but I am asserting that the male-centered critique of the male tradition still remains trapped within ontology and the ultimately identical and redemptive logic of an a- and un-historical dialectic. It remains incapable of divesting its negative self or its "other' self from its anterior ontological determinations and commitments. The "woman" question then gets invested in oppositionally and is thus made once again the victim or subject of phallogocentric inscription/representation. We thus have the Derridean insistence that feminism can only be a conjuncture within the presiding logic of phallogocentrism, a diagnosis that in my reading is a mistake, for Derrida here is resorting to a logic not unlike that of theodicy, for, if nothing by definition is a stepping-out of phallogocentric closure, then nothing surely is. But this argument is as duplicitous as it is magisterially tautologous. The will to a certain belief is ideologized into a cognitive truth, a tendency quite rampant in many post-structuralist quarrels about the meaning of texts. I will merely refer obliquely to the Lacan-Derrida dispute over the Poe text to suggest that here again we have a polemical situation where two readings, neither of which believes in the norm of "corrigibility," nonetheless go on to detect error in the other. What is astonishing, given the brilliance of both Derrida and Lacan, is the fact that neither philosophic reader attempts to theorize this basic incommensurability, i.e., the non-coincidence of truth as cognitive with reading as rhetoric. The consequent connotative internalization of "correctness" is left both unexplained and un-spoken for from the point of view of ideological preference.

To go back to the Derridean assertion about the status and positionality of feminist discourse, the question should be: who is making the adjudication? The perspectival incapacity of phallogocentric discourse, even in its non-identical mode, to differentiate feminist articulation from its own putatively overarching and inescapable identity is naturalized and axiomatized as the essential lack of feminist difference from that which it critiques, i.e., the phallogocentric economy. In other words, what male Post-Structuralist discourse has to say, in the moment of its self-alienation, about the reality of the feminist intervention is constituted ideologically as the truth-in-itself of feminism. The "unspeakability" of Woman or the "woman question" is thus sublimated into ineffability,i.e., sublimated out of the agenda. The woman who was once subjected to male constitution and representation for "cultural" purposes is now once again subjected to the same male will in the name of culture's self-interrogation. In either case,the protagonist or the antagonist is male, and in each case the lost cause is "woman": either lost by or lost out of history. The name of woman is converted into that absence or that name of a name which then serves the antinomian purpose of the male tradition's endless and Sisyphian flagellation of itself: woman maintained or kept as vessel. The thesis of woman's impoverishment is figured out obversely and interchangeably as the alienation of the male self from its-self. This syndrome has the same structure and temporal morphology as that other conjuncture where Imperialism/Colonialism attempts to lick its wounds redemptively and nostalgically by way of renewed thematic investments in what were once colonies. My question simply is: Does Imperialism/Colonialism have anything more to say that is worth hearing? Is that point of view viable, "conscionable" or even interesting any more? Similarly, does and can phallogocentrism have anything worthwhile to say about feminist projects?

In all the powerful male elaborations of the theme, for example, of Identity and Identity-critique, the issue of perspectivity is rarely, if ever, brought up. It is strange that male Post-Structuralist theory should keep returning to Nietzsche so extensively and yet remain so unresponsive to a decidedly Nietzschean theme: perspectivity. For example, in the case of the unspeakability of woman, the male theorist does not ask the question, from whose or what point of view? Woman is unspeakable, by whom? That "woman" is unrepresentable from, by, and within the male point of view is construed as the general and natural unrepresentability of Woman-it/herself. This reading is suspect for the following reasons: (a) Even as it launches an all out attack on Identity, male Post-Structuralist discourse stops well short of the critique of representation. While it succeeds in demystifying and denaturalizing "identity," it does not assume responsibility for the ideological and perspectival nature of this very critique; (b) It assumes that an ontological critique of identity discredits all forms of representation, thus failing to make distinctions between acts of representation that are indigenous and autochthonous and those that are coercive. That the very terms, "indigenous" and "autochthonous" are ideological sedimentations from a master-discourse is no doubt a valid claim, but these terms need to be semanticized and historicized differently even as they are claimed to be effects of the dominant discourse. [A point in question here would be an all too glib view of the structure known as "nationalism" from a pan-nationalist or inter-nationalist view-point. The internationalist critique of nationalism is convincing only because, and this is as paradoxical as it is ironic, the "internationalist" constituency has gone through and beyond the temporality known as "nationalist," and hence the misleading "internationalist" claim that "it" is a non-constituency.] Here too, post-structuralist discourse refuses to take seriously the notion of non-synchronous development. By characterizing the dominant temporality as synchronic, it derives oppositional strategies also as synchronic. To state this in terms of my present theme, male post-structuralist discourse generalizes the theme of its alterity and alienation and forces its temporality on the not-self of the feminine and its very different insertion into the identity as well as temporality of binarity. By insisting juridically that feminist semantics cannot be parsed into meaning outside the phallogocentric syntax, male post-structuralist theory fails to realize, even conceptually, that a feminist critique of the male tradition can be different from a male critique, or that it might carry a different charge and valence. The positionality of the critical subject is emptied of its polemical and historical specificity. Since male alienation is my theme here, I cannot resist the temptation of a meaningful digression here. I am thinking of Meursault and the philosophy of the "absurd" in Camus' *L'Etranger* where too the "other" as Arab has to be eliminated, literally bumped off, quite indifferently and meaninglessly so as to enable the Eurocentric philosophy of man's alienation by rationality. I wonder how the story might have sounded from the point of view of the Arab who had to die fortuitously and unhistorically so that the colonizer may rejoice in his negativity. My questions are: who is the author here and who the subject? What about the unspeakability of the Arab? Where and why is it unspeakable? Whose privilege is it to elevate unspeakability into an ontological category? Is Meursault's unspeakability and that of the Arab the same? Whereas the European point of view in its very alienation is historically dense and thus in control of its self and destiny, the Arab's unspeakability is deracinated from historicity itself. The Arab or Arab reality then becomes the signifier whose de-realization as a signified paves the way for the birth of a western philosophy of "Man." Just as the site of the Arab is the site of the "nameless," so with the site of "woman." She becomes the ultimate signifier, inflated beyond meaning, to be penned in the image of man's self-scepsis.

The dismantling of "identity itself," I submit, is a historical process whose many different projects, components, and phases are not synchronous with one another. Thus, when Lacanian psychoanalysis ordains that one does not speak for one's self, for one's self is always-already alienated through socialization, symbolization, and the acquisition of language, it is not immediately clear if this is an ontological thesis, a historical observation, or a supra-historical thesis that is intended to overlook the circumstantialities of history. Has not the "one" always spoken for "one's self" and consolidated culture and history on that univocal basis, and, moreover, has not this undivided solitary self or "one" been the unity of man as representative of humanity? And should not one account for this? The now ontologically discredited regime of the "one who spoke" has in history created a beneficiary man, and a victim, woman. The Lacanian thesis does not take into account this sedimented history and its very serious ideological consequences. To play a little on words, that exemplary Post-Structuralist device that barters away whole histories and constituencies in the name of a terroristic polysemy, it is little wonder that this particular psychoanalytic account of sexuality and identity offers no program of "affirmative action" or "equal opportunity" projects. The reasons for this abstinence are (a) that such projects are based on the acknowledgment of anterior realities and imbalances, an acknowledgment that Lacanian psychoanalysis will not make for it requires too much historicization, and (b) these projects, unlike Lacanian Praxis, are intended not as explanations and justifications *après coup*, but as intentional, affirmative and transformative practices.

I am quite aware of the profundity of the Lacanian revolution and how tellingly it displaces and dispossesses the metaphysical language of Self and Identity. After the Lacanian revolution it would be literally pre-posterous to claim to "have" and incarnate a self through speech. The self is a structural effect just as meaning and identity are dispositions or effects within the structure of language. As Lacan demonstrates in his seminar on Poe's purloined letter, the meaning of the letter is nor some semantic interiority but a relayed movement within the structure of the signifying chain or network. So far, so very good. However, the Lacanian overthrow of the Self of Ontology is exactly that, no more and no less, i.e., it does not take into account the ideologically entrenched and historically sedimented nature of structure itself. To be held accountable positionally or structurally may not be the same as being celebrated as the Self of Ontology, but this very occupation or inhabitation of structure or structurally ordained spaces is not innocent or indifferent, i.e., it is authorial of "identity-effects." The ontological dismantling of the Self does not automatically imply or achieve the historical obliteration of historical effects and imbalances. The self as structure is not any less ideologically susceptible than the self of ontology and metaphysics. We still have the problem of accounting for the specificity of different positions within the signifying structure, for positions are not interchangeable, and besides, some positions are vested with power and some with "lack." And this has nothing to do with the ontological thesis of the primordial lack or repression. Here again, I have no fundamental quarrel with the Lacanian line, but my disagreement is with Lacan's elaboration of structurality as that which operates preemptively of history, in algebraic abeyance as it were of the contents of structure. To prove my point concretely, in the case of the Purloined Letter, what if the "contents" of the letter had to do with, say, espionage, or information relating to a revolutionary movement within the country, or the queen's involvement with a pan-national insurrection? Of course, Lacan would be quite right in maintaining that his resolution of what the letter means would not be altered by the determinate contents of the letter; indeed, the elegance of the Lacanian heuristic consists in its lack of context-specificity. All that it requires is the generalized and tautologous piece of information that the letter has the kind of contents that could initiate blackmail: a kind of question-begging innocence of history. It is this indifference to context as content that constitutes the detective's expertise. Thus we have a contradiction at the very core of structure: structure as heuristic or epistemic device celebrates its success by de-realizing precisely that which it was supposed to account for. In other words, structure becomes the thesis of intelligibility itself at a level of rarefaction where there is nothing to be intelligible about.

The Lacanian perspective on meaning and identity can be celebrated as radical only as relative to the metaphysical *episteme* that it interrogates. The same is true *mutatis mutandis* of Derridean deconstruction. The question that feminist historiography asks is: Is the radicality of any theory or praxis to be evaluated exclusively with reference to the orthodoxies of the metaphysical regime? And if so, why? Could it not be the case that we are either flogging a dead horse or that our interest is not in achieving a "break," but in the eternal and timeless maintenance of a "tradition of opposition" that has perforce to keep alive the very tradition that it questions? Flog a dead horse, or to change the metaphor, fight with a phantom, revive the phantom through the fight, and keep on shadow-boxing with real and substantive intensity — is that the intention of feminist historiography and revisionism?

There is no doubt in my mind that the two themes that post-structuralist thought has brought home to us are: (a) recursiveness and critical self-reflexivity, and (b) the omnipresence of ideology. We cannot afford to make distinctions between history as content and empiricity and historiography as a grammatological practice, between history as reality and meta-history as an objective and value-free set of rules and prescriptions about the conceptualization of history. History is what historiography does, and meta-history is what is tacit in history. Equally and analogously, we cannot launch into a critique of knowledge with the assurance that objective and trans-ideological truth or knowledge can be arrived at by way of transcendent, natural, or *aprioristic* categoriality. Now does this mean that (a) critical self-reflexivity and historiographic and meta-historical self-consciousness rule out the very possibility of making and writing history, i.e., in Nietzschean terms, should we be so full of "remembering" that we forget to "forget," and thereby lose our sense of perspectival contemporaneity, or in Foucauldian terms, should our capacity for counter-mnemonic practice be paralyzed by the identically mnemonic? Or, (b) Must our concern for changes of the second order take such precedence and be so overdetermined as to prevent us from seeing the vital connections between the first order and the second, i.e., must our zeal for a "deep and structural" transformation force us to isolate "structure" from its dialectical implication with "history"? Or, (c) Should critical praxis, recoiling as it does from the regime of ideology, fail to make choices among different ideologies, thus trivializing the discovery that ideology is inescapable? And finally, (d) how should the revisionist will realize its capacity for auto-critique without putting in peril its own projects, i.e., without discrediting its own credibility? Which is to say, how should the feminist post-structuralist will envision its "own identical" time even as it sets in motion that "other heterogeneous time," that critical or post-historical temporality that calls into the question all languages of the self, the identical, and the proper? What I am hinting at here is a differential interaction between trajectories of identity and a politics of heterogeneity. Neither the absolute privileging of pure reflexivity and its other, heterogeneous, heteronomous, and post-temporality nor the the fear (exemplary here is Fredric Jameson) and suspicion that all decentering attempts merely serve to reinstate the center, but the differential enactment of the dialectic disengaged from its metaphysical *telos*.

Now that I have tried to express the eccentric relationship of feminist critical theory to post-structuralist theory, let me conclude with a few strong claims on behalf of a feminist historiography that steps beyond post-structuralist closure and orthodoxy; (a) As historiography, feminist theory is different precisely because it is still interested in creating and transforming history, i.e., historiography does not paralyze the history-making competence.

Rather than celebrate the static model of the second order in isolation, feminist critical theory aligns historiography and critical theorizing with the making and doing of history; (b) Even as it undertakes the critique of representation and the position of the subject, it does not abdicate the responsibility of the intentional/ agential production of meaning as change; (c) It attempts to create an axial connection between short-term politics and a radical indeterminacy so that even as contingent empowerments and reversals are achieved, the ideal of the non-authoritarian and non-coercive production of culture is kept alive; (d) It brings to reality the phenomenon of heterogeneity both as a lived expression and as a political coalition, i.e., a heterogeneity that will have achieved a break from the regime of "identity" and "binarity" towards a different future; (e) And finally, as a comment on my own position as subject as gendered male and feminist by persuasion: feminist theory makes possible the realization that positions such as feminism, ethnicity, lesbianism, post-colonialist politics are both expressions of boundaries and invitations to think beyond boundaries. It also invokes the ideal of a compassionate and a trans-denominational humanity in all its perilous indeterminacy, a humanity in the making. It allows me as male-outsider to be an insider to the feminist cause and at the same warns me that I should be wary of allegorizing the feminist cause. It teaches me that though as male I am "safe" as no woman is, I may yet try and seek membership among the oppressed through appropriate acts of divestment.

NOTES

1. In a recent essay, "The University in the eye of its Pupils," Derrida examines the deployment of such critical protocols in the context of the University and its institutional claims to rationality.

2. See my forthcoming essay, "Donald Barthelme's *The Dead Father* as Post-Modernist practice," for a narratological working out of the "break" and what lies beyond the "break."

3. For a specialized treatment of this notion of "over-sight", please see William V. Spanos' essay, "The Indifference of Difference," published by the Society for Critical Exchange. This essay, in its turn, is profoundly indebted to Michel Foucault's analysis of the "panopticon" in his *Discipline and Punish*.

4. I am referring here to a whole range of texts by Jacques Derrida that deal with the problem of temporal and epistemic traces.

5. Jacques Derrida (1982) in a recent interview ordains that feminism can only be a moment within the logic of phallogocentrism. This in my reading is a mistake, for here Derrida is

resorting to a logic not unlike that of theodicy, for, if nothing by definition is a stepping-out of phallogocentric closure, then nothing surely is. But this argument is as duplicitous as it is tautologous.

6. Elaine Showalter's anthology *The New Feminist Criticism* is full of insightful essays that deal with this question. I am also referring in particular to Sandra Gilbert's essay, "What do Feminist Critics Want? A Postcard from the Volcano" (29-45).

7. Ernst Bloch's notion of "non-synchronous development" deals with this issue. Eurocentric thought tends to impose its own synchronicity on the temporalities of its "colonies."

8. See my essay, "The Singular Event and the End of Logocentrism," in *boundary 2* (Fall 1983): 33-60.

9. See my essay, "Ethnic Identity and Post-Structuralist Differance" in *Cultural Critique* 6(1986):199-220.

10. For a thorough (but not always convincing) discussion of the relationship of ideology to meaning and interpretation, see Fredric Jameson's *The Political Unconscious.*

11. For an elaborate analysis of the "second order" logic, see my forthcoming, "Ideology versus 'Ideology': Towards a Post-Structuralist Ethics."

12. See my "Ideology versus Ideology" essay.

13. See Gayatri Spivak's critique of Julia Kristeva and of Eurocentric feminism in general, "French Feminism in an International Context."

14. At a recent conference, I was advocating decentering and decanonization and deconstruction only to be stopped short by a colleague in Afro-American Studies Whose entire mission was i1indeed to create a canon.

15. See Luce Irigaray's many projects as feminist, theorist, and feminist psychoanalyst for a complex understanding of the eccentric and non synchronous position of the subject.

REFERENCES

Althusser, Louis. 1976. *Essays in Self-Criticism*. Trans. by Grahame Lock. London: New Left Books.

Bloch, Ernst (ed). 1977. *Aesthetics and Politics*. London: New Left Books.

Cixous, Hélène, and Clément, Catherine. 1975; 1986. *The Newly Born Woman*. Trans. by Betsy Wing. Minneapolis: University of Minnesota Press.

Derrida, Jacques. 1982 (with Christie V. McDonald). "Choreographies." *Diacritics* 12:66-76.

———. 1983. "The Principle of Reason: The University in the Eyes of its Pupils." *Diacritics* 13:3-20.

Foucault, Michel. 1977. *Language, Counter-Memory, Practice: Selected Essays and Interviews*. Trans. Donald F. Bouchard and Sherry Simon. Ithaca: Cornell University Press.

———. 1979. *Discipline and Punish: The Birth of the Prison*. Trans. Alan Sheridan. New York: Vintage.

Irigaray, Luce. 1985. *Speculum of the Other Woman*. Ithaca: Cornell University Press

———. 1985. *This Sex Which Is Not One*. Ithaca: Cornell University Press.

Jameson, Fredric. 1981. *The Political Unconscious: Narrative as a Socially Symbolic Act*. Ithaca: Cornell University Press.

Jardine, Alice. 1985. *Gynesis: Configurations of Woman and Modernity*. Ithaca, NY: Cornell University Press.

Nietzsche, Friedrich. 1949. *The Use and Abuse of History*. Trans. by Adrian Collins. New York: Liberal Arts Press.

Showalter, Elaine (ed.). 1985. *The New Feminist Criticism: Essays on Women, Literature and Theory*. New York: Pantheon.

Spivak, Gayatri. 1987. "French Feminism in an International Context." *In Other Worlds: Essays in Cultural Politics*. New York and London: Methuen.

A response to "The difference within: Feminism and critical theory"

Gayatri Chakravorty Spivak
University of Pittsburgh

কথার সে ভার নামা রে মন
নীরব হয়ে শোন দেখি শোন

These words that I sing to myself in my mother tongue mean: "My mind, set down that weight of words. be silent and listen, listen."[1]

I should like to be quiet this morning. I speak against that wish because of my contract with you, in response to papers that have hit my passion as I think they have hit yours. The unease that these papers have produced in us reflects what Hortense Spillers marked out so significantly for us in her essay. As the "tragic mulatto/a" we are engaged *as* feminists, in making feminism itself a tragic mulatto/a. I should like, this morning, to digest and swallow that unease in silence. Because I cannot be silent, what I say will be marked by that unease.

There is a difference between the speakers. There are those of us who were engaged in feminism when it started as a fledgling movement in the U.S., when it was a passion, and those of us who have profitted from the other group's labors and quite appropriately speak about feminism *now*. The first group collaborates with the second group in turning its passion into a discipline. A discipline is the task of producing disciples so that they can be doctors — literally teachers — so that they can teach. A discipline is not the *business* of teaching; the discipline is not even the business of the production of teachers. A discipline produces disciples, appropriate feminists, vessels for the task of producing another generation of disciples. *Our* discipline would produce feminists, in other words, who can teach. As we are engaged in fashioning this discipline, we realize that we are marrying our passion to an alien, an alienating disciplinary formation. That is the subject position that the passionate feminists in this room occupy: the subject position of producing a mulatto/a — feminism married to critical theory. That is the difference within the group of essays: a difference that we have not been able to acknowledge. As Spillers pointed out, the mulatto/a is the site of a contradiction that cannot be spoken. What we cannot speak, the passionate feminists, is that we are involved in a contradiction that not only can we not avoid, but we don't want to avoid. That is the difference for those of us who are passionate feminists, not just speaking *on* feminism: we speak from within this contradiction that we cannot avoid. This is our subject position.

Quite often when we say "subject position" we reduce it to a kind of confessional attitudinizing. We say, "I'm white, I'm black, I'm a mulatto/a, I am male, I'm bourgeois." A subject position is not, in fact, a confessional self-description either in praise or in dis-praise. In *The Archaeology of Knowledge*, Foucault writes:

> So the subject of the statement should not be regarded as identical with the author of the formulation. . . . [It does not matter if the author is white or male or bourgeois or black or Indian or a feminist or anything.] She is not in fact the cause, origin or starting-point of the phenomenon of the written or spoken articulation of a sentence. . . . it is not the constant, motionless, unchanging focus of a series of operations. . . . It is a particular, vacant place that may in fact be filled by different individuals. . . . If a proposition, a sentence, a group of signs can be called "statement," it is not therefore because, one day, someone happened to speak them or put them into some concrete form of writing; it is because the position of the subject can be assigned (95).[2]

It is because the position of the subject *can be assigned*, and "assigned" is rather a poor translation; "assigned" means, I think, that it can and must become a sign; not for the person who speaks, but for the person who listens, not for the person who writes, who can say what she likes about who she is, but for the person who reads. When, in fact, the responsible reader reads the sign that is the subject position of the speaker or the writer, it becomes the sign, let us say, of an ethno-politics, of a psychosexual reality, of an institutional position, and this is not under the control of the person who speaks. She cannot diagnose herself; we are given over to our readers.

"To describe a formulation," to continue with the quotation, "*qua* statement does not consist in analyzing the relations between the author and what she says (or wanted to say, or said without wanting to); but in determining what position can and must be occupied by any individual if she is to be the subject of it" (Foucault 95-96). And in that sense, the person who will be the subject of the discourse that we have produced is our students, the generation that can now be caught in that movement of disciplinarization which is much older than feminism and which bears the mark of history. Whatever our color, whatever our gender, whatever our national origin, this is an authoritative, Western-European structure within which, whether we *want* to or not, we are *willingly* placing our passion: feminism as the production of the tragic mulatto/a. We must take responsibility for our students, if they as proper disciples, will not necessarily assign us our confessed subject position of unease, and yet we must not, as we give to our students this particular gift, we must not pretend that we do not exist as disciplinarians. We want to create a discipline; we want to marry feminism to critical theory.

What is the burden of critical theory? It is part of the unease that the best *disciplinary* definition comes from a Western man. The burden of critical theory, or of *critical* philosophy as it is opposed to a dogmatic philosophy, as Kant would say, is to look at the structure of the subject that produces the theory. Once again, the burden is to look at ourselves, as we do what we do, but not in those confessional descriptions that we can all too easily produce ourselves: saying we are female, male, heterosexual, gay, black, white. We must be responsible to the trace of the other, the future, the reader, our generations of disciples that is inscribed in what we are about to do.

We are not, then, involved in a happy act; on the other hand, we *must* do this, and that's the subject position that we must not ignore. We cannot forget that all of us are in this room together because we *share* only one possible subject position, provided by the fact that we are in an institution. It is an institution that has a history, whether you are untenured, whether you are a student, whether you are black, white, whether you are a distinguished professor. It is an institution with a history that enables us to be in this room and that obliges you to sit quietly while I speak. We are academics or fledgling academics in the most opulent university system in the world. Therefore, before we start describing ourselves as anything, we must acknowledge that something is going on here which produces a certain kind of unease.

Let us not pretend that passionate disciplinarizing feminists are the only group that feels this unease. I walked up to an upper-class African gay male friend of mine, in fact a mulatto, on his birthday and asked him to tell us his name. He gave us the string of his names, the sixth name, as he said was the name of his ancestor. Undoubtedly somewhat troubled by the burden of hyperbolic admiration because of the color of his skin, the other side of racism, he added quietly, "A slave trader." Collaboration with the enemy does not depend on the color of your skin or on your gender. Although we are feminists, we are negotiating willingly with the enemy as we marry feminism to critical theory. It does not mean the marriage should be annulled. It is that responsibility that all of us should acknowledge before we set ourselves apart from others so that we can be loved.

What could some other subject positions be, apart from the institutional one? Barbara Johnson and I were talking together yesterday about our houses. We have both bought a house recently. We were talking about the problem of making changes on the house. As houseowners, we occupy a subject position that is much more effective within the structures of exploitation, than as feminists when we speak against capitalism, or against Marxism, as it might happen. The housing industry is the one index that is given in the business pages to indicate how the economy is doing. It's the one industry that, in fact, is in the investment sector, but is presented as in the consumer sector. It's the one industry that has the same kind of contradiction that I'm talking about here. There is the passion of owning a house, having one's own space, a dwelling place, a home. On the other hand, there is also the economic fact that every time we buy a house, releasing so much money into the circuit of capital, we are inserting ourselves into the economic structure that exploits large groups of those very people in praise of whom we speak when we speak as feminists at a podium. Barbara's and my subject position as owners of houses is much more important, much more effective in keeping alive a structure of exploitation, a defense program, than anything that we can say by coming up and claiming a subject position as black or white, or as a feminist.

A subject position is a hard place, and we cannot read it ourselves; we are given over to others even as we make inevitable public attempts to read our subject position. A subject position can be assigned; it is a sign. From the perspective, then, of the fact that we inhabit different kinds of subject positions, and we are engaged in this unhappy marriage and that, in fact, feminism is now emerging as the tragic mulatto/a. I will ask a few questions, and I will offer a brief summary.

I noticed as the speakers went through their speeches, the speeches that have moved me so much that I wish to be quiet, that a certain kind of enemy was emerging. This enemy was variously named "post-structuralism" or "post-modernism" within a subject position that also appropriated the verb "to deconstruct," quite often. All the speakers, nearly all the speakers (I was counting) claimed that she or he was deconstructing something or the other, or something or the other was not being deconstructed. In these speeches, at the same time the noun "post-structuralism" or "post-modernism" was being used as a kind of enemy; an enemy that had to be changed into something else so that feminist historiography could use it; an enemy that was such a nay-sayer that is had to be left behind so that secular humanism could be celebrated, an enemy that had done us such harm, that we must think of a new consensus so that we can appropriate it in some new way. Therefore, I thought, perhaps speaking not only for the movement. but for some absent friends, I should give a little lecture on what I understand deconstruction to be, and how deconstruction does not enter this discourse of diagnosing an enemy, even as we want to cover over the unease of what we are actually doing.

What is the trace? The trace is like this: whenever you construct any kind of a discourse, describing feminism, describing the slave experience, describing being white, describing whatever, whenever you construct any kind of a discourse, if you look at it you will see that at the beginning of the discourse, in order to be able to speak, at the beginning of the discourse there was something like a two-step. The two-step was the necessity to say that a divided is whole. You start from an assumption which you must think is whole in order to be able to speak. There is no one who can speak if she does not presuppose that there is something at the beginning which is a unit. If you look carefully, you will see that this unit is itself divided from something it seems to repeat. This leaves something like a mark, a thumb print, a little design at the beginning of a discourse which is covered over; that is the trace. The trace is the mark like a bird's print on the sand, which seems to inhabit the beginning of any discourse, and the trace must be covered over in order to be able to speak. We must cover over the trace of the history of the Western institution in order to speak as feminists.

Now, what does the deconstructive philosopher do? She looks at the trace and she says, "This here trace is, in fact, the mark of an absent presence. I can see that, in fact, the origin was not a unit. I can see because I'm a deconstructive philosopher, that, in fact, what I'm calling a unit, in order to be able to speak, is the mark of a division. I decide to read this thumb print or this step of a bird in the sand or the shit of an animal who's in the jungle, I decide to read this as the sign of an absent presence. As I decide to read this, I've undone the trace because, in fact, the trace might also be not the sign of anything at all, but I cannot, as a deconstructive philosopher start my discourse if I don't assume that it is the sign of something else. This is what the trace is."

This kind of thing has nothing to do with the disappearance of the subject, or the fragmentation of the subject, the decentering of the subject, the absence or presence of truth. This decision to read the trace as the sign of an absent presence is what deconstruction is. The decision, in fact, immediately undoes the possibility that the trace might mean nothing. It looks like it means the presence of an absent subject, but that is only because I have decided to decipher it. This innocent self-criticism that we cannot have a method that we can present to anyone as fully justified, because of the trace-covering situation within which we are placed, is being turned into a storyline by the anti-post-structuralist chorus — the line being that *today*, as a result of capitalism, or the result of bad politics, the subject has been fragmented. In fact, deconstruction is not a narrative of a fall. If you look carefully at Derrida's writings, you will see that one of his strongest critiques of Heidegger is that Heidegger turned this, the finding of a bird's footprint in the sand, and deciding that it is the footprint of a bird that has flown, that inhabits any discourse, into a story of a Fall in the history of philosophy.[3] In fact, what I am describing here is the acknowledgement of vulnerability in us because we are inserted into the history of language. It is a self-critical position that cannot lead to a final correction. There can be *no* fully deconstructive politics, not even a fully deconstructive feminism. Even when you are being a deconstructor, you acknowledge that the beginning of anything, even of deconstruction, is based on a mistake, a covering over of a negotiation with something other. This cannot lead to a confident, full-fledged politics. It is *after* this persistent self-critique that a deconstructor takes her stand, asymetrical with her theoretical position, following the old rules of coherence and contradiction. The fact that Derrida is taking a position only in terms of Western metaphysics, and only in terms of the institution, and only in terms of being a man who must not speak of women, does not invalidate him as a teacher because those are the areas in which he feels he can be; that is his perceived subject position. He is within those three structures: the institution, the tradition of Western philosophy, and that of a critic of phallogocentrism, which bears a relationship, however oblique or disavowed with a note that we hear here, of a man who wishes to be *for* women. If we want to engage in other political practices, that is our responsibility. The problem will not be solved by turning this into a story, and then saying the story behaves like white *males* or *white* males.

In the essay of that name, "differance" is discussed through the very structure that it denies, the institutional structure of the philosophical proposition. In that essay, Derrida keeps punctuating his critique of the proposition with the litany of a (pro)positive negation: *differance* is *not* a word, it *is not* a concept. Surely he is inviting us to read his text as without absolute justification even as it negotiates with what it critiques: as feminists with critical theory. There is no way that a deconstructive philosopher can say "something is not something" when the word is being used as a concept to enable his discourse. The project of *differance* succeeds in its failure because you can only describe it or perform it through that structure that it critiques, just as we in marrying feminism to the discipline, and to the production of disciples, differentiate the project of feminism from whatever woman as such might be in her radical otherness. Perhaps she is not a concept or a metaphor, but we are involved in a structure that we must persistently critique. As we must inevitably sell our passion into the institution, we must also watch out for succeeding in our failure. The word *differance*, for example, has entered the great French dictionary.

Let me carry my allegory a little way beyond, suggesting that feminism *as* critical theory, which is what our title inevitably suggests, is also a "translation" into, in our case, the U.S. institutional language. The word *differance* in French was supposed to be a neo-graphism, not a neo-logism. A word which, when re-written, could not be read aloud in a different way. You notice no one, speaking in English, speaks this word as "difference." In French, there is no difference between difference and *differance*. *Differance* remains the same word. We, Anglo-U.S. academics, have turned it into a *French* word that we *hear*. When someone says, "Of course, the argument from *differance* disproves that a white male can be a feminist," and undoes the neo-graphism, she turns it into a spoken word, the common French word, that can be heard because of the authority of English. Let us beware of the authority of the institution canonizing our feminist difference.

Deconstruction, as I see it, can only take place if you love what you are deconstructing.[4] Deconstruction is not an exposure of error. Deconstruction notices how we produce "truths." Deconstruction is the move that notices that we must produce truths, that we as communicating subjects must produce meaning, that in fact there *is* always something *like* reference. Deconstruction, as we turn it into a negative metaphysics, does not say that there is no meaning, there is no truth, there is no subject. It says, in fact, what I began with when I sang to you: it says, when you are looking at yourself and distinguishing yourself from others to say that you are better, stop a minute, unload and listen, listen and look at your subject position. If you are distinguishing yourself from that other thing through hatred, stop a minute, remind yourself that the only way in which you can deconstruct is to love the thing you are critiquing. You know it so well, that you cannot not make the structures of that thing the structures of your own discourse. You cannot *not* present your discourse through the structures that you are critiquing. This involves a change of attitude, a mind change, which is not celebrated when we turn deconstruction into a facile method of exposure of error, into a facile method of de-mythologizing simply, over and over again, to say that my message is better and you better listen. That is not the relationship between that which is criticized and the critic when she is deconstructing.

It is only a friend that you love in this way. This is the "love," knowing from the inside, that you give to an enemy your respect, so that the clear-cut distinction between friend and enemy begins to shift and blur. You must learn to know your enemy so well that you borrow the very structures of his discourse. This is, *in fact*, our relationship to patriarchy. We must deconstruct it because we "love" it in that broader sense; without it we are not in fact able to utter. If this is difficult to accept, look at it this way. Barbara Johnson and I couldn't be homeowners, she a professor at Harvard, I at Pitt, if we did not love the structure that we criticize. Deconstruction teaches you that you must acknowledge that the only way in which you can criticize is by so loving your enemy; this is also why deconstruction cannot by itself be a political position. In the first wave of deconstruction, Derrida suggested that deconstruction was "guarding the question," keeping the question alive. In one version of it, where you as a critic are not outside the system, it could lead to the following position: everything you do, you pause and you ask this question — what did I do in collaboration with the enemy in order to attitudinize? That's guarding the question. As things changed, he changed the name of this program to a call to the wholly other, "*appel à tout autre*" not simply "*garder la question*" — guarding the question — anymore. That's when deconstruction contaminated itself by becoming affirmative, again Derrida's word, around 1974, although the place of that move was implicit in the earlier material. Even when the death of the subject was being celebrated in other quarters, again I'm quoting, if you've read the text you will know, that was when deconstruction recognized that it must say "yes" to everything, and it was marked by saying "yes" twice: "yea, yea."[5] It must say "yes" to everything, even the thing that undoes its subject; even as we are saying "yes" to the discipline, even as we are saying "yes" to patriarchy as we can stand and criticize it, deconstruction is obliged to say "yes" to its enemy. Therefore, if it were taken as a political project, it would become nothing but pluralism. Political stands can be taken only after it has been acknowledged that deconstruction by itself cannot be a politics, yet without it all politics mire themselves in a self-congratulation that the period of struggle only imperfectly postpones. Deconstruction is like the skull in the corner of the drawing room which reminds you that you must die. It is not something that you can leave the politics out of, and you certainly cannot trivialize it by turning it into a story of the subject under capitalism becoming fragmented, or the white male killing the subject and denying identity, and then saying we will do something else.

I would like to make an aside here in terms of feminist historiography and Radhakrishnan's brilliant speech. What I missed in his speech was any specific reference to feminist historiography. Feminist historiography is basically positivist in its inspiration and it would be hard to say that it undoes deconstruction. Do you remember Mary Beth Norton's piece for the *New York Times Book Review* some months ago, perhaps it was last year, about the feminization of Clio, the feminization of the spirit of history? It was a very, very well-documented piece, and I refer to it here to bring the specificity that Radha's text lacks. There is a certain authority in feminist historiography which has refused the gift of deconstruction and it will go as it goes. That was one of the questions that I wanted to ask Radhakrishnan because his talk was so powerful. There is also the fact that there is historiography of the oppressed which uses deconstructive methods. I was talking to him about this group of historians with whom I work, a collective which is trying to rewrite colonial Indian historiography, not in terms of nationalism, but in terms of peasant insurgency. That group, in fact, has been using deconstructive methods for about ten years, and from that position, it's getting is all kinds of criticism from the established left in India.[6]

The fact that hegemonic feminist historiography in the bosom of the super power in the United States, even when articulated by disenfranchised individuals, does not use deconstruction, and is, in fact, an authoritative discipline or sub-discipline of history (Mary Beth Norton certainly was suggesting that the discipline itself has been feminized); and that deconstruction, as used to re-write the history of the oppressed in a Third World country is criticized by the established left, once again tells you that where deconstruction hangs out is not very much dependent on what kind of passport you carry. It does not really have to do with deconstruction being white, male, or anything. Not to acknowledge that a non-deconstructive feminist historiography exists, and that a deconstructive historiography of the oppressed exists in the Third World, even as this particular characteristic of deconstruction is ignored, may be symptomatic of the fact that Radhakrishnan and I are both green card holders. We live in a First World country, but have kept ourselves clean from citizenship so that we can have a voice that we can suggest you cannot hear. It is those kinds of articulations that are *assigned* subject positions, not merely whether you are white, or male, or female, or gay or straight.

It is time for me to remind myself that I want to be quiet. These contradictions that I critique I myself inhabit. I am speaking because of a contract; I have accepted a fee; I am in an institution. If I could speak my desire, I would not speak. It is from within that predicament that I am going to criticize what I criticize in the next few minutes.

It was suggested during the question and answer session after a very powerful paper that the question of intention is a trap and we should not allow ourselves to fall into it. We cannot not intend; language is intended. That does not mean that we, as characters, are *identical* with our fully grasped intentions. It is like the difference between making a confessional declaration and inhabiting a subject position that is assigned to you: as a houseowner, as a professor, as someone who is involved in turning passion into a discipline. You carry the responsibility of intending even as you speak. It is a problem, but that doesn't mean, that, therefore, it should be forgotten, and we must find ways of not talking about the dirty word. Even *that* is an intention, the intention to avoid talking about intention because it is a problem. Because it is a problem we must love it and look at its production in language which we are supposedly producing, not talking about it. It is the dirty secret that we must love in order to speak. As we are sitting here, all of our bodies are producing excrement; we can't talk about it. It's somewhat uncomfortable to be at speeches, especially if you are of a certain age, after dinner because there's a lot of flatulence in the room, but no one wants to do it; on the other hand, without it, you cannot live. It's the dirty secret that must be denied in order to pretend that we are only minds. Intention is like that. You can't get around it by saying it's a trap. You are caught in that trap. When you are playing tennis, you are not playing just by the laws of tennis; you are also playing by the laws of thermodynamics. The difference between the two laws is: one you think you can control by declaring I'm Indian, I'm not white — love me. And the other plays you. The way in which the institution, the history of the institution plays us, the way in which being a houseowner plays us — these are a much bigger circuit. The one we declare is the laws of tennis; we master those; we play well; we defeat our opponent. But the one we don't declare, the one we don't learn, is the laws of thermodynamics as it plays us, because even as we learn them, *we are in them*. Intention, being in the institution, those laws play us. That is what is meant by not putting faith in a narrative because the narrative that we can produce — for example, here the story of the unquestioned excellence of feminism — is only a narrative. But the narrative within which we are written, here the history of the institution or the circuit of capital within which the housing industry in the United States is one of the strongest indexes, or the enabling power of denegated patriarchal discourse, those laws play us; we can't narrate them. If we were to narrate them, we would have to say "yes" to our enemy, but if we are, in fact, saying "yes" to our enemy, then we would become deconstructors. That is what I am trying to do now; saying "yes" to our enemies so that we acknowledge that the unease in this room which has obliged us to present ourselves either as better than the rest, if we happen to be gifted with a dark skin or with the right sex, or worse than the rest, if we happen to be cursed — used to be a gift, now a curse in benevolent radicalism — with the other kind, so that the unease can become productive. In fact, in taking the responsibility of saying that there *is* a relationship between feminism and critical theory, we graduate ourselves into the responsibility of having to become self-critical in our subject position as academics, teachers, students in a capitalist country. If Marxism is our enemy, perhaps we want to knock Marxism because we happen to be American. We are written by the narrative of the United States that, in trying to find something better than Marxism (inevitably conflating the history of Marxism with Marx), we go back to ethnicity and "my folk." We are written by a narrative which is bigger than we are; that is our subject position and there is no loss in accepting that.

One last thing about feminism and the discipline. When we talk as we have been talking, using the language of a critical theory which we also want to trivialize, we should also ask — those of us for whom feminism was, and is a passion, and neither just the discipline, nor an object of investigation — we should also ask, are *we* not involved in the kind of upward class mobility that critical theory bestows? Critical theory is the most developed gift of the humanist academy. It is dangerous because it is genuinely powerful. By defining and describing feminism in terms of critical theory we should be aware that we are using a powertool that is also dangerous at the same time. We are academics within English and American literature; we have to think about the fact that the discipline of English, the teaching of English, hangs out in places that are very far from the United States. I will now slip into the subject position that you like. As you know, the teaching of English literature began first in the colonies. Let me give you a few figures.

The United States has give or take 230 million people. There are today nearly 3000 four-year colleges and universities, degree granting, engaged in the production of "doctors," in the general sense — teachers if not necessarily PhDs — in that move of "*discere/doctore*," disciplining/teaching. In India, for example, there are over 720 million people and there are 162 universities. Some of these universities have affiliated colleges, but if you look at the figures in the *Commonwealth Universities Yearbook*, you will see a college with five teachers has also been put in as *one* college. You compare the college with five teachers to the University of Pittsburgh where I teach and you see it's an unequal comparison. So even the numbers are not quite correct. The trans-disciplinary models that we draw from our disciplinary practice and experience in the United States, mostly at good colleges and schools, will not be carried over to the teaching of English or feminism elsewhere. That is also the burden of critical theory, and that is not a difference within, that is a difference outside. I don't want to give up the project of marrying feminism, marrying my passion to critical theory, because that project can't be given up. We are obliged to do it as academics in this country. We are written by that disciplinary demand, but as we do it, deconstruction would oblige us to see that at the origin of that endeavor is, in fact, a division — a division between ourselves and the rest of the world into which we are written because, for example, we own houses in the U.S. Yet, it is that circuit that is writing us, as much more powerful subject positions than our declared intent to say feminism is against capitalism. In such a situation finding in deconstruction a whipping boy is not going to add to anything but our relative complacency.

Because I feel that what we unnecessarily see as our opposition should not get trivialized as we congratulate ourselves, I have been trying to show how becoming responsible for our subject position would involve deconstruction in a certain way. I hope that what I've said has not been too incoherent. I always have my excuse: I would rather have been silent.

NOTES

1. This text is an only slightly edited transcription of taped remarks in response to the conference.
2. I have changed the gender of the pronouns in Foucault's text.
3. In the interest of my defense of deconstruction, I no doubt do Heidegger's subtlety an injustice. I have in mind a passage like, say, "Letter on Humanism," in *Basic Writings*, ed. David Farrell Krell (New York: Harper & Row: 1977), p. 200-201.
4. I quote here a footnote from a subsequent paper, "Feminism and Deconstruction, Again," in Teresa Brennan, ed. *Between Psychoanalysis and Feminism* (London: Methuen, forthcoming): "The paleonymic burden of the word 'love' for a feminist is to be distinguished rigorously from the gentlemanly or belleslettresistic attitude of 'love for the text'." I have recently learned much from Derrida's meditation on friendship ("Friendship: Of Democracy," unpublished lectures, Univ. of Pittsburgh, 28-29 September, 1988). For the moment at least, across sexual difference, I will stay with love.
5. For the most extensive play with the two "yes"-s, see Jacques Derrida, *Ulysse grammophone. Deux mots pour Joyce* (Paris: Galilee, 1987). Incidentally, Derrida's reading of Molly Bloom in this text is a curious case of "feminism" in critical theory.
6. See Ranajit Guha and G.C. Spivak eds., *Selected Subaltern Studies* (New York: Oxford Univ. Press, 1988).

REFERENCES

Derrida, Jacques. 1973. "Differance." In *Speech and Phenomena and Other Essays on Husserl's Theory of Signs*. Trans. David B. Allison, 129-60. Evanston, IL: Northwestern University.

Foucault, Michel. 1972. *The Archaeology of Knowledge and The Discourse on Language*. Trans. A.M. Sheridan Smith. New York: Harper & Row.

Norton, Mary Beth. 1986. "Is Clio a Feminist? The New History." *New York Times Book Review* (April 13, 1986):1.

In the CRITICAL THEORY series the following titles have been published and will be published during 1989:

1. DÍAZ-DIOCARETZ, Myriam and Iris M. ZAVALA (eds): *WOMEN, FEMINIST IDENTITY AND SOCIETY IN THE 1980's.* Amsterdam, 1985.
2. DÍAZ-DIOCARETZ, Myriam: *Translating Poetic Discourse: Questions of Feminist Strategies in Adrienne Rich.* Amsterdam, 1985.
3. DIJK, Teun A. van (ed.): *DISCOURSE AND LITERATURE. New Approaches to the Analysis of Literary Genres.* Amsterdam, 1985.
4. ZAVALA, Iris M., Teun A. van DIJK and Myriam DIAZ-DIOCARETZ (eds) coordinated by Bill DOTSON SMITH: *APPROACHES TO DISCOURSE, POETICS AND PSYCHIATRY: Papers from the 1985 Utrecht Summer School of Critical Theory.* Amsterdam, 1987.
5. HELBO, André: *Theory of Performing Arts.* Amsterdam, 1987.
6. SEIDEL, Gill (ed.): *THE NATURE OF THE RIGHT. Feminist analysis of order patterns.* Amsterdam/Philadelphia, 1988.
7. WODAK, Ruth (ed.): *LANGUAGE, POWER AND IDEOLOGY. Studies in political discourse.* Amsterdam/Philadelphia, 1989.
8. MEESE, Elizabeth and Alice PARKER (eds): *THE DIFFERENCE WITHIN: FEMINISM AND CRITICAL THEORY.* Amsterdam/Philadelphia, 1989.